QUARTER HORSE BOY

Movement at the back of the horsebox made Tod and Kelly turn their heads. A glistening bundle lay at the Palomino's heels. She knew what to do. She freed from the shining membrane the smallest, most wonderful foal Tod had ever seen. Tod could not believe his eyes. Even Kelly was shaken, for he too had never seen a newly-born white foal before.

3 cde

Mary Patchett

Quarter Horse Boy

Illustrated by Roger Payne

CAROUSEL EDITOR: ANNE WOOD

CAROUSEL BOOKS
A DIVISION OF TRANSWORLD PUBLISHERS LTD
A NATIONAL GENERAL COMPANY

QUARTER HORSE BOY
A CAROUSEL BOOK 0 552 52019 5

Originally published in Great Britain
by George G. Harrap & Co. Ltd.

PRINTING HISTORY
George G. Harrap edition published 1970
Carousel edition published 1972

Carousel Books are published by Transworld Publishers Ltd,
Cavendish House, 57–59 Uxbridge Road, Ealing, London W.5
Made and printed in Great Britain by
Hazell Watson & Viney Ltd, Aylesbury, Bucks

CONTENTS

YOUNG TOD

IT WAS a hot, hot day. Somewhere in the West a bush-fire burned itself out, smouldering so that the fierce gusts of wind raised clouds of ashes. Fine ash came down like a mist from forty miles away over the withered grasslands. It sifted down onto the Booramby homestead buildings, and on to the Aboriginals' camp a quarter of a mile away on the banks of Mooti Creek. Mooti Creek was too small to be called a river, but it ran deep and strong and gave year-round water to the man fortunate enough to own the land through which it flowed.

Sunlight coming through the ashen mist acquired an orange, oily quality of intense heat. Old Jim Greer, whom the Aboriginals called "Nakimer", the "Great Old One", stirred restlessly in his veranda chair. He rose, cursing a little at the hot wind that stirred the thick, green creepers curtaining the veranda, and let spots of burning sunlight pierce the leaves.

Yelling voices came from where the main building of the homestead was joined to the kitchen buildings by a short, wooden bridge. Old Jim, massive, frosty-eyed, his face as brown, as pungent and bitter as a twist of tobacco, lifted his body from the chair. Gnarled hands on the wooden sides raised him lightly on heavily-muscled arms made strong by controlling many a powerful, half-broken horse, and by throwing the great wild bullocks that wanted no part of man.

Nakimer was irritable, but then it was seldom that he was not. Now he was surly with his housekeeping sister, Cora. The Aborigines and the station hands called her "missus"; Nakimer called her "Korina", after the white cockatoos, when he wanted to annoy her, but not when he wanted an answer. Miss Greer never shrieked as the cockatoos did, but she did her share of scolding. Often anger twisted her thin face into furious lines in her hatred of feckless servants, a difficult brother, and life in general.

The hard, unceasing work of making a home in the far-off Australian bush was a bitter occupation. It was made worse for Miss Greer because she allowed neither love nor friendship to invade her privacy. She grew old in an environment she did not want, tending a brother of whom she disapproved. She had not the capacity for extracting affection or beauty from the world about her. Even her nickname annoyed her. She saw no beauty in a sky filled with her namesakes, drifting treewards, the last rays of the sun touching their sulphur crests so that the wind seemed to be carrying a flight of great white flowers waving their golden stamens across the sky.

Nakimer mumbled to himself, wanting the large cup of tea Cora usually brought him about this time. He set off towards the kitchen, walking lightly for such a big man, his small horseman's feet in elastic-sided boots moving with animal silence across the wooden bridge between the buildings.

The kitchen veranda was also walled-in by greenery. He reached it and roared like a bull. It seemed a strangely angry sound to be connected with the shadowy veranda and the hot, orange light glinting through the gap in the leaves. The surrealistic sight of a meat-safe against the wall in the coolest place aroused this wrath.

A bullock had been slaughtered the night before so that the station folk could have all the red meat they craved. The top shelf of the safe was filled with the choicest cuts, hanging from meathooks, swinging there, slabs of crimson flesh, dripping slow red blood onto the white enamel of the dish below. That was fine, and the clouds of flies buzzed against the fine netting, whining in impotent fury and frustration: house flies; blue flies of a beautiful, putrid iridescence; large sinister blowflies; all defeated, and all furious.

It was the lower shelf that upset Nakimer, for on it, looking out at him with round, solemn eyes framed by a small face of dusky cream, sat a half-caste baby. It was probably not more than five months old, but it was far more active than a white child of twice its age, able to crawl on the wooden floor of the big safe, and so exercise muscles that would allow the baby to walk in another couple of months. It put its pink-lined fist in its mouth when Nakimer roared. It was not frightened; on the contrary, it was stimulated, and smacked its knees with its small monkey-paws in appreciation of the fine noise he made.

Nakimer was rather disgruntled; the baby should have yelled, or crouched in the corner, small and compact, and still in the way a baby wild animal would have done, defending itself by its immobility.

This was not the first creamy baby that had been thrust into the fly-proof meat-safe by its busy, or lazy mother. It was one of the few practices frowned on alike by Nakimer and the missus.

Nakimer's roar brought the young mother, Addie (the missus' name, for she disapproved of the house servants having outlandish Abo names), running on silent, naked feet, giggling nervously and fumbling at the catch on the safe, to the joy of the assorted flies, as she snatched her baby out of it. The little naked body clung to her in the instant curves assumed by every young animal when it touches its mother. Addie stood nervously moving from one leg to the other, pushing one hard-soled foot, undistorted by shoe-wearing, up her shin to rub her knee, hanging her head, ready to burst into giggles or to run away.

But the young animal in her arms curved its body close to her and held up its little round head. It looked at the angry old man and broke into a disarming grin, holding out a pink-lined paw. Nakimer was astonished. He felt nothing for these small native creatures. They were born, grew up on the station between walkabouts, were absorbed into the bush one way or the other, he did not know or care. The best of them remained on the place, working about the stables or the homestead or as stockmen. When someone remarked, "Booramby has the best bunch of stockmen in Queensland," another replied, "They ought to be good. Nakimer's bred them up himself for fifty years!"

Nakimer shouted at the Abo girl. "Get those bloody flies out of the meat-safe, and put that kid somewhere else!"

The girl giggled without looking into the tough old face, but the baby looked squarely at him and continued to smile and hold out its hand. Reluctantly Nakimer put his horny forefinger into the small palm. It was entirely against his code to pay the slightest attention to it. The gins got food, their kids got a job if they were worth it. What more did they want?

This one, it seemed, wanted to be noticed. Grudgingly he left the tip of his finger in the fat bud of a hand. Feeling foolish he lifted his head and caught sight of the buzzing, gorging spots of black against the red meat in the meat-safe. Again he shouted.

"Get those bloody flies outer the safe—here, gimme the kid."

The baby, transferred, curved like a small, hot possum about his massive forearm. He looked down at it with hostile eyes. It merely patted his mahogany-tough cheeks. The flustered gin laughed and yelped and flapped at the flies, squashing those she could catch in her black fingers, and Nakimer stood helplessly by while the baby solemnly poked at his nose, his eyes, gurgling and crooning to itself. Then he heard steps and knew the missus was coming.

"Shut that door—'ere, take the kid," he said, and the small boy went back to his mother. She managed to slip like a black shadow round the end of the veranda before the missus reached the veranda door.

"What's all the noise? I wish—"

"One of those damned gins puttin' the baby in the meat-safe. You'd better look, she's sure to 'ave left flies inside it."

The missus' face took on its look of tight-drawn disapproval for her brother, her contempt for Addie and indifference for the baby. She opened the meat-safe cautiously, to his truculent, "An' where the 'ell's my tea?"

The cold, white face turned to him. "The tea's in the kitchen. Pour your own."

She expected him to tramp by her and turned back to go on with her war against the flies. But the big man paused, and asked in a gruff voice, "That Addie's kid?"

She nodded.

He grunted angrily. "What's she call it?"

Cora put the latch on the door and rose to her feet, gaunt, almost as high as his shoulder and he was a tall man. She looked at him with unbending hostility.

"How should I know? Some outlandish Abo name, I've no doubt."

Still grunting like an angry buffalo the big man went on to the kitchen. Addie sprang up nervously from where she squatted by the stove, feeding it with chunks of wood from the well-filled box beside her. Clinging like a small sloth to its mother's underside, the baby appeared pale against the darkness. Nakimer poured himself a cup of scalding tea, then, looking over at her, he stabbed his finger in the direction of the baby, asking, "What name that fellah?"

For an instant mischief touched Addie's face as she answered, "Titchilcumbin."

" 'Willywagtail!' What kind of a name is that?" he said angrily. "Give the boy a name I can remember, not your confounded yabber."

"You gibbit name, Nakimer?"

For a moment he searched for a name, but nothing suggested itself and he burst out furiously, "Call 'im 'Tod'."

So Tod he became, and the name stuck because it seemed a part of him, for he was a solitary child who played alone—"on his tod", a bushman would have said. So something lasting came to Tod from his first meeting with the Great Old Man.

Like all Abo children, Tod returned to his mother to be fed long after his first birthday, but not for five or six years as some of them do. By the time he was a year he was an old hand in the stable, and by his second birthday he was able to do many small tasks about the horses. Old Kelly, the head man, mulberry black and grown old in Nakimer's service, was proud of Tod. He said the boy was getting to look like a foal, and certainly smelt like one.

The missus drove Addie hard, and while Tod returned to his mother whenever he was hungry, a situation developed between the missus and the baby in which Tod neither asked nor gave quarter. To her he was a continual reminder of things she would rather forget. She refused to notice how valiant the small creature was over knocks and bruises; she ignored his disarming baby smiles and the appeal of tiny outstretched hands. He was, to her, just another nuisance from the nearby blacks' camp, and while she was never actively unkind to him, she always behaved as if he was not there.

Gradually an antagonism developed in the baby. Once, when Addie was busy and Tod came in to be fed, the missus did not call his mother. Instead she half-filled a tin mug with fresh milk and banged it down on the table before him. She hesitated for a moment uncertain whether he, like most Abo children of many times his age, did not know how to drink from a cup. One tiny paw still gripped the rim of the table. The other stretched out and shakily tried to lift the mug. It was too heavy, so he took both hands to it. The missus stood just behind him, and the baby turned while she still struggled with herself over the question of helping him.

Tod lifted the mug levelly enough with both hands, his black eyes travelling slowly from the substantial shoes on a level with his own wee bare feet, up the front of the limp cotton dress, over the flat bosom to the disapproving face. He raised the mug a little higher, dropped his eyes, and poured the milk in a steady stream over the nearest shoe.

Surprise made Cora stand still. The baby turned and put the mug on the table. Again he looked up at the austere face towering above him, his black eyes as brightly dark as a bird's, and as hard, then he walked away, a quaint little naked figure, spare-hipped and erectly balanced as befitted a man of his mother's people.

The missus stood there and did not move until he was out of sight. Then she began automatically mopping the milk from herself and from the floor, her face a mask. Strangely enough, the calm independence of that small, retreating back gave her the first feeling of tenderness she had known for the innocent half-breeds of which she had seen so many over the years.

It was difficult to get the money out of Nakimer for repairs to the homestead, but the stables were always kept in tip-top order, and woe betide a stableman who was slovenly over the care of the horses! The stables were roomy and far-spreading, for Nakimer's passion was horses. Stock-horses, thoroughbreds, racers—they were all one to him, providing they were the tops in their own class, and horse-breeders in Australia, and all over the world, coveted his stock. Really fast horses went to his trainer in Brisbane, and all his absences from Booramby were on horsey business of some kind.

This passion came to Tod in full strength. He spent his life in the stables from the time he could toddle. A civilized mother would have had a nervous breakdown at the sight of her child earnestly polishing the hooves of some great fractious animal whose hocks were taller than his own head. But the mares stepped as carefully around him as if he had been one of their newborn foals, and few horses nipped at him when he climbed laboriously up the sides of the loose-boxes until he was on a level with the beautiful heads of the frequently unpredictable thoroughbreds. No horse ever kicked at him, nor stepped on him when he was in the straw at their feet or passing under their bellies.

Once, when Tod felt hungry and did not want to leave the stables, he stood fondling and crooning to a new-born foal, a little soft-haired beauty, still damp from the birth-fluid. The mother nudged the tiny creature to its hooves, and turned her head. She pushed it gently rearwards where it began to drink, straddling its tiny hooves on the straw, waggling its absurd tail and looking surprised at its own success.

Tod, whose instincts made him stand quietly by, came forward now, reminded of his own hunger, and he tried to join the foal at its meal. The mare stood still. She was an old lady and birth was no new story to her. She obligingly turned her head

and pushed Tod, but he had not the advantage of the foal's longer neck, and he stood frustratedly parting the soft damp hair covering the foal's ribs, waiting for it to finish.

With care for her own offspring and for Tod, the mare lay on the dry straw, moving her body so that the clean hard stems rubbed against her hide, snorting a little very softly, resting after her labour. The foal, its instinct to feed still paramount, waited reluctantly until its mother ceased her lazy movements, then it went forward followed by Tod. Both young things fed from the mother until she decided to get to her hooves and then child and foal dropped from the mare's body like a couple of well-fed leeches.

If Addie worried that Tod's appetite was failing, then she never showed it or attempted to find out if he had any other source of food. His diet became more varied, with cows' as well as mares' milk. He ate the chunks of almost-raw meat his mother gave him, clutching and chewing at it, and he searched about the old orchard for windfalls. The horses were given treats of raw vegetables and sometimes fruit, for it was Nakimer's strict rule that they should never be given scraps of bread or lumps of sugar. Carrots and other coarse vegetables were grown round the homestead and the old orchard produced various fruits. Tod ate what the horses were given, cheerfully spitting out dirt and grit when it bothered him, but with no fancy ideas about the occasional grub found in the fruit.

Kelly, the head stableman, came from the west with Nakimer to settle on Booramby. In those days Kelly was so mulberry-black that Jim Greer christened him after the bushman's name for the crows, whose shining black plumage was no deeper in colour than was Kelly's skin. In return, Kelly gave his boss the title of "Nakimer" from the speech of his western tribe.

Kelly, and Nakimer too, were old men now, and both men knew more about horses than most men learned in their lifetime. He was probably the only person in the world whom Nakimer trusted fully. Nowadays, old Kelly enjoyed visiting the wildly untidy blacks' camp on the Mooti bank below the homestead. There he sat around with the elders of whatever tribe was in residence, talking to them, smoking his foul pipe, lying under gum-trees whose speckled shade fell like confetti sprinkled by some divine hand.

Kelly accepted any promising youngster who wanted to help in the stables. From these he chose those who were to become stockmen, and those whom he would keep as his own men. Many of the youngsters went walkabout, a migration of humans that is rather like the migrations of birds and animals. It is a mysterious hunger-urge that has been with the black men from away-back, and civilization cannot still it within its few puny years.

The black man of old migrated because a primal instinct urged him to. Walkabout was a journeying to where certain foods waited for him that were necessary for survival in his lean, sparse land; lily-roots in sleepy billabongs that in three months would be dry and rotted; yam patches to be dug by the gins with their pointed sticks. Yams were as important to the Aborigines as potatoes were to the Irish, and not unlike them in their tuberous growth. Wild fowl, migrants themselves, at certain seasons covered a complex of billabongs, and meant good eating for the hunter, ankle-deep in ooze, who took his prey from beneath the water, his dark hands closing on their feet in swift silence, unseen in the opaque water.

Kelly thought of these things as he lay in the half-shade, his old nostrils impervious to the reek of the camp and the unwashed bodies, although able to enjoy the clean, pungent scent of the sun-heated bush. Among the many excellent horse-boys Kelly had had over the years there was none quite like Tod. Others had had Tod's way with horses. Being half-wild themselves the best of them seemed to the old man to become horses of a different shape, but with the added benefit of hands that could carry, feed, groom and water the four-legged kind.

As soon as Tod learned an independent existence from his mother, his nights as well as his days were spent in the stables. The old mare from whom Tod often fed had had many foals before the little bay, entered in the studbook as "Swy Boy" and usually shortened to "Boy", who was Tod's constant companion. Tod became a creature of the stable, sleeping on the straw, warmed by the great body of the mare or against the velvety baby hide of the foal.

Kelly was happy enough to leave the care of both mother and foal to the tiny boy. When Tod was still too small to groom the mare to his satisfaction, Kelly took a hand himself, and allowed the boy to consider the foal entirely his responsibility, along with the mare's hooves and legs as high as hocks and knees. The mare's head, too, Tod groomed meticulously by climbing onto the top rail of the stall. He went to work with the brush held in both tiny fists. The old mare was placid, and Kelly was old. He could not bend as easily as he had twenty years before and it was a temptation to lie back on the straw and watch the absurdly small imp taking his work so seriously. In Kelly's mind the thought was born that here might be a worthy successor to himself.

Tod was blissfully happy; he ate as and when he felt hungry and rarely visited the camp to play with the other youngsters. His own people found him strange, and to white people he was an alien, but he did not notice either of these things. The mare, Lucky Bess, and her foal, Swy Boy, were all his world. He needed no other.

At first, when mare and foal were put in the paddock, Tod went with them. He took them out after the morning grooming, and brought them in at night and stayed himself. There were other mares and foals in the paddock, and Tod played with them all.

Most of the day Tod spent around the stables, trying to copy the horse-trained men's work, climbing onto any hide-covered back he could reach, sometimes riding out on the front of one of the stockmen's saddles, for the men were amused by the little boy's persistence.

It was a healthy life, and Tod grew and developed the flat, steely muscles of his race. On his rare visits to the camp he sometimes joined the small boys making spears to hurl at the sticks and leaves floating down the creek. Sometimes he followed in the wake of the elders, or the warriors, who showed the children the bush lore that must be taught beside that which is largely inborn in all Abo children.

Kelly encouraged Tod to handle the fast-growing foal until, in time, Tod with his light weight rode the youngster about the paddock or sat astride the mare, urging her to move with a tattoo of his small sharp heels that hardly reached the maximum curve of her ribs. He had a cat-like ability to land on his feet, and his frequent falls meant nothing to him.

The first shock to disturb these happy days came when Swy Boy was thrown, branded and castrated. Tod snatched at the branding iron and had to be held by one of the men. When he was let go he hurled a stone at them in a frenzy of hatred that anyone should dare to hurt Swy Boy, not knowing yet that he himself must learn these tasks, and perform them as efficiently as the trained men he was watching. In time he had to learn to accept such things, but his first experience scarred him deeply.

The foal's intense fear, the white-rimmed eyes and the struggling of the strong, young body that had never before known pain or fear, brought torture to Tod. The final effort when the colt rose to its feet, shocked by terror and shaking with pain, and moving away from Tod who loved him, was a moment of bitterness such as the little boy had never imagined in the happy-go-lucky life that was his.

After a time, Swy Boy once again accepted Tod as his trusted friend, but it was never quite the same for Tod. His sense of betrayal went far deeper than it did for Swy Boy who had suffered it.

As the foal grew away from Lucky Bess, so Tod grew away from Addie. She never worried about him, and in time a little half-brother appeared and Addie and Tod scarcely noticed each other. It was the natural drifting apart of all wild creatures. Addie did not drive Tod away as a dingo, an eagle or any other mother of the wild drives her young out of her life, knowing that if she does not, then her young will always be dependent on their parents and their parents' territory, and all would starve. Instead, Addie accepted that Tod lived his own life in the softened conditions of semi-civilization and needed her no longer.

Tod went to the kitchen when he was hungry. He and the missus eyed each other warily, but there was always food for him on the special shelf of the drip-safe. Because of this he was better fed than most small Aborigines. He knew that the missus must have authorized this food cache of his, but neither ever spoke of it.

In his second year the missus presented Tod with two tiny pairs of shorts. She did this for all the small boys around the homestead in an effort to give them a more Christian appearance. Tod wore them without protest. They gave him a dim feeling of grown-up pride, and occasionally he put on a shirt.

Bathing was an irregular affair, but when he was hot he went under the showers that were attached to the stable. Then, with the boys from the camp, he swam in the deep pools under the overhanging creek bank, diving and squirming like a young eel among the tree roots. Swimming came as naturally to Tod as walking.

Kelly, wise in the ways of stable boys, did not entirely approve of the child's single-hearted devotion to Swy Boy, but he knew that at three years the break would come when Swy Boy would be sold to one buyer or another. He had already given Tod the care of Lucky Bess, who was due to foal again, and the old man decided to enlarge the number of Tod's charges.

Things did not turn out quite as Kelly anticipated. Swy Boy, frisking and playing with his mates, often went down to the creek to drink. On one occasion he waded out into the water, and stood gazing at a strangely-moving black stick floating down the current towards him. The movement brought the strange thing almost under his nose. He reared and struck at it with a fore-hoof, slapping the water and drenching his chest with spray. His hoof missed the living stick with its hard black eyes. Swy Boy bent his graceful head, snorting a little, and the head of the swimming snake touched the soft skin of the colt's nose. He leaped backwards, and for an instant the long red-bellied body dangled there, until a swing of Swy Boy's head flung it onto the bank at the edge of the water and it crawled quickly into the grass.

The other colts crowded inquisitively around. Swy Boy, with unseeing eyes, backed out of the creek and stood with his head hanging. The others looked at him curiously, almost fearfully, and moved away. Swy Boy's head went lower, he straddled his hooves on the sand and shudders ran through his body.

It was an hour later when Tod, having finished his stable duties, set out to look for Swy Boy. The other youngsters had drifted back to the paddock and were cropping the grass and Tod was surprised not to see Swy Boy among them. From the top of the bank he caught sight of the shining body lying on the sand, the lovely head stretched upwards in an unnatural way, as if to protest at death which had come so treacherously when the colt's youth and strength were at their greatest.

The child moved the head into what seemed to him a more comfortable position. He lifted a front leg and it fell heavily back again. Tod had never seen death; instinct told him what it was. He squatted down and put his small hand flat on the smooth, hard bone of the forehead and he sat there, silent, unmoving, not crying as a white child might have done, only feeling that this thing that was death had passed into his own heart.

The other colts came streaming back to the stables at sunset. Kelly, watching his charges trotting into the yard, missed Swy Boy and Tod. He pulled his leathery old body into the saddle of his own horse which stood nearby, and cantered towards the creek. There, looking down from the top of the bank, he caught sight of Tod, motionless beside the shining head. Already the terrible venom had sent blood seeping through the veins and tissues it had made porous. The once taut, muscular body was beginning to swell. Soon lovely Swy Boy would be a hideous travesty of his own elegant body.

Kelly dismounted. He pulled the reins over his horse's head and left him and went down the steep bank, digging his heels into the soft earth. The seamed old face was expressionless. In his heart the old Aboriginal, who loved only Nakimer and horses and, perhaps, young Tod a little, understood the boy's sorrow. The old man had seen many horses die of untreated snake-bite. More often than not a bitten horse died whether it was treated or not by the old method of cutting out the fang-marks—if you could find them. The new method of using serum was more often successful.

Kelly touched Tod's shoulder. "It's too late, boy. Was 'e dead when you found 'im?"

Tod looked up, his eyes blurred and dry with the tremendous ache behind them. Kelly bent down and saw the fang-mark's on the delicate skin round the colt's nostrils. He did not say, "If you had found him earlier the serum might have saved him," because it was too late. Tod knew about the serum; it was one of the things all the stableboys were taught to use.

Kelly straightened up. He was a spare old figure, his thin, corded arms protruding like sticks from the rolled sleeves of his shirt, arms as stringy and powerful as twisted tree-roots. He stood looking down at the child's head, noticing that the hair was still streaked with the yellow dead-leaf colour it had been when Tod was a baby. He said gently, "Come on, boy, you've got the mare to see to."

Tod heard Kelly, but his voice seemed to come from far away. The pain behind his own eyes turned their vision dark and he could not make the effort to move.

Kelly's voice became a growl. "Get a move on!" he said harshly. "See to the mare, then get the trace chains and bring old Barry down here. Tom or I'll 'elp you. We'll bury Swy Boy down by the old willow in the top paddock."

Tod gave a cry like an animal in agony and the

old man bent and pulled him to his feet. He went on remorselessly. "It's too late to help Swy. Come on, boy. Lucky Bess'll foal in a few weeks, then you'll have plenty to do."

Kelly heard his own words with a kind of surprise. He wanted Tod to get away from his possessiveness, to work among all the horses, and here he was promising him another foal!

Tod stumbled up the bank behind the old man. The world was crowding in on him. He knew what he had to do, but first he went to Lucky Bess and stood with his face against her warm-smelling hide while she whickered at him softly and nibbled his shoulder. He attended to her, and the everyday work made it possible for him to go on with what he had to do.

When the whole thing was over Tod returned to Lucky Bess's stable and lay down in the corner as he always did—only this time Swy Boy was not beside him. Lucky Bess moved her hooves and snorted and made small whinnying noises, and in time Tod slept.

By the time the old mare foaled Lucky Boy, Tod regained his heaven. Like Swy Boy, Lucky Boy, son of Lucky Bess, flourished, and Tod loved him with every beat of his heart.

The years passed and Tod was seven before he had his first memorable encounter with Nakimer since his meat-safe days. The old man was an everyday figure around the stables, and Tod never looked up from what he was doing even when Nakimer stood for a little time watching him.

But when Lucky was coming up to a strong, fleet three-year-old, with Tod almost as at home on his back as in the stables, Nakimer stood one day watching the boy ride the colt out of the stables into the paddock. Using neither saddle nor bridle the boy turned the horse in through the gate and the horse, now grown to a big, rangy bay, responded to every touch of the small knees.

Clover sprang, green and juicy, between the clumps of withered grass. The paddock's twelve acres flowed away into the distance, and other thoroughbreds moved about, cropping the sweet young green stuff. The paddock was kept exclusively for blood stock. It gave them room to gallop and sweet water to drink from the creek approached by a narrow sandy beach. Clumps of shady trees made the whole paddock a horses' paradise.

Nakimer leaned on the top rail, his foot on the lower rail, and watched the boy ride through the gate. He looked tiny on the tall black. The old man chewed on a grass stalk, his felt hat pulled down over his eyes. It was a sweet sight, a thoroughbred ridden by a child who knew how to handle him. Nakimer called Kelly over.

"Looks good, don't 'e, boss?" said Kelly.

"Yeah. We'll give 'im another year; the By Chance stock mature late. Meantime—"

He stopped. Tod became conscious that the two men were discussing Lucky and his pride in his horse overflowed. He turned him from the gate, bent low on Lucky's neck and sent him skimming like a flying bird across the grass. The boy's knees tightened. Lucky stopped in a few strides, reared and tossed his head, and Tod clung on like a monkey, one small fist gripping the mane. The old man grinned at Kelly.

"Flash little bastard, ain't 'e?"

Kelly heard a note of pride in the harsh voice, something he had not heard in reference to a stable boy in all the years he had been with Nakimer. He drawled back, " 'E's not flash, boss, 'e's proud. Tod thinks the world of Lucky. 'E's not showin' you how 'e can ride; 'e's showin' you how Lucky can gallop."

The old man grunted. He looked down at Kelly, "Lucky's 'ad more handlin' than most. It's time 'e learned to carry a saddle and bridle. Think you can teach the kid to ride 'im on a bit and in a saddle?"

"That kid can learn anything when it's to do with an 'orse, boss."

"Then teach 'im."

So Tod learned to bridle Lucky, and his heart mourned for his horse's soft mouth. He used the reins as sensitively as he used his knees on the warm hide. Lucky was unafraid of the saddle, but he was puzzled. Just as he had been mouthed without pain or difficulty, so he learned to carry the light saddle, and Tod learned to ride in it. At first the saddle and stirrups seemed to throw him forward when the horse cantered, but that passed until he rode the horse equally well in or out of the saddle. Tod loved best to ride with the horse's warm hide against his own bare legs, to feel the strength of the rolling muscles, the sense of his own domination over a powerful beast.

Tod never asked nor expected more of life than that he should be left alone in his single-minded devotion to Lucky.

Anyone, man or child, who asks so little from the gods he favours, is also asking for complications to come into his life. The other stable boys soon discovered that he could be turned into a miniature fury when a handful of feed was snatched from his horse. But Tod was fortunate, in a way, that these louts did not dare to do anything that would harm Lucky. Kelly was too alert for that, and they all feared Kelly. But the big bay was a thoroughbred, and as such he was touchy and flash-tempered. Tickling his ear with a long straw, letting the hose in the next loose-box slip so that a stream of water hit him while he was dozing, brought displays of fury from the horse that were very secondary to Tod's.

Finally Tod really lost his temper and chased two of the boys with a rake. One tripped as the other ran off laughing, and Tod leaped like a tiger at the fallen one. He raised the rake in both hands and brought it down on the boy's back. The boy stopped laughing. A white boy would have yelled for help, and would probably have been taken to a doctor. The black boy washed away the blood and returned to work, and, in his happy-go-lucky way, he did not hold it against Tod. As for Tod, he was neither pleased with himself, nor ashamed. He had protected Lucky in the only way he knew. Kelly spoke his piece, and Tod's horse was left alone. To Tod himself, Kelly said nothing.

Nakimer stood on his veranda eyeing his string of horses as they streamed up from the creek for their evening feed. They drifted rather than walked towards the stable. In ones and twos they went slowly up the slope sniffing the air, bending their beautiful heads for an occasional pull at a sweet root of clover, nipping a flank here or there so that small squeals pierced the sluggish air above the long pale finger of sunlight lying on the grass, and the grotesquely elongated shadows spread across the land. With each munch, each playful nip, the horses drifted a little nearer to the stable yard.

Lucky was the last to leave the creek and Tod made a small black blot on his back. The horse stood fetlock-deep in the gently rippling water, dipping his mouth into the stream, letting it run cool and sweet over his tongue, lifting a large hoof and pawing the water so that the little boy was clothed in diamond-clear spray, and the shining hide darkened as the spray sank in. Tod remembered Swy Boy, and his sharp eyes kept a look-out for the living death that must not touch Lucky.

From the distance Tod heard the sound of a car pulling up at the homestead. He was not interested. Cars came and went fairly frequently, so there was nothing strange about it. When Lucky topped the bank, Tod saw a dirty station wagon drawn up before the homestead steps. Nakimer stood between two strange men, all three leaning on the veranda steps. The little boy felt a thrill of pride when he saw the strangers straighten up when their eyes strayed to Lucky.

Riding bareback, Tod gave his own kind of message to the horse. Lucky broke into a long-paced, lazy gallop, moving beautifully. Nakimer's hard, old face broke into a smile, he cupped his mouth with his hands and shouted, "Bring 'im this way, boy!"

"What's *that* ridin' your horse, Jim?"

Nakimer chuckled as Tod wheeled the big bay and cantered slowly towards the three men. "That's Lucky Boy's groom, and they don't come any better. Been with the colt ever since 'e was foaled. The boy can do anything with 'im."

"Risin' four, is he?"

"Yeah, an' the boy's risin' ten, an' you better not get any ideas about either of 'em! The gelding's by By Chance out of Lucky Bess. Lucky Boy's goin' down to Frank Howell's stable pretty soon. Would've gone before this, only Frank's 'ad trouble in the stable. Come on down, 'ave a good look at 'im—and hands off!"

The men laughed and followed Nakimer. They stood looking at the horse with admiration, at the boy with amusement. Tod was thrilled at the attention Lucky was getting. Nakimer ran his gnarled old hand against the hair so that the men could see the dark hide of the Arab strain. When they finished their inspection Nakimer put his hand on Lucky's neck and looked up at Tod.

"Boy, I want Lucky given a good work-out every day, never less than twenty miles, more if 'e needs it. I want 'im hardened up over distance—"

One of the men broke in, speaking in an amazed voice. "Are you goin' to let the kid take on the gelding?"

Nakimer nodded. " 'E'll come to no harm with Tod." It never occurred to the old man that the question might have applied to Tod's safety. "Take 'im away boy, 'e's all yours."

Tod's heart swelled with pride. He turned Lucky towards the gate and took him through in style. Nakimer had said "he's all yours", and Tod took that quite literally. Lucky was his, his to train and look after, all his, Nakimer had said so.

Tod had so little to do with the other stable hands that in his ten years he had learned very little about the financial workings of a stable. Never having handled any money himself, he had no realization that it was a necessity for Nakimer. It did not occur to him that if a horse was beautiful, as Lucky was, that beauty was not an end in itself. It did not enter his head that Lucky would not always be with him, as he was now, fit, beautiful, a part of Booramby—and his. Nakimer had said so.

That night, lying in the straw only a few feet

from Lucky's polished hooves, Tod fell asleep the happiest boy in the world.

Tod's first contact with a world beyond the confines of Booramby was when he began riding Lucky over the brown paddocks. Then, perhaps because Aborigines are the children of movement, he began to crave for the land that instinct told him lay beyond the horizon he could see. He was interested in every gully, every rock. He discovered great craggy formations that rose from the plains. The biggest of these was known to white men as Red Rocks; to the Aborigines it was Jungaburra, the Place of Spirits.

Red Rocks rose in the surprising way of Australia's rocky formations, straight from the level of the creek's banks, and in one place straddling the water. It looked as though some enormous monolith, four times the size of Ayers Rock, had been forced upwards by fierce internal fires to burst through the primeval earth. The pressure that caused the birth of the great rock had also shattered it, spreading boulders for five miles over the land, leaving the centre heaped into a hill of flaming red rock surrounded by other great pieces, some now worn and mellowed by wind and rain, all enormous like some giant's playthings.

Rocks spanned the creek in a big arch and turned the banks into tall red precipices that shadowed a narrow-beached Eden, a place of sand and red walls and blue water, secret and still, touched only by a narrow band of sunlight at midday.

Strange footprints marked the morning sand, lively rock wallabies and euros, those kangaroos of the heights, sat grooming themselves on the topmost rocks against a changing sky. For the Aborigines Red Rocks was a place of great magic and fearsome spirits, and no Abo would go there at night. The wandering tribes gave it a wide berth, and only sometimes when it was growing dark after dusk, would elders go in among the red magic.

Tod had been so little with his tribe that such superstitions had passed him by. He had never heard of Jungaburra. Riding across the flat paddocks until the curve of the world came to meet him and the horizon moved on, the secret places were no longer hidden from him. He would ride among the fallen red giants, then leave Lucky in the shade and explore on foot.

He rode out day after day, and each day Lucky rested and Tod searched for he knew not what. He found tribal pictures, the outlines of animals he knew. He chanced upon a narrow defile forming the entrance to a rock-walled sandy strip where the river divided and made a long slim island between two forks. Here Tod would lead Lucky across to feed on the fresh, sweet, green grass of the island.

Tod became possessed by Red Rocks. He explored every foot of them. When the heat beat down he discovered an underground entrance to caves formed by the splitting or movement of rocks not quite born, sunken in earth cooled by the summer rain while above there was a kind of jagged

city, a flowering of primeval fires. There were partially torn and exploded rocks that even the savage fires could not force to the surface, a place of great hollows, damp and cool and vast.

Tod felt a certain nervousness about losing his way, so he carried his knife in his hand and cut and scraped at rocks so that he could retrace his footsteps.

It was after a month of this that Perina Greer, great-niece of the missus and Nakimer, arrived at Booramby to stay a while. Her arrival was not with the missus' consent. Perina, whose name was the Aboriginal for "Kingfisher", and who was only twenty, should not, in the missus' view, be allowed to stay in her great-uncle's company, even though chaperoned by the missus herself.

But Nakimer had insisted that Perina must come when his nephew, Perina's father, died and left her an orphan. So she came for her long holiday from her Teachers' Training College when she no longer had a home to go to, and the missus could not refuse to have her.

So one hot day when the dust-devils were whirling across the plain, Perina travelled as a passenger in Mick the mailman's old car after leaving the plane at Longreach, taking a second plane to Gilgi.

Perina was blonde like all the Greers, an even paler blonde than Nakimer and Cora. Her long, straight hair seemed almost white in contrast to her round, sunburnt young face and very blue eyes.

Tod, riding Lucky back from Red Rocks in the cool of the evening, saw the stranger in the mail car when he was three or four miles from home. Perina saw a small boy on a big horse and said to Mick, "Good gracious! Look at that tiny fellow on that great horse!"

Mick laughed. "That's Tod ridin' Lucky Boy. That kid's as much of a horse as Lucky himself. 'E's been around the stable ever since 'e could walk. Nakimer's sendin' Lucky down to the trainer and I don't think Tod knows about it, not yet."

"Poor little boy. Will he mind?"

"Reckon 'e will."

As they drove on Perina thought uneasily about Tod. She knew what it meant to lose a loved horse, and she felt that, unlike herself, an Abo boy would have so little with which to fill the empty place it would leave in his heart.

A dust-devil, whirling dry earth, leaves, sticks and anything else it could gather in its dancing dash across the plain, chose to veer erratically and whirl itself over the car. Its giddily turning column was broken, dry detritus almost choking the two in the mail car. Perina forgot about Tod. Mick stopped the car and they got out and shook themselves before driving on as the shattered whirlwind gathered itself together twenty yards away and waltzed off into the distance.

Nakimer and the missus were on the veranda to greet Perina. She laughed over the rivulets of dust that still coursed down her clothing and shook herself like a dog before she joined her great-aunt and uncle on the veranda.

Aunt Cora took her away to unpack and shower but Nakimer stood looking towards the plain, away over the tops of the casuarinas and paperbarks lining the banks of the creek. Beyond them he saw the slow-cantering shape of Lucky, and the featureless dot that was the boy riding him. He watched Tod ride across the creek and up the hill to the stable, and he was well satisfied. The long rides were giving the horse durability. In a few weeks he'd send him to Frank Howells' stables in Brisbane to begin training and to have the fast gallops that would put an edge on him. It would be time enough to tell Tod when the day came for the horse to go.

Nakimer glanced back at the distant plain. Five of his stockmen were riding their weary horses homewards. It might be a good thing to send Tod out to learn stock work when Lucky left. He left the railing and went to shower for dinner.

Perina towelled her newly-washed hair vigorously and twisted it up into an old-fashioned knot on her neck, put on a thin frock and open shoes, and left her room. She had never been to Booramby before; her parents had discouraged the idea, probably for much the same reasons as those that aroused the missus' disapproval.

The girl looked about her, guessing the long buildings on her right to be the famed stables, where the horses would be feeding in their loose-boxes. She had seen her uncle's horses race and a

Booramby stockhorse had once wiped the board at a country town rodeo. She had all her family's feeling for horses, which was why she had been so determined to visit the source of so many beautiful thoroughbreds.

Aunt Cora called to someone from what Perina supposed was the kitchen, and she crossed the wooden bridge onto the other creeper-covered veranda. In the distance she could hear the pulsing of the dynamo that ran the electricity. Over against the veranda wall and next to a big generator stood a large meat-safe and at that moment Tod appeared round the corner of the veranda, clearly on his way to the special place where the missus kept food for him.

It never occurred to Tod to be grateful to the missus for his plentiful food, any more than Lucky gave a horse's thanks to Tod for his care.

Tod stopped when he saw Perina. She looked at the child and wondered if he were Tod. She smiled at him and Tod stared in astonishment at the pale shining of her hair.

"Hello, you're Tod, aren't you?"

Tod removed his eyes from her hair and looked down, putting one hard-soled foot on top of the other in a gesture of embarrassment as she went on, "Won't you talk to me, Tod?"

Tod did not have many words with which to talk, but he did say Hello, very shyly.

"Are you looking for anyone?" she asked.

Tod shook his head, and Perina went on, "I saw

you on my way here. You were riding such a beautiful horse. I was told his name is Lucky."

Tod's face lit up. Perina did not have to be told that Lucky was the way to Tod's heart.

"How old is Lucky?" she asked.

"Risin' four, miss." Tod was surprised at the "miss". He had never spoken to a strange white girl before.

"I hope you'll let me come to the stable to see Lucky again?"

Tod tried to hide his pride. This girl with the strange hair asked *his* permission to see Lucky! Well, she should. Hadn't Nakimer said Lucky was *his* horse? Then the missus came from the kitchen and took Perina back to the house, but not before Perina smiled at Tod again and said, "Good night, Tod, I'll see you tomorrow."

Tod was secretly thrilled. As the two reached the veranda opposite, he went on to the edge, parted the creepers, and watched them out of sight. Then he went to the safe and took out his dinner. He carried it back to the stable to eat, and sat on the straw in the corner, talking to Lucky as he ate.

"I bet you'd like a hide that colour, Lucky," he told his horse. "No, it wasn't grey, not really," he argued with himself, "it was kind of goldy-silvery," and with his limited vocabulary that was the best he could do.

The missus disapproved of Perina's friendship with Tod, and Perina, being of a more honest generation, had a good idea why. She looked at her uncle, and thought of Tod's small creamy face, and refused to let Aunt Cora interfere. As Aunt Cora could not give any good reason why Perina should not make friends with Tod, she merely looked her disapproval when Perina left for the stable to see her friends, Tod and Kelly.

Kelly chose a lively chestnut mare with two white feet as Perina's mount. She won Tod's heart by pretending to know less about the care of horses than she did, and asking him to teach her to look after the mare herself. She cheerfully carried her own horse's feed and water, and groomed Charm as carefully as if she had been Tod himself.

Often Perina rode out with Tod, and for the first five miles they would jog along together. Then she would notice that Tod was becoming restive. He would say that he must take Lucky along at a pace that would be too fast for Charm, and Perina understood that she was not wanted. She never pressed the boy to give her reasons, but turned her horse and cantered back home. Tod liked her for this almost more than he liked her for her admiration for Lucky.

PERINA

SOMETIMES Perina rode out with her great-uncle to where he wanted to look over his stock in the far paddocks. They would take their lunches in their saddlebags, stop near water and boil the billy, and ride on again. And all the time Nakimer's sharp old eyes took in the condition of his cattle clustered under the sparse trees, drinking from the creek or from troughs fed by the windmills, or just scattered about, feeding.

At other times, when cattle- or horse-buyers arrived, Perina joined them to drive out where the cattle had been mustered by the stockmen early in the day. They would be held on a cattle ramp, a piece of flat land where a half-moon of sturdy fencing held the cattle within its curve, and a sleepy man on horseback patrolled the open front of the half-circle and kept the cattle in position.

It was rather a surprise to Perina, interested in education, that no provision was made for schooling the handful of Aboriginal children from the blacks' camp on the creek bank. She was less surprised when she walked past the littered, deserted camp one day. The tribe had gone on walkabout. All the same, a school inspector should have visited Booramby, isolated though it was.

Nakimer treated the idea of Aborigine education with lordly disdain. "Don't do the blacks any good. Much better leave 'em alone."

"I'm teaching Tod to read and to do little sums. He's quicker than any child I've ever taught.' '

"Don't go spoilin' 'im, Perina. I know Tod's pretty bright. He only wants horses; he can get those here."

"Are you sending Lucky down to the trainer soon?"

"Yeah, as soon as Frank Howells gives the word."

"But losing Lucky'll break Tod's heart. He told me once, so proudly, 'Nakimer says Lucky's *my* horse'."

" 'E'll get over it. Lucky's goin' as soon as Frank can 'ave him."

Perina did not answer, but she worried for Tod. Lucky's going would strip Tod of the one thing in his world. Kelly told her the tragedy of Swy Boy. That had been a kind of death for Tod. Now he must die a little again, and there was nothing she could do, except understand.

Perina opened new worlds for Tod. It started when they leaned on the stable fence and watched the youngsters coming up from the creek. Lucky and another big fellow began a playful fight, pawing at each other with their forelegs, extending their necks to bite and squeal, manes tossing, eyes wild.

This made Perina tell Tod how the knights of old trained their horses in battle movements, how to war with each other while their masters fought.

She found she had first to explain to Tod what she meant by "of old", and then what "knights" were. Poor Perina struggled to make him understand. When she mentioned the courage and endurance of the white horses of the Carmargue that were first bred by Caesar, she found herself really in the soup! What with France and Caesar she never really got it all ironed out to Tod's satisfaction.

With the aid of a small atlas in the back of a note-book, she tried to give Tod some idea of the world that lay beyond Australia, and the "tribes" that lived in the various countries, but she was never sure how much the world took the place for him that fairytales would for another child. How could this child understand when he had never seen the sea, or even a train—though, paradoxically, he had seen planes flying overhead, and cars were an every-day event for him.

A plane flew over during Perina's stay. Tod heard the droning of the engine long before she did, and she followed him out of the stable and watched the little boy's awed face as he watched the most enormous bird, with the insignia of the Royal Flying Doctor Service on its wings, flying overhead. Perina tried to tell him that it was man-made, and that the giant "bird" carried people in its belly, and then she stopped. It was obvious that as something made by man it had little value for Tod, but as a bird, greater and swifter, stronger that the finest wedgetailed eagle, it was filled with magic for him, so she left it that way.

Perina felt the tension of the passing carefree days that must end when Tod lost Lucky Boy. She worried whether she should tell him now, or leave the telling as long as possible. She decided it was kinder to give the boy fresh interests, but Tod's single-mindedness defeated her. She persisted, going through all the papers that came by the weekly mail car and cutting out any items she thought might interest Tod. These items were always, in one way or another, connected with horses.

Nakimer was sitting surrounded by newly-opened papers when Perina came up from the stables.

"Take a look 'ere—" He held out a photograph of a row of eight horses. "Ever heard of Quarter Horses?"

"Of course," Perina said promptly. "I've seen them at work; they're wonderful stock horses. The Armstrongs of Pintara have five of them."

"Well *I've* not seen them, but I've 'eard about them. Sounded like a lot of tommyrot to me. But these pictures look pretty good, eh?"

Perina laughed and leaned over the back of her uncle's chair. She had a great affection for the old ruffian, and she respected his knowledge of horses. Anything else about him she did not consider her business.

"Aren't they lovely?" she said. "Why don't you buy some, they're marvellous after cattle. You know they're called 'Quarter Horses' because they're the fastest ever over a quarter of a mile?"

He nodded, and pointed at a side-view of one of the Quarter Horses. " 'Ave they all got couplings curvin' down like that?" She looked at the short, strong curve of the horse's back, and muscular loins as he went on, "I s'pose that's where they get their speed?"

"All the ones I've seen have those lines. They're so sturdy, and they're good-tempered, too—not cranky like your Thoroughbreds," she teased him.

He grunted and took the paper back from her, studying the pictures.

"May I have those pictures to show Tod, please?"

"Take the lot, but let me have them back. I might make a few inquiries."

"Might? Just let anyone try to stop you!" And Perina went off to get dressed.

The daily rides went on until, one day, Tod said nothing about Perina turning back. She rode beside him until the homestead disappeared over the curve of the world. The sky was filled with the black, floating forms of big kites; scavengers moving in an endless pattern against the blue of the sky, above the red blot of a dead beast on the vast, sunburnt plain.

Perina looked away from the mesmeric, moving shapes in the sky. Just appearing over the far edge of the world was the top of a hill of broken rock, blazing redly in the sunshine. Minute by minute a strange, miniature world of colour and harshness unfolded before them, a world so vivid that it hurt her eyes, so stark, so infinitely strange, that she felt frightened.

She glanced at Tod's face. It wore an inward expression as of some mystery about to unfold, and she did not ask where they were riding. The kites were mere specks against the sky, a stillness, a dryness, surrounded them, and the heat reflected back from the rocks intensified.

The flaming redness made it seem that they were riding into an inferno as they passed through great broken arches, until at last they went in single file down a slope so steep that the horses dragged their hind hooves like brakes. There below lay the creek, its cool greenness reflecting the red cliff-sides.

Tod led the way through the last opening. A long narrow island clothed in blessed green split the water. It was edged with sand, red as the rocks from which it had been ground by the ages into infinitesimal grains crunching beneath their horses' hooves.

Charm and Lucky were soon stirrup-deep in the water, and then climbed onto the strange wedge of bright green grass that made the red landscape even more bizarre. The horses cropped the grass with relish.

"What a beautiful place, Tod, I didn't know—"

Tod broke in, smiling proudly, "No-one really knows but me. The men say 'things' come out of rocks and get you. They won't get me, Lucky's too fast!"

"Why hasn't Nakimer brought me here?"

"It's too hot. Nakimer doesn't like caves, no-one does. Besides, I think Nakimer's afraid of the—things. Kelly is. Two men got lost here once. No-one ever found them."

"Aren't you afraid?"

Tod looked surprised. "No, why should I be?"

Perina reflected that Tod had never seen or read anything designed to make his skin creep.

Soon the sun would be over the narrow gorge. Tod and Perina unsaddled their horses, and ate their lunch on the shadowy side. Then Perina kicked off her boots and swam in shirt and shorts and Tod joined her. Their bodies cooled, they stretched out and fell asleep in the shade near the rocks whose substance held the fires of aeons of sunlight. Tod woke first and when Perina opened her eyes he said, "Come on, I'll show you some pictures."

Perina followed Tod deep into a great pile of broken rocks and through an opening hidden in rocky folds, just big enough to admit a horse. She found herself in a dim labyrinth of caves where for an hour Tod showed her the pictures on the wall, crude drawings of Aborigines and animals. She was half sorry and half relieved when Tod led her outside again.

It was a measure of Tod's trust in her that he never actually asked her not to talk about Red Rocks to Nakimer or Kelly, but Perina knew instinctively that Tod trusted her to be silent.

After that first day, Tod and Perina paid many visits to the caves at Red Rocks. Perina enjoyed seeing Tod's pliant little figure riding beside her on the big horse. Tod was fascinated by Perina's colouring, her pale hair, brown face and very blue eyes. She once described a Palomino to him, and he became obsessed by the idea of a horse with a mane and tail like Perina's hair. They ate picnic lunches, swam and dozed in the coolness of a cave, and the girl was glad that no-one showed any interest in the destination of their rides.

Nakimer announced that he was thinking of having a weir built across the creek, and that an engineer was coming to stay for a few days to determine the best site. He was also to look at the Windmill Dam, twenty miles from the homestead, to see if it could be enlarged. Booramby was lucky in having Mooti Creek, which seldom dried up, but water in the far paddocks was a dicey question, as it always is in Australia.

Donald Mackenzie, the engineer recommended to Nakimer by the firm to which he sold his wool in Brisbane, arrived one evening. Perina looked with interest over her uncle's shoulder at the rough map of Mooti Creek he was showing Mackenzie. The map was spread out on the dining-room table beneath a pool of light, and Perina looked curiously at the place marked "Red Rocks" about which Mackenzie was questioning the old man.

"That? We call it 'Red Rocks'. The Abo name is Jungaburra. Never go near the place. Hot as the hobs of hell. Nothin' much grows there. It's too big to cart away so we just leave it."

Mackenzie was solemn and middle-aged, but he enjoyed the company of young people, and he suggested that Perina might like to go with them the next day when he wanted to get an over-all view of Mooti Creek.

Perina went to the stables to find Tod early the next morning. She found him grooming Lucky and playing a game with him. Tod tickled Lucky with the end of the brush, and Lucky bided his time and gave Tod a brisk nip when he caught him off guard. Both were so obviously happy and absorbed that Perina found the idea of parting them unbearable. She tried to forget it while she told Tod about the new dam. Tod was disappointed. He had looked forward to a day's exploring with Perina, and now he would have to go alone, and in another direction.

"I hope they don't touch the Rocks," Tod said anxiously.

"I don't think they will. Uncle just wants to keep away from them. I should think they'd make the dam before the creek goes through Red Rocks."

In a way, she proved to be right.

Perina enjoyed the day out. She loved the vast plains brown beneath a sun that seemed as warm and as solid as beer, and once stopped to watch the rustling of a patch of long, pale golden grass until a perentie emerged like a small alligator. It was seven feet long and wheeled its way slowly through the dry stems, head up, sensitive forked tongue tasting the air, hoping to find a ground nest, or to climb the nearest tree and look for young birds in hollow boughs.

Sometimes kangaroos broke cover. A herd of the charming red ones came up the Mooti's bank and bounded off across the plain looking like a flight of low-flying birds. Red kangaroos are the most graceful of their species, skimming along in leaps that are perfectly balanced by their long tail which never touches the ground as they "fly".

The creek curved and twisted, and Mackenzie often stopped to examine the banks. It ran for nearly forty miles through Booramby, so tracing it was a slow process. It had meant an early morning start with kookaburras laughing in the trees, and movement among the animals which had not yet gone into hiding after the early-morning drink.

Mackenzie lingered longest on the bank about a quarter of a mile above Red Rocks. He returned to the car and they skirted the fantastic, rocky world and went on. It was five in the afternoon before they turned back towards home. Mackenzie had his sketch of the creek, his assessment of the best place for the weir, and that evening he and Nakimer chose two sites for further reconnaissance.

Next day Mackenzie made a more detailed examination of the sites they had chosen, and then drove across country to look at the Windmill Dam that Nakimer wanted enlarged. It was evening when they returned to the homestead, and Perina went down to the stables to find Tod, and to thank him for taking care of Charm. He was curled up drowsily on the straw in Lucky's stable. Lucky was drowsy too. He snuffed at Perina, and she rubbed his ears until he shook her off impatiently. She said goodnight and walked back to the house.

The next day Mackenzie left to organize his gang and the materials he needed. Perina and Tod resumed their rides, and the day of her departure drew nearer. She worried about Tod, and questioned Nakimer about the date when Lucky was to be sent to Brisbane.

"Funny you askin' that, girl. This letter that came today's from Frank Howells. He's ready for the horse, so I s'pose 'e'll be on 'is way in a day or day."

"I will have to go soon. Will you let me travel in the car that pulls the horsebox?"

"What d'you want to do *that* for? You'll have a much longer journey."

"I don't mind that, I think it might comfort Tod if I was with Lucky. Or will you let him go too?"

"The boy stays here," the old man said sourly.

"All right, then let me go. Kelly won't mind."

"Sounds daft to me, you goin' by train instead of plane. Anyway, you do what you like." He looked at the girl's distressed face and went on, "Don't waste yer pity on Tod. 'E's got to learn I breed horses for profit. I can't 'ave the stableboys breakin' their 'earts every time a horse leaves 'ere."

"Tod can't help loving Lucky the way he does.

Be gentle with him, please. He's going to be so unhappy."

"Mackenzie's takin' Tod out to the dam with 'im. Says 'e needs a useful nipper. But first 'e'll be campin' out with the stockmen when they start bringin' the cattle in. Time 'e learned stock work."

Perina nodded. "Yes, I suppose that's the best for Tod."

Nakimer scowled at her. "I'm not bein' kind to Tod. I'm bein' practical. A boy moonin' over a horse is no use to me. You can tell 'im, if you like, I'm gettin' three of those Quarter Horse mares you were talkin' about. They'll be 'ere next time you come. They're in England at the moment in quarantine. Howells is fixin' it for me. I only 'ope they're as good as you say, or you look out! The mares 're in foal—appears there was some kind of slip-up. They're part of a consignment of ten, an' I got 'em cheap because I'm takin' the risk over the sire."

"You'll let Tod look after them, won't you?"

"If 'e grows up and realizes a horse is just a horse—"

"But it isn't—not to Tod. And it never will be, so you'd better make up your mind to that. You'd better just accept that Tod has a kind of genius with horses, and no-one will ever care for those mares of yours in the way he will!"

"You'll be runnin' Booramby next!" the old man grumbled, but he gave her a strangely loving smile.

Perina found Aunt Cora sitting at the kitchen table darning socks. She kept house for her brother and joined him at meals, but she kept away from him otherwise. Perina thought how sad this was, for these two old people were really more apart than if they were living in different countries.

She slipped into a chair opposite the missus who, after years of almost silent living, found it difficult to open a conversation. Perina smiled at her.

"I do hate leaving. I've loved being here with you."

Miss Greer's face reddened with the effort as she said, "It's your home now. You must come back whenever you can—for good, if you want to."

"Thank you, Aunt Cora. I'll be back for all my holidays if you'll have me." She rose and went round the table and put her arms round the old woman's shoulders. "Dear Aunt Cora, you do worry so terribly about things that don't matter at all. I wish you wouldn't."

"Decency does matter."

"D'you know, what you call 'decency' doesn't seem to me half as important as the kindness you and Uncle Jim've shown me since I've been here." The old woman was silent. Perina went on, "Aunt Cora, will you do something else very kind for me?"

Aunt Cora gave the impression of a frightened horse shying, but she managed to ask, "What d'you want?"

Perina went back and sat in her own chair and leaned her elbows on the table. "Well, when I go back I want to write to Tod, and although he's learning to read he couldn't get through a whole letter about horses, which is what I want to send him now and again. I want to send him magazines and cuttings, too, and I'd be so grateful if you'd read them to him."

"Why don't you ask Nakimer?" The old voice was harsh. "He's the one who ought to read to the boy."

"No, he's not. He can't feel the way you do about things, so why should poor Tod be penalized for something about which he had no choice? You will do it for me, won't you?"

"I might."

Perina left her aunt and went down to the stables. She found Tod grooming Charm, while Lucky stood by gleaming like silk and stamping impatiently to remind Tod that it was nearly feed-time. Perina helped Tod, and then sat on the straw and talked to him.

"Tod, shall we take our lunch to Red Rocks tomorrow? I have to leave the next day."

Tod turned towards her, his small face filled with sorrow.

"You'll come back?"

"Yes, of course I will, and I'll write to you and send pictures and things all about the three Quarter Horse mares Nakimer is getting, the ones you are going to look after."

"I won't have much time if I have to exercise Lucky every day."

Perina's heart misgave her, but she only said, "Oh you'll find time. Think of those lovely mares, a new breed that nobody you know has even seen, and those three little foals that'll need you so much. Now listen while I tell you something. I've asked the missus to help you read my letters until you can read them all yourself."

Perina stopped talking, thinking to herself, "I am a coward, I just can't tell him about Lucky. Someone'll tell him tomorrow and he'll have one more night's happy sleep."

Tod did indeed have a peaceful night, and he had a happy day at his beloved Red Rocks with Lucky and Perina. On their return, when they were still far from home, Tod's keen eyes picked out the horsebox drawn up before the stable.

"The horsebox is out," he said uneasily. "I didn't know Nakimer was sending any of the horses away." He turned his head and looked at Perina, and she could not meet his eyes. She was torn by an unbearable misery. Tod, who had so little, must lose even that! Why couldn't Nakimer tell him? It was his doing. Or Kelly, or a stableboy—anyone! But she had always known that she must be the one to tell him.

"Tod, I think I should tell you something, and I can't bear to. You know that Lucky is racing stock and must go into training sometime. Well, that time is now."

She forced herself to meet Tod's eyes as they looked from his stricken face and he said unbelievingly, "But Nakimer said that Lucky was *mine*—"

"Tod, try to understand. Nakimer didn't mean it that way. Just think that Lucky's going to a good life. He'll be given everything. I asked to go with Kelly, and I'll look after him, and I'll go and see him and write to you about him."

"You knew—you knew they were taking Lucky!"

"Oh, Tod, don't! I couldn't tell you before."

In the silence she heard the faint creaking of the saddle, the silvery sound of the bit being jangled in a horse's mouth, and the air was full of the brave smell of healthy horses. Perina struggled with her tears and forced herself to look at Tod. She knew that nothing really mattered to him any more, nothing registered, except that after tomorrow he would not see his Lucky again.

* *

Clouds moved up over the clear, night sky, where an hour before stars glowed against the deep blue of space. Now they were blotted out one by one, eaten by the dark mouths of the advancing clouds. Tod lay on his folded blanket and gazed upwards at the disappearing worlds. His twelve-year-old body was very weary and he was glad of this, even if it meant that he was too tired to sleep. Weariness dulled the pain that was always with him because Lucky, his Lucky, was not on the greenhide line that held the night horses a few paces away. The moaning of the cattle rose and fell like the surge of the sea on a lonely shore.

Night brings man his saddest memories. The man-child Tod thought of the day when he had stood alone on the hillside and watched Lucky being taken away in the horsebox. Perina had been there; she had leaned out of the car and waved. He had stood very still but it was only his body that stood there; his spirit had been with Lucky as the horsebox became smaller and smaller in the distance.

When it returned it was as empty as his own heart, and Kelly, who had taken Lucky, no longer seemed his friend. Tod was unconscious of the fact that Kelly and Nakimer had come to stand behind him. In spirit he was totally alone. Then Nakimer put his gnarled old hand on Tod's small shoulder, and Tod's spirit had come back into his body in one fierce, painful thrust. His face was a mask of grief and hatred, and one hard little fist struck at the hand on his shoulder as he stumbled away.

"Let 'im go boss," Kelly said. " 'E'll be back."

Kelly was right. The next morning Tod came back to the stable. In silence he had gone about the work of attending to his string of horses. Now, lying there in the fading starlight with the boneless dark closing around him, the boy tortured himself with memories.

Within three days Tod and a bigger stableboy, Alf, were made horse-tailers to the droving plant that was to go to the farthest reaches of Booramby to round up Nakimer's great herd of cattle, so that the boss could make his own selection for sale or for slaughter.

Tod and Alf were to look after the stockmen's remounts. Tod had never been on a drove, and when he learned he could choose his own horse from the spare ones, he chose an old fellow with a box-like head and no particular merits. Tod lavished love and care on his strange choice, feeling that here was one horse Nakimer would not want to take from him. Jake was a strong, ugly beast, and he was happy and a little bewildered by a care and affection he had never known before.

Tod turned restlessly in his blanket and his hip touched a hard grey object. It was a rather ancient dictionary. It reminded him of something else. In those grim days before the men had ridden out leading a droving plant consisting of five stockmen, a cook in a small wagon laden with food, blankets, spare saddles and other necessities, and followed by the string of thirty horses kept in line by Tod and Alf, Tod had always found something extra nice to eat left for him. He hadn't been able to eat very much just then, but out of the wilderness he lived in had come a faint pleasure that the missus had thought of him. Some instinct made him take the food and discard it later.

Then, on the last evening before the drove, a letter came from Perina, posted at their first stop. The missus gave it to him, and Tod stood looking blankly at the envelope. He had never had a letter before. He knew this one would be about Lucky, and wanted with all his heart to read it. He held it out silently to the missus.

Miss Greer, her voice rusty from lack of use, read it, and Tod heard Perina had just given Lucky a feed and brushed him down. Both she and Lucky missed Tod and thought about him. Lucky was going to make him very proud when he won his first race. And all the time the harsh old voice had gone on reading, sorrow and longing closed over Tod's head in the way that water folds over a drowning man. Perina had finished by writing that she would send him a long letter later on. She added how she wished she could be with Tod when the three little foals were born. Then she sent her love to Aunt Cora and Nakimer, but Tod stopped listening. His misery and longing had gone so deep that the outside world was just not there for him.

The missus returned the letter to the envelope and then she thrust it into his hand and he held it automatically. From far away her voice had begun to disturb him. He stood there listening to life flowing turgidly back into his body as the missus went away and then reappeared holding out a small, scruffy book to him. Tod looked at it without touching it. Then she had spoken crossly because she could not bear to look at that small face exhausted by sorrow.

"Take it! Take it, boy. Then perhaps you'll be able to read the next letter yourself."

He looked down at the thing in his hand. It was the dictionary that now, three weeks later and thirty miles away, he felt lying hard against his hip. At first the dictionary seemed just a great big muddle, then he attacked it determinedly. He began at the "A's", skipping the big words and picking out the words he knew, learning how they were spelt, and what they really meant.

When they stopped through the day to rest men, horses and cattle exhausted by the heat, he took out his dictionary and struggled with it. Progress was slow, but it was *progress*! How, starting from almost nothing, could it fail to be? After a few weeks he was rather proud of the number of words he recognized and could spell. He was quick to learn and he had a visual memory as well as an ear for sound. At first he worked doggedly, then he began to enjoy it.

Gradually, long days in the saddle and nights under the stars hardened Tod mentally and physically. It was not that he loved Lucky less; it was simply that life does not stand still. Now it seemed to him that he had known and loved Lucky in another life. He never lessened his care for all the horses, and he became more friendly with the men. They knew that he was the best horse-tailer they had ever known. Their mounts were better cared for, and so their days were less tiring. Their approval warmed Tod.

Jake, Tod's old horse, nibbled and nuzzled him, greeting him with a small, snuffling whicker. At night Tod fastened Jake on the end of the horse-line, and put his blanket nearby so that Jake could blow and snuff round his neck to reassure himself that the boy was really there. Often Tod opened his eyes and saw the square, ugly head a black blur against the shining sky, and he would put up his hand and rub the old ears lovingly.

Jake was neither young nor beautiful, but he was strong and experienced. His heart, that had never known the love there can be between man and horse, became centred on Tod. He even acquired a certain sleekness, tried rather clumsy curvets, or gave Tod playful nips with his yellow teeth. Tod bore the nips stoically; the old fellow's affection, his obviously increased pleasure in living, warmed the boy's heart as nothing else could.

Tod had always slept near horses. He liked their sleepy movements and stirrings, and the warm smell of hides mingled with the ammonia pungency of damp grass.

As the new Tod emerged from the shell of the old, he and Alf, the other horse-tailer, became friends. Tod's absorption in the horses made Alf more interested and he groomed and examined hooves with a zeal second only to Tod's.

Alf came from the camp on the banks of the Mooti. He was fifteen, veteran of a dozen walkabouts, a true member of his tribe, and a full Abo. He was more friendly, if less intelligent than Tod.

Often when Tod sat frowning at his dictionary, his lips trying to form words, Alf sat on the same log and made boomerangs or spear-hafts. When Tod was tired of "studying", he watched Alf and sometimes copied what he was doing. Then the boys would try out boomerang or spear, and Alf would show Tod how to shape and throw a returning boomerang, or how to mould a spear-shaft so that it turned like a bullet shot from a rifle as it whistled through the air. In the competition that followed Tod learned something of the ancient ways of hunting still used by the tribes. He learned far more than a white boy would have in the same time, for he had the inborn knowledge of his race, which is something no-one can teach.

Every couple of days, the growing mob of cattle would be spelled somewhere near water, while a couple of the stockmen scoured the plains, searched under clumps of trees, visited waterholes and creek beds, and brought the cattle they found back to join the big mob.

Once the night air vibrated hollowly to the drumming of hooves as in the half-darkness, a herd of galloping creatures plunged furiously through the camp and away. The horses on the night-line reared and whinnied and it was all Tod and Alf could do to quieten them. Tod thought a herd of brumbies, the wild horses of the Australian bush, had rushed through the camp, but when it was light he saw by the imprints of the small, unshod hooves that the galloping creatures had been a mob of wild donkeys.

A few nights after this, the leader of a brumby herd, a great, wild bony stallion came sweeping in from the plains, leaving his own forty or more mares miles away while he plunged among the camp's tethered mares. He nipped their rumps, urging them to break away, and finally went off with one of them. Like the Aboriginal, the wild stallion knows a great many things without being taught. Taking mares is the only way a wild stallion can bring new blood into his herd, and a good herd needs new blood. Drovers, and lone travellers sleeping in the bush with their riding mare or a pack-mare hobbled nearby, must be on the alert to stop these one-horse forays.

Tod was furious at losing the mare, but the stockmen dissuaded him from following her. The stallion, his old wives and his new, would be far away by dawn, perhaps hiding in some red-walled cranny in the hillside that appeared to have been sliced apart by a giant's sword, a cranny large enough to hold a regiment. Brumbies know all these and every narrow gorge leading to freedom.

The men drove the cattle slowly before them, inwards from the vast perimeter of Booramby. Gradually they came within the fenced land where the grass was fresher, and long troughs led away from the windmills whose tattered sails wheeled against the sky, making sudden rushes of water spill over the troughs until the air was delicious with the scent of damp earth.

Tod learned something of cattle work. He learned to shoe horses with the best of them; to line saddles; mend halters and bridles; to cope with a hundred emergencies inseparable from the massed movement of animals. He grew taller and stronger, and the affection between Jake and himself became something special for them both.

Gradually Tod looked forward to returning to the stables, but he enjoyed this healing world of wind and sunshine. He began to think of the promised Quarter Horses, and to look forward to their arrival. Of Nakimer he thought with reserve. He could not forget the way Lucky had been taken from him, and he returned to Booramby bigger, wiser and tougher. He seldom thought of his mother, Addie; their relationship was much as it might have been had she been a mare and he a foal. They scarcely recognized each other in their brief passings.

The wind blew from the west. Nakimer stood on the Booramby veranda and looked towards the infinite splendour of the setting sun. He heard a sound that was scarcely a sound, a low, continuous murmur. It became a moaning carried to him by the steady force of the wind. The last exhausted rays of the sun touched the old man as he waited, turning the hairs on his brown arms to golden dust as he gripped the railing. He listened, making certain that what he heard was the sound he had been waiting for. He turned away and went down the steps and on to the stable to tell Kelly that the cattle were coming.

Nakimer passed the missus giving a flower bed its evening watering, and he told her the cattle were coming, but she did not answer. She was surprised to find herself grudgingly pleased at the sudden thought that Perina's letters awaiting Tod would give him the welcome home he most wanted. She treasured her own letters from Perina, but never shared them with Nakimer. Perina had known this would happen, so she also wrote to the old man now and again, smiling sadly at the thought that she must write separately to three people living in the same small world.

Next morning the old man stood again on his veranda watching for the dark line that he knew would soon be pushing its way over the curve of the world, growing, spreading, carrying its own orchestra. He enjoyed the sharp, high cries that rose like trumpet calls above the incessant moaning. Then he heard the stockwhips crack, the high, yipping calls of the men, saw the tossing horns gleaming in the sunlight. He listened to all the sounds, and saw the movements of a great herd that would fill the heart of any cattleman with joy. He went as lightly down the steps as a man half his age. From the stables he and Kelly, who had their horses ready saddled, rode out to meet the drovers.

The wide paddock into which the men eventually drove the herd of half-wild cattle stretched for many miles, and the grass and water had been left to lie fallow for this invasion. The cattle had access to three miles of winding creek. They would be driven into the half-moon stretch of the post-and-rails fence in mobs of about five hundred. There the boss would look them over and indicate his choice of those that were to be driven away on the first leg of their journey to the sale yards.

When all the great beasts were in the area of the paddock the men left them to scatter. Men, horses, tucker wagon, came on towards the homestead. Kelly and Nakimer rode near enough to be able to note the condition of the herd before they reined in their horses and waited for the stockmen to separate themselves from the cattle for the ride in.

Presently they came towards them, unshaven, dirty, weary. The head stockman appeared, and the two men rode to meet him. They greeted each other. The half-caste in charge of the drove sat with his thigh across the saddle. His long stockwhip was curled about his shoulder, he pushed his felt hat up from his sweaty forehead and his fingers scrabbled at his scalp under his lank, black hair. He spoke laconically.

"The cattle look pretty good, eh boss?" And the dirty, unshaven face he turned towards Nakimer was, underneath all this, no darker than Tod's.

Nakimer nodded and looked curiously at the rangy horse the man was riding, asking, "Horse-tailers do all right, Charlie?"

Charlie nodded. "Don't come no better than young Tod. Never seen 'orses stand up to a drove like this lot. There 'e comes now."

The two men followed his pointing, tobacco-stained finger. Tod and Alf, having let their string free, rode slowly out from behind the mob. Nakimer noticed Tod's horse.

"That old Jake the boy's ridin'?"

Charlie laughed and nodded. "The old feller goes like 'e was a colt again with young Tod."

Nakimer grunted and turned his horse, the others following. Behind them the cattle, weary after the day's journey, broke up into slow-moving clumps. The men on their horses and then the wagon moved off in a ragged line towards the homestead.

Tod rode on silently. Sometimes his small, horny hand dropped down onto Jake's big shoulder as if to comfort himself by the feel of his friend's warm hide. He rubbed him gently with his hard palm. The pain he had felt at parting with Lucky touched

him again in the familiar surroundings. It was not so fierce now; it flickered over him as a flame touches burnt-out wood, but the fuel was not there to turn it into the fire it once was. He wondered if there was any news of Perina; and Alf, tired of Tod's silence, rode on with the drovers.

Later, when Jake and the other horses had been attended to, Tod walked over to the house. The missus, watching for him although she did not admit it even to herself, thought how he had grown, matured. His small figure was as straight and lithe as ever, but she felt that whereas a child had ridden away, a man had come home. They greeted each other briefly.

"Here, there are two letters from Perina for you," said the missus. "Your supper's on your shelf. You can read your letters in the kitchen."

Tod felt a quick pride touch him. The missus had not said, "Do you want me to read them to you?" She had known he would try to read them himself. He pulled the tattered little dictionary from his pocket and said, "I've learned some words every day."

This was the longest conversation he had ever had with the missus. Now she nodded and turned away so that he would not see the gratified expression on her face. Tod took his letters into the kitchen.

He ate his supper quickly so as to get all other things out of the way. Then he sat down on a wooden chair, put the two unopened letters in front of him and examined the address. *Tod, C/o Miss Greer*. For the first time Tod wondered why he had no other name. Then he opened the fattest envelope and pulled out several sheets of paper wrapped around something. He unfolded the paper and inside he found a snapshot of Perina standing by Lucky's head. Tod's heart leapt with excitement.

In all his life the boy had owned precisely nothing. Now he had two letters, a photo and an old dictionary. He knew immediately that he wanted a book so that he could practise reading. Tod was well on the way towards the civilized mania of owning things.

Perina had written in a clear, round hand, but it was handwriting, and Tod's only reading had been in print. He bent his head and struggled doggedly to read the first page. Here and there he deciphered a word, but because so many were unrecognizable the page made little sense. He felt humiliated, and he began again. Before he reached the end of the page he felt, rather than heard, the missus come into the room. She carried a cheap, lined writing pad in her hand, and several pencil stubs. He said nothing, but he looked up at her and his dark eyes were shadowy with despair. She did not speak either as she drew up a chair beside him. She put the pad on the table in front of him.

"You don't know the alphabet," she said. "You can't read or write until you know that."

She wrote it out for him, then pushed the pad in front of him and watched in silence as he copied what she had written. She drew Perina's letter beside the pad and began writing the hand-written letters beside the capitals. When they had worked for about an hour the missus said, "Now would you like me to read the letters to you?"

Tod nodded. She took the letter and began to read. Tod listened to the dry voice and the tiredness of the day fled. He was back with Perina and Lucky as she told him how she had been reading a book about Arabs. It said the perfect Arab must have a neck curved like a crescent moon and a nose small enough to fit in a teacup. She added that she thought Lucky's nose was more of the breakfast cup size. Tod only half understood what she had written, but he sensed a joke and smiled a little.

When that letter was finished they began on the other. This one was about all the things that Perina had been able to find out about Quarter Horses. The missus paused to tell him, "Those horses are on their way here, so you'd better learn all you can about them."

She went back to the letter. "'Quarter Horses are descended from Thoroughbreds, Tod, like Lucky. They began when an English stallion called Janus was taken to Virginia, in America (I'm sending you an atlas, so that you can find these places), just about two hundred and ten years ago. Janus was exceptionally fast over short distances, and in those days most races were short ones. Then the races became longer and people forgot the Janus strain. Only the cowboys, who are American stockmen, sometimes bred them. So, Tod, remember when you are looking after Nakimer's Quarter Horses, that they will be half Thoroughbreds and half mustangs. Mustangs are wild horses like our own brumbies, and have just as mixed blood. I can't really explain to you, Tod, because you don't know any history, but you do know about Arabs and Thoroughbreds, and Arabs were taken to America by the Spaniards, and so that is where the fast, strong mustangs got their Arab blood.

"'In America, Quarter Horses are usually called "cutting horses". That's easy for you to understand, because you know all about stock horses, and how they "cut out" the beast they want from the herd. And you've heard about rodeos—that word comes from America too, by way of the Spaniards who brought over the Arabian horses. Our stock horses compete in our rodeos, and it's a good thing for you to know about stock horses, because some people say that Quarter Horses are the best stock horses in the world.

" 'Now, about fifteen years ago a Quarter Horse mare called "Marion's Girl" in Arizona (atlas!) was judged the best "cutting horse" ever, and I *think* that one of the mares Nakimer bought is descended from "Marion's Girl". So you may have a real champion when her foal is born. Some Quarter Horses are so good working cattle that their riders can just show them the beast they want cut out, then get off and the horse will follow it and cut it out from the rest of the mob. This is clever the way cattle dogs are clever, but it's not usual with horses, I know.' "

Miss Cora paused, then went on without comment.

" 'Tod, don't be sad about Lucky; he's very happy and well looked after, and he's doing what he was born to do. You made this possible for him by looking after him so well. So just be proud of him, and wait for your Quarter Horses. I'm sending a book about horses showing where the different ones come from, and your atlas. The two sort of go together, I think. I'll write again soon. I'm sure Lucky misses you, and I do too. . . .' "

Miss Cora paused, mechanically folding the letter and putting it back into the envelope. As she handed it to Tod he thought that her lined old face was less severe than he had ever seen it. Something of Perina's affection for Tod touched her. She could never forgive him his birth, absurd and unjust as she knew herself to be, but she realized dimly that in Perina's eyes Tod had a kind of genius with horses, and a faint stirring told her that she, too, could find pleasure and fulfilment in helping the boy. She rose and for a moment stood looking down at Tod's dark head.

"If you like, Tod, you can come back here in the evenings when you've finished dinner and I'll teach you to read."

Tod looked up at her wonderingly. "I'd like to read."

Miss Cora nodded and left the kitchen and Tod sat on thinking of many things, unfolding Perina's letters again, and trying to read them once more. He turned off the light and went down the steps towards the stables. The beauty of the night was all about him. The moaning of the cattle came from far away. That night he had heard of other lands, and he wondered about them.

All his short life Tod had imagined that the world was simply Australia. Now he knew that this was not so. His curiosity stirred. In an intangible way Australia was coming alive for Tod as *his* land. He did not know that "the old days" meant the time when men bought a kingdom for a quid of tobacco in a land of sun and sweat and sorrow, of glory and gold and grief, but something told him this was *his* land and his "today".

Tod found that a party of horse-buyers had come to Booramby in his absence and bought a consignment of horses. The boy mooned about, missing old friends, conscious that Lucky was absent. He worked well, he was incapable of neglecting any horse, and he was comforted by the love and care he gave Jake, but old Kelly, watching him closely, realized that the hole in his heart was still there.

Because Nakimer had tacitly agreed that the Quarter Horses were to be cared for by Tod, Kelly hoped they would arrive soon. Nakimer told him there had been delay over the English quarantine regulations and Kelly frowned disapprovingly.

When the engineer, Mackenzie, and his men arrived to begin the combination of dam and weir that had been decided upon, there was still no definite news of the new horses. Donald Mackenzie brought only a nucleus of trained men, for Nakimer was to supply the others. So when Mackenzie asked for Tod to be his own boy to fetch and carry for him personally, Nakimer agreed to his going.

Tod liked Mackenzie, but he knew Nakimer's decision would have been the same whether he wanted to go or not. So off he went with half a dozen other Booramby men, amazed and interested in the big mechanical lifters and diggers, and all the mass of paraphernalia stacked by the site.

As Mackenzie's boy he went with him in the

Land Rover ahead of the rest of the team. Tod led Mackenzie and the foreman downstream to the high-walled gap, orange red in the afternoon sun, where the creek divided and the cliffs rose remote and unscalable except for the single-file path that was the only way up or down the scorching rocks. This was the place that was always associated in Tod's mind with Perina and Lucky, and those long happy summer days. Tod made no mention of the elaborate complex of caves he had found, and the entrance was so cunningly contrived that it was unlikely to be discovered.

The only real regret Tod felt on being sent out with Mackenzie was that his reading lessons had to be deferred, for he felt he had learned a lot in a couple of weeks, Mackenzie liked Tod, he was quick and conscientious, and he was amused and rather touched by his "luggage"—Perina's letters, the tattered dictionary, the thin school atlas and paperback on horses that Perina had sent—and he occasionally helped him over a word or a sentence as they both sprawled outside the tents when the work was over.

The only electrical or mechanical things Tod had ever seen were cars and the electric light plant at the homestead, and he had no notion how these things came about. To him the most thrilling part of the construction was the blasting that sent up fountains of red earth and rocks, for the site lacked the high banks needed to dam the water. Mac's foreman was the expert on this work, and because

Tod was quick and nippy he often borrowed him. Tod learned how to set a charge, and to relate the size of the blast to the cavity needed. He learned, too, how to stop an explosion by dismantling a lead.

"I'd take the kid in my demolition gang any time," Casey, whose talents were more often used for destruction than construction, told Mac. "I've got 'im settin' the charge now, an' 'e can damn near do the whole job himself."

"Well, don't let him blow himself up," Mac said. "I could do with havin' him around a bit more."

It was a happy time for Tod. He discovered that the earth went down a long way, something he had never thought about until he saw great mechanical shovels burrowing into the ground. It was very dry, and for once no-one wanted rain until the catchment was finished.

Once, kicking at the excavated soil, Tod bent down and picked up a strange object. It seemed to him to be man-made from the smoothness of what he thought was a piece of white rock. It was heavy too, heavier than rock of comparable size. He ran down the man-made hillock and showed it to Mac. The Scotsman peered at it.

"That's a shell, Tod. It's fossilized; that makes it heavy. You can see it's a shell by the spiral curves."

Tod stared at it. He had no idea what "shell" or "fossilized" meant.

"D'you know what the sea is, Tod?"

Tod shook his head. He thought the sea might be something to do with water.

"Well, it's salt water that lies over about two-thirds of the earth's surface. Fish swim in it, ships sail on it, and there are thousands of shells like this on the beaches. Millions of years ago all the centre of Australia was an ocean where it is desert now. This shell seems to tell us that this land was once covered by ocean, and if we were to dig deep enough, we'd find shells and the skeletons of fish."

They found more shells and Tod took a large one to give to Perina. He hesitated a little about taking one for the missus, and then decided he would. The thought gave him a good feeling, for it was his first experience of the pleasure of giving.

When he lay on his blanket that night he thought about the sea, but he could only visualize it in terms of the waters of Mooti Creek breaking its banks, flooding out to lie in shining, grey-green stillness over all the land. Nothing of the eternal restlessness of the ocean, the changing colours and spume-topped waves, came into his imaginings, only a glassy stillness spreading to the horizon with, of course, the tops of the trees showing above it.

Mac told Tod to hold his shells to his ear and he would hear the roaring of the sea. Tod was not disappointed, because he half suspected that Mac was pulling his leg. His ancient calcified shell no longer had sounding chambers. It had existed so long in dried-up earth that it was dead indeed, so Tod listened in vain. When he asked what kind of sound he was listening for, he was told, "A murmur that never stops, like a great mob of cattle at night without the high sounds."

Tod thought about this, but his imagination was never able to give voice to the glassy sheet of creek water that was his imaginary sea.

To Tod the weir was a miracle. He looked forward to the sluice gates being fitted, and then to the first rain that would fill the dam and perhaps make it necessary to open the sluice gates to hold the water at the right level. Mac told him a big flood from the opened gates would send the water racing over the island in the gorge, but that the island would reappear again when the water reached its level.

Then, before the construction was quite finished, Kelly rode out to take Tod back with him. The Quarter Horses were due in four days. Excitement at the news revived Tod's horse-hunger, which grew and grew as he rode old Jake back to the stables.

THAT night Jake had an extra petting, then Tod prepared the stalls for the three mares. Nakimer and Kelly were taking the car and the big horsebox that had ample room for six horses in it. They were to drive sixty miles to the train siding where the mares would be off-loaded, and the stableman who brought them would return to Brisbane.

Tod's last job was to put feed and water and plenty of bedding in the horsebox. Round the sides he put specially padded rolls to protect the horses travelling over the rough roads, in the way that fenders are hung round small boats to prevent them crashing against other boats or wharves. The bush track was rough, and Nakimer's precious mares, so near to foaling, must not be bumped against the hard sides of the horsebox.

They meant to leave early, and Tod was to have everything ready to receive the mares at Booramby. But when Kelly stopped in the morning to collect Nakimer, he did not appear. The missus came out to say that Nakimer had lumbago and could not even get out of bed. She added he was very angry, but quite unable to move, and that Tod was to go with Kelly.

A "cooee" from Kelly brought Tod racing up the hill. He was delighted to be going, and they set off while the sun was cool and pale and illumined the earth like candle-light.

Tod was very excited. Car trips were a rarity in his life, and he had never seen a train. Kelly sat behind the wheel like a wizened old monkey feeling nearly as excited as Tod. He was boss of the Quarter Horse operation and he loved it. Tod had not seen Kelly alone since his return and now he brought Perina's letter out of his pocket and showed off by reading the letter to Kelly when a stretch of road permitted, which was really not important as he knew it off by heart.

It was heady stuff for the young half-caste; hours of motoring, a train to see, and three new mares to collect, and Tod let his imagination run riot. Kelly said nothing to bring him to earth, driving as fast as it was safe to do. He wanted plenty of time for the return trip, so that the mares would not be shaken up. They started about five, and it lacked a few minutes to nine when they saw the roofs of the little siding with its dilapidated wood and corrugated iron huts, visible for miles across the dried-up plain.

When they were still a couple of miles away, Tod sat up with excitement. Something like a black, furiously smoking caterpillar was racing across the plain before them. Tod clutched the door as its shrill "wooh awhooh awhoo" drifted across to them. He was seeing his first train, hearing its voice and the screech of its brakes as it pulled into the siding and stopped with jangling, grunting sounds, its black, segmented body jerking angrily as the still moving back wagons fetched up against the immobile front ones.

"It won't do the mares much good if they've been in that thing for long!" Tod said.

In a few minutes they stopped in the yard. The train steamed and made wheezing, creaking noises, and Tod wondered nervously what it would be like to be near the thing. It was an ancient train, black and dirty, and with a high-funnelled engine that looked more like something out of a child's picture-book than usable rolling-stock. But to Tod it was an amazing piece of civilization, quite as wonderful with its thirty-two inch bust as if it had been a great, chesty continental model, pouring its glittering body along the rails.

"Come on, boy," said Kelly. "We'll see about those mares."

The two walked towards the train. Tod kept a tight hold on himself, not wanting to show Kelly his somewhat fearful thoughts about the puffing monster that had come to such an uneasy rest on the stretch of rail facing the shed and the earthen platform.

Tod lagged behind as Kelly went to meet a man wearing a stetson who had jumped to the ground and hailed him. But Kelly beckoned Tod over. The boy gritted his teeth and went to where Kelly stood a couple of yards from the black, wooden box that so lately had seemed part of a long, angry caterpillar.

"Tod'll be lookin' after the mares," Kelly told the man casually, who looked with amazement at the boy. Then, perhaps indignant at the man's sceptical glance at Tod's size, Kelly added defensively, "Nakimer's bred a good 'un there. Best 'and with horses I've ever seen."

He stopped, not wanting Tod to hear his praise, but he need not have bothered. Tod was far too worried at the thought of *his* mares somewhere in that long segmented body, to bother about a discussion on himself. Kelly turned to him.

"Ringer 'ere, says the ramps're in the truck with the mares, so come on. We'll take a look."

Ringer jumped up into the truck and took the old man's clawlike hand to help him in. Tod, his heart in his mouth, clambered up like a monkey. It was gloomy inside the truck, seeming dark after the brilliant light outside. Inside there was the comforting horse-smell Tod loved, and he saw the solid bodies, the lifted, intelligent heads of the three mares. Then he saw something else.

"Kelly! Two of them've foaled!"

It was true. Ringer was surprised they did not know. He went to a mare whose vivid chestnut hide shone out of the gloom, and put his hand on her flank.

"Bronze Star here had her foal ten days ago." He moved and patted the shoulder of a black mare with one white sock, and went on, "This is Stormcloud, she's the one that delayed us. She foaled the night before we were to leave, so the boss said we'd keep 'er a few days."

The tiny foals looked like velvet toys beside their mothers. Stormcloud's small, handsome colt had two white stockings and a star on his little black forehead. He stood, his four small legs apart, balancing himself on his minute five-day-old hooves. Bronze Star's baby lay contentedly on the thick straw, and the mare bent her head to give her a reassuring sniff. It was the third mare, due to foal at any time, that held Tod's gaze. He had never seen a horse like her, and even Kelly looked a bit dazed at Ringer's words.

"She's a Palomino."

"But isn't she a Quarter Horse?" Tod interrupted.

Ringer laughed. "She is; she's a Palomino Quarter Horse, a real pale chestnut with silvery mane and tail. Looks good, doesn't she? Her name's 'Fool's Gold'."

Tod was speechless, but Kelly just grunted. He was not admitting that Palominos were anything new in his life, thought actually he had never seen one. For Tod the mare was something quite new.

"Quarter Horses come in all colours," explained Ringer, "and they can learn anything, clever little devils!"

Tod put his palm on the mare's swollen side, using enough pressure to reassure her; he knew all horses hate fingers trickling over them like crawling flies. Her coat was silken and smooth, and as she moved forward a little the light fell on her side. Tod saw that the strange, pale golden hide was faintly iridescent; it seemed to ripple in the light. The splendid mane and flowing tail were frostily white.

"She—she's a beaut!" he said softly.

"Come on, git the ramp down."

"Will the train go on?"

Ringer laughed. "It will in the driver's good time, boy. Depends on 'ow much beer's in the station master's office! 'ere, build 'er up to a good slope and the mares'll go down easy."

Tod undid the halter and led Fool's Gold to the ramp.

"We call 'er 'Goldy'," Ringer told him and Tod whispered, "Come on, Goldy, I'll take care of you."

The mares followed Goldy and Tod, while Kelly and Ringer carried the tiny foals after them, and put them down on their unsteady young legs on the earthen platform. They followed their mothers towards the horsebox.

Tod turned to look at the foals. He knew all about young Thoroughbreds, but these were different. The mares, too, lacked the nervous movements, the dislike of strangers, that is so noticeable in the Thoroughbred. The mares with their enchanting foals, and the third, so soon to have one of her own, were alert but placid, like contented cats. The difference was like that between the inbred aristocrat and the man so sure of his position that he feels no need to assert it.

This self-assurance was remarkable in mares that had been travelling for seven months, and had been so much handled by strangers. They went lightly up the ramp into the strange horsebox. The black colt's undisciplined hooves made him trot after his mum with much shaking of his little starred head, and perpetual wriggling of his small tail.

Tod's eyes took in the general outlines of the mares. They were shorter-legged than Thoroughbreds, and their eyes held an entirely different expression, a placidity, rather than the white-rimmed wariness he knew so well. He noticed too, that they had small, fox-like ears, strong forelegs with flattish knees, well-defined tendons and well-angled pasterns. The distance from the stifle to the hock promised the leverage that gives speed, as did the strong downward curve from coupling to tail. Yes, they were beautiful, all three of them. As for the foals—he looked at the small heads and the legs that were longer in proportion to their bodies than were those of their parents; he looked at the velvety beauty of them, the intelligent, friendly eyes, and his heart rejoiced.

Tod adjusted the rolls of padding and offered water. The mares drank thirstily. Kelly looked in and nodded.

"We'll pull up in an hour or so and give 'em a feed." He turned away and called back, "Here's Ringer. He's off now."

Ringer put his head in and said goodbye to Tod.

"Look after them mares, boy. The boss paid

plenty for 'em, and 'e's been a long time gettin' 'em. So long."

Kelly left the foals to finish their feed and lie down to doze on the springy, well-covered floor. Tod moved them away from their mothers' hind legs where they would be in no danger from the rough road. Chestnut and black lay against each other, giving sighs of repletion. The long lashes curved upwards from the closed eyelids and they both slept.

Tod tethered Fools' Gold in the centre of the horsebox where she would get the least jolting. They were ready. Kelly started the engine and they went down the red, dusty track at a steady pace. Tod's head nodded and he dozed, lulled by the mesmeric humming of the engine. An uneasiness crept through his sleep, and he pushed himself upright in the seat and rubbed his eyes.

"How far've we come?" he asked Kelly.

"About fifteen miles."

"Kelly, let me take a look at the mares."

"Not yet, boy."

After they had gone another couple of miles Tod burst out, "Kelly, I'm sure something's wrong. Let me look."

Kelly drove down a steep dip and up the other side. The dip was the dry bed of a creek, russet red at this season. A treeless plain spread around them and the heat pressed against them. He stopped the car and Tod jumped out and ran around the back. The heat was oppressive and the sun like a flame touched the top of Tod's head and his shirt-covered back. He opened the top half of the door and looked in. The foals still slept and the mares stood quietly with sleep-drooped heads. All the same, Tod was anxious. He opened the whole door and slipped inside to where he could see the Palomino mare. In a second he was out again and running round to Kelly's side of the car.

"Kelly, the Palomino's started to foal!"

Kelly greeted the news with silence, then he said, "We must have shade, an' we ought to get the other mares out. How near's the foal?"

"Just starting, I think."

"Jump in."

Tod went round and obeyed. Kelly started the car and backed slowly and carefully down into the creek bed. Then he turned in a wide circle and the red banks rose on either side of them. He drove at one side of the pebbly creek bed, the banks rising higher as they moved forward. Presently the bank curved inwards like a towering wave of red earth. The curve had been made over millions of centuries, when the occasional floods had swept down the waterway around the curve of the bank, carrying rubble and treetrunks, and perhaps rocks, when the current was fast enough. The water half-way up the turning bank had flung all this detritus against it, scraping, bobbing, pushing until it had made this splendid hollow wave of earth.

Now Tod saw why they had come. There was no shade for miles, but the angle and height of the inward curve threw a wide, deep shadow almost to the other side. At sundown the shadow would narrow, but now it would remain a black stain across the red, sharp-edged where it met the sunshine. The creek itself formed a kind of funnel down which blew a faint breeze, making it several degrees cooler than on top of the banks.

Kelly stopped the car. "This'll do."

Together the two set about getting the mares down from the truck and walking them a little way off in the shade. They carried the foals which behaved like sleepy puppies, opening long-lashed eyes and closing them again, probably enjoying the faint breeze.

Now only Goldy remained in the horsebox. Tod spread the door wide, and opened the sliding panel at the back that was kept closed when the horsebox was in motion. Now that the body-warmth of the other mares was removed, it was reasonably cool inside the big box.

The Palomino stood patiently. Tod offered her water and she sipped a little. He stroked her lovingly, then went and joined Kelly nearby. Kelly, who had presided at so many foalings, knew that a healthy mare is better left alone so neither he nor Tod worried her with unwanted attentions. The sturdy mare, given the best conditions possible, went about the job of producing her first foal without being in the least bothered about it.

To Tod the time crawled by, but he knew that Kelly was right to do nothing. He fed the other two mares. The tiny colt woke and got to his hooves. He pranced over to Tod, shaking his small head and nipping at Tod's hands. Then he felt the pangs of hunger and returned to his mother.

"Nakimer'll think something's happened," said Kelly.

"So it has."

They were silent. Movement at the back of the horsebox made them both turn their heads. A glistening bundle lay at the Palomino's heels. She knew what to do. She freed from the shining membrane the smallest, most wonderful foal Tod had ever seen. Tod could not believe his eyes. Even Kelly was shaken, for he too had never seen a newly-born white foal before. Both had seen foals that turned white later, but these were a smoky colour at birth. This tiny creature was dark-eyed and enchantingly white all over. Tod's heart thumped with excitement. He was filled with a warmth of love and possession towards the fairylike creature lying at its mother's feet.

Goldy nudged it very gently until it stood up, wobbling, almost collapsing, its soft silky hide still damp from the birth-fluid. She nosed it gently towards her hind legs and the miniature tail wriggled ecstatically as the baby animal began to feed.

Tod longed to touch this infinitely beautiful creature, but he knew better. So the men sat where they were until Kelly judged it was time to offer the mare food and water. She took both placidly, apparently unimpressed by her fairy-princess daughter. She whickered lovingly at her, gently sniffing until the baby lifted her tiny head and rubbed noses with her mother.

After another long wait Kelly announced, "Come on, we'll go now. Let's get the mares in, Tod. You stay here in the box. Watch the foal and let me know if I'm driving too fast."

So they set off on the last lap for Booramby and the waiting Nakimer.

The heat-filled world revived a little as the sun, an orange ball in a haze, dipped to the horizon. Nakimer, grunting and cursing, struggled from his bed and dragged himself onto the veranda. Miss Cora, carrying a cup of tea, looked at the contorted figure of her brother.

"You old fool," she said coldly. "Why can't you stay in bed until your back's right in a couple of days."

Nakimer glared at her, clutching the back of a chair, and she relented. She put the cup down and pulled a long veranda chair to where he could see the road winding away into the distance. She helped him into the chair and gave him his tea. He drank greedily, exertion and pain making the sweat pour from him so that his pyjama coat was limp and soaked.

"Kelly and the boy ought to've been back hours ago. Somethin's happened to the mares."

"Nonsense," Miss Cora said firmly. "They can look after the mares, so stop worrying."

"Those mares between 'em cost me more'n sixteen thousand dollars, plus gettin' them 'ere and all the delays. I got 'em cheaper because some fool let 'em out an' no-one knows which stallion got 'em in foal, but they were still mighty expensive." He stopped and then added gloomily. "The foals might be real drongos, fer all I know. They'll 'ave to stand or fall by what they are, not by who their sire is."

"They won't be the first to do that, and there'll be more foals," Miss Greer said drily, then relented and added, "On the other hand, they might *all* be champions. You won't lose, you never do." When Nakimer continued to look gloomy, she went on tartly, "Anyway, Tod'll make them the best of whatever they are."

Nakimer bucked up a little. " 'E's all right, that boy."

"Well, see you do fairly by him this time, or Perina'll have something to say to you."

"When's she comin'?"

"Soon, now, I expect. There were letters for Tod and me today, when you got yours."

She walked to the steps and peered across the land. "They're coming now," she said calmly. "Stay there. You'll see just as well as if you stood up."

Kelly drove straight to the level ground in front of the steps, and Tod set about getting the mares out as Kelly went up the steps to join Nakimer. The old man eyed him crossly.

"Where you bin all this time?"

"The third mare foaled on the way, so we 'ad to take it slowly."

"Foaled? She all right?"

Kelly nodded. "Tod's gettin' them out to show you. The other mares foaled earlier. The colt's ten days old, and the filly five."

The old man glared as if Kelly was to blame, and Kelly hopped down the steps like a lively black crow as Tod appeared with Stormcloud who walked calmly down the ramp, undisturbed by all the crises of the day, and stood looking around her. Kelly took the halter and led her up and down and Nakimer nodded approval. His eyes lit up when the little colt galloped up to his mother, frisking around her before drinking eagerly.

"Nice youngster," was Nakimer's comment.

Bronze Star followed by the even smaller filly, also found approval. Like Kelly, the old man was struck by the quietness and poise of the mares. But it was when Tod led Fools' Gold out that Nakimer forgot his lumbago and tried to sit up, only to collapse with a groan. He tried again and ended up swearing loudly as Tod came up the steps carrying the fairy-like white filly.

Tod stood proudly beside Nakimer, who put out his hard old hand that could touch a horse so gently, and stroked the tiny foal. The missus looked wondering at the dark eyes, the delicate, lovely limbs, and she smiled at Tod, coming forward to touch the baby silk of the hide.

"How beautiful they all are, Tod."

Tod almost burst with pride at the astonishment and admiration on the faces before him. Nakimer found his voice.

"Take 'em to their stables, Tod. The white foal and the mare first. Bed 'em down. Kelly can lead the others. They don't look a bad lot."

Tod grinned at the grudging praise, and he and Kelly started for the stable with the mares and their foals, leaving the car and trailer until later.

It was late by the time the mares and foals were all comfortably settled for the night. Tod went up to the house for his supper before returning to the stables to sleep.

He sat at the kitchen table and tucked in. The missus came in carrying Perina's letter and Tod took it from her. The habit of silence was difficult for them both to break. He just managed to say, "I can't read it now, I must get back to the mares."

The missus nodded. "I had a letter too. Perina'll be here in two weeks, for a fortnight. She'll love the foals."

Tod nodded, shoved his letter in his pocket and returned to the stables. He could have sung for joy on this, the first night of such a period of happiness as he had never known.

It was not long before Tod was riding the mares bareback, taking them gently across the paddock, and he knew that he had never ridden any horse, not even Lucky, with the same quick responsiveness to knees and hands and voice as he found in all three mares. He longed to try his Quarter Horses after cattle, but for a time the foals were too small either to follow or to be left behind.

Then Perina arrived. Her Brisbane weekends had been spent at Surfers' Paradise, and she was Indian-brown. The salty sea and bleaching sunlight and wind blowing through her naturally blonde hair had turned it to palest gold. As she came into the stable that first day, Tod stood transfixed.

"Perina! You're just a girl Goldy!"

Of course Perina fell hopelessly in love with Fools' Gold's baby, not only for her frost-white mane and tail, and her tiny body that had not yet begun to darken into the pale gold of the mature Palomino, but also because of her funny playful little ways, almost as if she was as much a cat as a filly. Tod found her so easy to teach that he had already taught her to bow, and she bent one miniature front leg and nodded her head at Perina, who was enchanted. Tod was very proud.

Perina joined Tod in the care of the Quarter Horses, and Nakimer, anxious to enter names in the stud book, called a meeting at which Aunt Cora, Kelly and Tod sat down with the old man and Perina and discussed possible names. Nakimer had decided to try to register his three Quarter Horse foals in the stud book, arguing that it certainly looked as if their sire was the desired one and that, anyway, no-one could prove that it was not. Kelly looked rather amazed at this reasoning, but he knew better than to question it.

So Bronze Star's baby went down as "Russet

Miss", Stormcloud's son became "Jet", and, much to Perina's delight, Aunt Cora suggested that Fools' Gold's filly be called "Golden Perina", and "Little Goldy" for short.

Perina had lots to tell Tod about Lucky, who was happy, beautiful and well-cared for. She had also saved up some hard facts for him about Quarter Horses; how they had not been recognized as a breed until about 1940 because, unlike the English Thoroughbred, whose blood-lines came from the eighteenth-century stallions, Quarter Horses sprang from a great mixture of horses. Most people had long forgotten Janus, the first sire. Spanish conquerors had taken Arabian horses to America, and some of these had gone wild, just as the Australian brumbies did, and mated with later European breeds. The granddaddy everyone remembered was called "Old Sorrell", and from him, and from mares carrying a great mixture of bloods, had sprung what the Americans called the "short horses", strong and speedy creatures over short distances. The Mexicans, when the Texas frontier opened, needed fast cow-ponies, and their small, strong ponies mated with the "short horses" whose offspring were soon to be known as Quarter Horses, a breed with the desirable qualities of speed and strength and equable temperament. In Texas there is a vast ranch run by Robert Kleeberg, that is worked by 2,000 Quarter Horses, and Kleeberg's King Ranch had sent three superb stallions produced by selective breeding to Australia in 1954 when the Australian Quarter Horse Association was formed.

Now Nakimer wanted Booramby to join the select half-dozen studs breeding Quarter Horses, and the fire in his old eyes matched Tod's when he told him, "We want a stallion like 'Pronto Mio'. 'E sold for over eleven thousand dollars."

The fire in Tod's eyes did not have the same origin as the fire in Nakimer's, since Tod was unimpressed by money. But he was so absorbed in his horses that when Donald Mackenzie came in to the homestead to announce the completion of the weir, the fact that the work was finished scarcely registered with him.

The foals developed rapidly as the days went by. Jet was a splendid little colt, and Tod was immensely proud of him. The little filly, Russet Miss, whose name was shortened to "Missy", was Jet's willing slave, allowing him to dominate in all their games. But little Golden Perina was different. There were days when Jet could boss her about and she would squeal and jump when he nipped her, but there were other days when she simply ignored him, and then she lived in a world of her own. If Jet bothered her she merely lay down in the grass and treated him to disdainful shakes of her head.

On one of these days, Tod finished his work in the stable and went into the paddock to play with the foals. He found Jet and Missy, but he could not find Golden Perina. He went to look near the creek, for the memory of Swy Boy's death was always in his mind when a mare or a foal was not in its expected place. Now he hurried to the top of the bank and looked over, and held his breath at the beauty of the sight below him.

A weeping willow grew on a broad ledge half-way down the bank. Its slender, whip-like growth had been cut a few feet from the ground because horses going to drink would tear at the swaying leaves and leave them ragged. Goldy, the baby who liked to play by herself, stood below the old willow. Her hide was still white, her mane and tail like spun floss. In spite of her elegance she was no weakling, yet she was so exquisitely built that an almost fragile look went with her disdainful air.

As Tod looked down she was rising on her hind legs, pawing the air, trying to catch the trailing ends of willow in her mouth. She leaped and curvetted, shook her head and sprang sideways as if to surprise the willow. She stood on her hind legs and whirled round, striking at the tantalizing trails, twisting her lissom body and making her elegant hooves dance.

Tod watched her at play until he sensed that she had become tired of it. He whistled to her, very softly. She threw up her head, turned and saw Tod and came up the bank to stand blowing softly at his neck while he whispered in her ears and stroked her velvety muzzle. They went across the paddock together and the other two foals raced to meet them. Tod fondled them and they went back to their playing, but Goldy's solitary mood was still upon her and she lay down on the grass, closed her long-lashed eyes and dozed.

Tod trained the foals to come to his whistle. He put saddle-cloths on their backs, and surcingles round their bodies. He taught them to spring away at the command, "Go!" As an extension of their natural play, they rose on their hind legs for mock fights with Tod. They threatened him with their pawing hooves and counteracted his moves as boxers do.

Little Goldy picked up this game more easily than the others, just as she learned most things more easily. Her reactions were lightning swift: she would begin to play at Tod's signal, and stop when he ordered her to. Often Tod received a bad bruising from glancing hooves, or he carried the marks of solid horse-teeth about him, but he bore it stoically because he enjoyed the game as much as the foals did. It had started when Perina sent him a cutting which told about the dancing horses of the Sybarites. He learned how the wily Crotonians, battling against the Sybarites, began to play music, whereupon the Sybarites' horses started to dance, causing their masters to lose the battle.

Who and what "Sybarites" and "Crotonians" were, Tod did not know, and dancing, other than the occasional corroboree, was for him only a matter of vague movement done to the kind of rhythm that can be beaten out by stick-on-log; but the game evolved as they went along, and Tod's reactions become almost as fast as those of his foals.

Always, deep down in Tod's subconscious, was the comfortable feeling that his mares and his beautiful foals were foundation breeding stock and would never be taken from him.

Perina persuaded Tod to go with them when she drove her uncle out to the weir during the time Mackenzie and his men were preparing to leave. They found Mac rather disturbed. Several sticks of dynamite and a battery box had disappeared. There were always wild men on walkabout who might know how to use the dynamite to throw in the creek to stun fish, but it was unlikely that they would know how to use the battery.

Lawless white men were often reported as suspected of hiding out in some part of the sheltering hills or uninhabited places, but as far as anyone knew there had been no strangers about the camp. Nakimer's advice was to forget it and, as there was nothing else he could do, Mackenzie agreed.

Tod was delighted with the weir he had helped to build, and he showed Perina with great pride where he had helped to dynamite the dam basin. Mackenzie explained how the weir worked, and pointed out the precautions he had taken with chains and locks so that no merely mischievous person could open the weir gates. Then he gave Nakimer all the keys, and the old man looked with satisfaction at the half-filled dam, and with approval at the gathering clouds, and they said goodbye and went home.

When Perina left Tod missed her, but he was so absorbed in his Quarter Horses that Aunt Cora and Nakimer missed her rather more than he did. But as the weeks passed and Perina's holidays came round again, Tod's delight in seeing her and her own pleasure at being back again never lessened.

Eventually the three Quarter Horse mares were sent away to be mated again to a splendid sire that had only just arrived in Australia. Like Tod, Nakimer's greatest pride was in the Palomino mother and daughter, probably because of their rarity, and they hoped for another foal like Goldy. Kelly went with the mares, and Tod gave all his time to his youngsters, taking great care over mouthing them, and over all the preliminary stages of their training.

The testing day for his three foals, Jet, Missy and little Goldy, came when each one was to be ridden by Tod to face their first mob of cattle. This was what they had been born for: this was the Quarter Horse's heritage. Stockhorses must learn, but Nakimer hoped that his Quarter Horses would have an inherited mob-knowledge, and his anticipation of the day was only second to Tod's.

Tod rode Jet first. He rode him to where Nakimer had ordered a small mob of cattle to be placed. The beasts stood or lay around and Tod cantered Jet quietly towards them. He stopped him twenty yards from the herd and walked him towards what he knew was the first bunch of steers the horse had ever seen. Jet's raised head told him he was interested. The intelligent head went down and Nakimer, watching through his field-glasses a little distance away, swore softly as Jet moved his small ears, sniffed the air, and turned his head round for a look at Tod as much as to say, "I'm ready; are you?"

The boy's hands were light on the reins as he rode Jet across towards the mob held by the half-moon fence on one side, while the stockman who had put them there sat quietly on his horse some distance away. Tod made small yipping noises at the cattle to start them moving, and he glanced towards the clump of trees a quarter of a mile to his right, which was where Jet had to put the beasts he cut out. The cattle moved, grunting and grumbling, and began to mill slowly together. The boy rode Jet forward using his knees to guide him, and half a dozen steers began to move.

Tod increased the pace for he wanted to give Jet the feel of the moving beasts. One broke away. Tod sent Jet after it. The Quarter Horse drove his shoulder against the beast and worked him back among the mob, as unperturbed himself as any seasoned old cow-pony. Tod urged him to move the beasts from left to right, to manoeuvre them away from the trees for which he was aiming, and then to bring them back again. There was much for Jet to learn about the vagaries of single beasts, but he had the feel of the cattle, and Tod sat motionless on his strong back, riding with the grace peculiar to the Australian horseman who does nothing by numbers but everything by instinct. Tod used only the lightest touch to show Jet how to place the cattle by the trees, and how to circle them to keep them there.

Then he rode Jet into the big mob and began cutting single beasts from it. Once or twice the stallion's quarry escaped back into the herd, but he needed no urging to go after it again, and when the sixth beast had been dealt with, Nakimer called it a day.

Perhaps because little Goldy meant so much to him, Tod left her to the last. Missy did well in her turn, and then it was time for Tod to try out his treasure.

Tod put a fresh saddle-cloth under the light stock-saddle and changed the sweat-frothed girth. He stood at Goldy's head, whispering to her, running his hand proudly over her silken body. He mounted and rode towards the replaced mob, which, because the day was so hot, was becoming rather cantankerous at all this running about.

A curious or a grumpy beast came trotting towards them, shaking his great head on which the long horns glinted in the sunlight. It was making grumbling noises in its throat. Tod just sat quietly there, wondering how little Goldy would greet this great red and white beast, and not wanting to give her any hints on how he thought she should do it.

Nakimer, watching through his glasses, saw the movement of the muscles through the silk of the pale golden hide, shimmering, lit by the frosty whiteness of mane and toil. She was a beauty all right! Then he sat up. He had never seen a stock-horse behave like that!

Little Goldy stopped as the big steer lumbered before her. She lowered her head and her sharp fox's ears twitched. Then she began to dance around the bullock! The bullock was as bewildered as the men; it bellowed and raked at Goldy with its long horns. She danced out of the way, rearing onto her hind legs, while Tod grinned and kept his body parallel with her neck. She snaked her neck out and nipped the great bony shoulder, so that the bullock bellowed furiously.

She was a dancing horse, a Sybarite horse, and for a few minutes she played with the lumbering disgruntled beast, and not for worlds would Tod have shown her that this was not the way cow-ponies behaved! Then, with no urging from Tod she became just a gold and white, supremely beautiful and orthodox cow-pony. She advanced in a business-like way on the steer and shouldered him back towards the herd. Then she took the small bunch of bullocks away from the trees and deposited them under the next piece of shade. She was playing a game and loving it!

They cantered towards the mob and Tod's heart was big with pride. Goldy needed no telling. When Tod moved towards the selected beast, she moved in. Once, when a beast broke from the mob and went thundering over the dry earth, Tod held Goldy back, then he leaned forward a little and she went, a streak of gold and white lightning, a Quar-

ter Horse at full stretch after its quarry, beautiful as the stoop of a falcon.

Again Nakimer sat up as if someone had shot him. Speed! Fast horses were his life, and he had never seen anything like *that*! Little Goldy turned the beast and sent it galloping back into the herd. She cantered sedately back, and faintly, from the distance, Tod heard Nakimer's roar, "Good on yer, Boy!"

But for Tod it was, "Good on yer, Little Goldy", and he believed that she was a rarity even among Quarter Horses; a stockhorse that, when shown a beast, goes into the mob and brings it out, unmounted. Perina had told him about these horses, and Tod was sure that he could teach Goldy to do the same thing.

Nakimer did not try to disguise his excitement. The mares, the mothers of these three remarkable horses, were in foal, and soon Booramby would have Quarter Horses trained for stock-work, and he would get new blood from another stud. Goldy's speed confounded him. They would have trials by the stopwatch. Goldy was his trump card. No-one would forget her having once seen her; she would be worth her tucker even if she never foaled; and she would be Booramby's spearhead in the publicity he planned. For two years Tod had been teaching her tricks as he might have taught an intelligent dog; to come when he whistled, to go when he told her, to wait, to find hidden objects, to fight on her hind legs at his command, and to stop when he told her. He taught the other two foals tricks too, but Goldy required so little teaching that she was his pride.

Tod came towards Nakimer, riding Goldy with Jet and Missy following, not on leads, but as dogs follow their master. There was a boy who knew horses! How old was Tod? Must be about fifteen. Not too tall, five feet seven or eight, maybe. Wouldn't grow much more—all sinew and horsemanship. Knew how to train 'em, too. That Goldy! Dancing about the big steer. . . . Must get a movie cameraman up from Brisbane. Must get the press—yes! That was it! Show the Quarter Horses next time Perina came up; she could arrange the publicity. Smart girl.

Tod stopped by the station wagon and waited, hiding the bubbling elation inside him.

"Not bad, for beginners," said Nakimer cautiously.

"Not bad if they'd been workin' stock all their lives," Tod said flatly, in defence of his loves.

Nakimer chuckled. "Not bad at all, boy. Wait till Kelly sees them. 'E'll be back next week. We'll 'ave a few trials with the stopwatch. Then we'll get some of the press boys up 'ere, and the blokes with their own studs, and give 'em a bit of a show. Think you can do it?"

Tod nodded. "You've only got to get my three to understand what you want, and they can do it," he said simply.

Kelly returned with the three mares, and Nakimer drove alone to the siding to pick them up as Tod could not leave his charges. With the mares back he had plenty to do, and it was some weeks before Nakimer arranged for the speed trials or wrote to Perina about his plan to show his Quarter Horses to breeders and the press. He asked her to see his trainer, Frank Howells, and get from him a list of people who should be invited. About fifteen visitors were all that could be managed at the homestead, so these must be carefully selected, and Nakimer wanted his trainer along with them. Perina fixed it to coincide with her long holiday, and she planned to arrive early and give Tod a hand.

Meantime the gallops took place over the distance of a mile with Tod riding all three horses in turn. One morning Nakimer himself stood outside by the track, with stopwatch in hand and Kelly beside him. Tod would ride Jet first, then Missy, now a glowing chestnut, and lastly Goldy, the pale blonde. Jet was to stand as a sire the next season. Telling Goldy and Missy to wait, Tod rode Jet up to the starting-line.

Nakimer held up his hand to signal the start. Tod, who had been watching him, saw it come down like a knife cutting string and Jet was away, galloping powerfully and easily. Nakimer's finger pressed the stop on the watch as Jet passed the quarter-mile post, and his eyes met Kelly's.

"Pretty good. Twenty-two point three."

Jet was scarcely sweat-damped and breathing easily when Tod rode back. The boy slid to the ground and saddled Russet Miss who then trotted amiably to the starting point. Her speed was rather less than the stallion's, but good enough for Nakimer, as she passed the post at twenty-two point five.

The sun was warming up and Tod went to Golden Perina's shimmering side. He put his face against her inquiring nose, and she nuzzled him while he whispered, "Come on, girl."

Nakimer turned to Kelly meanwhile. "They're all so placid," he complained. "That's good up to a point, but when they're up against it, will they have fire in their bellies like my Thoroughbreds?"

"They say they will, boss. I been talkin' to plenty Quarter Horse blokes since I bin away. They say that when they need it they're all heart. Look, Tod's ready."

The boy and the beautiful Palomino made a wonderful picture as they turned at the starting post, with Golden Perina moving continuously on her elegant little hooves. Nakimer's hand came down and Goldy's mane and tail streamed in the wind like spume blown back from the top of a wave. She came towards them, flashing in the sunlight, a magic horse of fire and frost, her neat hooves thrusting the ground away beneath her belly. She flashed past the post and Nakimer looked at his watch and whistled.

"By God, Kelly, she's fast. A flat twenty-two!"

"The boy wasn't pushin' 'er too much, boss."

"She's a real good 'un, Kelly. We'll show 'er around for a few years, then put 'er to stud. She'll make 'em sit up and notice the Booramby strain! Hello Tod, want to know the times?"

Tod nodded. He did not really mind much about speeds. His whole instinct for horses spoke of soundness, of easy handling and intelligence; those were all he cared about. He glanced up the hill where the current crop of Thoroughbreds ate and played and squealed. They were beautiful, as long-legged and temperamental as ever, and then his eyes came back to the shorter horses beside him. He was content.

At Howells' suggestion, Nakimer let him charter a plane to bring the guests. The whole Abo tribe, at present in camp, cleared a runway. The weir was finished, the dam filling nicely, and the mails ran hot with Perina's letters and the answers. She and Frank Howells found they could not cut the guest list to less than twenty if it included, as it should, important breeders, a couple of Government officials, and the leading sportswriters. They were to fly up early one morning, inspect the horses and stables, see the gallops, the cattle cutting contests and any special Quarter Horse activities that could be devised. They would lunch at the homestead, take a look at the new weir, then return to the homestead to dine and sleep. All of them would be flown back next day.

Miss Cora made no objections. She chose half-a-dozen women from the camp and brought them to the house to learn the rudiments of sweeping, washing-up, bed-making, vegetable peeling and other rather simple jobs. Then she sat down and made out a list of the stores she wanted sent up from Brisbane. Booramby killed its own beef, so a quantity of food was no great problem. Behind the kitchen was the old brick oven, little used now, but well-suited to large-scale cookery of joints, poultry and vast great pies.

The influx of visitors was only what many station homes coped with for the yearly Picnic Race Meetings of past generations. Miss Cora knew how to manage, and Perina would be there to help her—when she was not helping Tod. Trucks arrived laden with goods, with cases of drink, bundles of sheets and blankets lent by neighbours, the nearest of whom was forty miles away. These people had all been invited for the day. Nakimer's stud was well-known, and the fact that he bought and bred Quarter Horses, which some of them had never seen, convinced the neighbours that the show would be worth seeing.

By the time Perina and Frank Howells arrived, the preparations were well under way. Her welcome warmed the heart; even Aunt Cora looked pleased when her great-niece in her cool dress, with her brown skin and pale gold hair, made everyone feel it was apt that the showpiece was to be Golden Perina.

That night Nakimer called Frank Howells and Perina in to talk with Kelly and Tod, and to draw up some kind of programme of events. Every time the Quarter Horses came into it, Tod's name was coupled with theirs. Perina frowned and chewed her pencil, trying to get some sort of order down on paper.

Frank Howells leaned back and lit a cigarette. He was a small, wiry man, an ex-steeplechase jockey who was known as a fine trainer. He and Nakimer had been friends, as well as in business together, for many years. He smiled through the smoke.

"A bloke told me about an event at the Quarter Horse Show at Texas—in the States," he added, remembering that Australia also has her Texas. "They had a two-twenty yards between a Quarter Horse and a Cadillac. They raced from a standing start and the Quarter Horse whipped the pants off the Cadillac every time! Think yours could do that, Tod?"

Tod smiled, then said gravely, "If their horses can do that, then so can mine."

Nakimer sat up, his face red with enthusiasm. "We'll do the same thing! The blokes'll 'ave a few bets on that! We'll try it out tomorrow."

Perina looked thoughtful. She sighed and said, "Something looks awfully funny about this programme. Tod seems to be everywhere, but that shouldn't matter." She stopped as Aunt Cora handed her a cup of tea.

Frank took his cup saying, "I'll tell you what I think it is. You have all the horses down in their double stud-book names, 'Golden Perina', 'Bronze Star' and so on, and as Tod handles them every time, I think you should give him both his names. What's your last name, Tod?"

Tod looked at him, his eyes wide with surprise. It had never occurred to him he might have another name. White people had two names, but at the camp there were "Charlies" and "Gibbers" and "Bootlaces", and no surnames; in fact, he had never heard the word "surname". Perina laughed.

"Of course. What's your tribal name, Tod?"

Tod looked blank and the missus stood behind Nakimer's chair and gazed strangely down at him.

"I don't know. I'm just Tod. I've always been just Tod."

"Then we'll give you another name," Perina said promptly. "*I* think as you've always lived on Booramby and you're practically one of the family, you should be 'Tod Greer'."

There was a moment's silence and Tod smiled; a small boy's smile of delight at a happy idea. Before he could speak Aunt Cora, her face flushed, turned angrily on Perina.

"Don't you *dare*—"

She turned and left the room. Perina looked bewildered, Nakimer said nothing but his face wore a small, rather sardonic grin. Perina glanced at Tod and it hurt her heart to see the bewildered expression with which he looked back at her. She was grateful to Frank for breaking in.

"Come to think of it, Tod doesn't need another name. Men and women who're the tops at their jobs often use only one name, and Tod's the best there is with horses. I think 'Tod' looks pretty good, however often it's used."

Perina looked at him gratefully. "Of course you're right. 'Tod' it is, and I just wish 'Perina' could mean as much, and mean *me* instead of 'Golden Perina'."

So the subject was changed and they went back to the programme, but in her heart Perina found it difficult to forgive Aunt Cora for her unkindness to Tod.

"Tod rides everything and does all the showing," Frank complained. "People'll think no-one else can ride the Quarter Horses."

Nakimer glared at him. "Tod trains 'em, he rides 'em because he knows what they can and can't do, and that's how it's goin' to be."

Frank knew better than to argue.

When the meeting was over Tod returned to the stables, and the men went off to bed. Perina walked to the kitchen and found Aunt Cora sitting at the table staring before her, her face grey and bitter as Perina had not seen it for years. She sat down and asked gently. "Aunt Cora, why were you so cruel to Tod?"

Aunt Cora was silent. Perina sighed and walked

round the table to kiss the old woman goodnight.

"I—didn't mean to hurt Tod," said her aunt. "Don't ask that again, please."

"I won't. Why should Tod want our name? I just thought—"

"You don't understand." The old voice was harsh, but Perina forced a smile.

"All right, let's forget about it. I won't ever ask it again, and I'm sure Tod won't."

"There—how's that?"

Perina in slacks and a checked shirt streaky with sweat stood back, curry-comb in hand, and admired Goldy's shot-silk hide, soft and gleaming like a light in the shadowy stable. Tod looked up from where he was polishing her hooves, and nodded.

They had worked on the horses since early morning and now everything was shipshape. Tod pushed the door wide open and sunlight flooded in. The Thoroughbreds were out in the paddock, playing second fiddle on this day. Everyone had been deeply disappointed when Fools' Gold had given birth to a chestnut foal instead of another white Palomino, but secretly Tod had been glad; he wanted his Goldy to be the only one until, in her turn, she produced a Palomino.

Perina brushed a damp streak of hair from her forehead. "Come up to the house, Tod. We'll have a long, cool drink before I begin helping Aunt Cora. I've brought you a new atlas and a picture, and some cuttings about Quarter Horses and Palominos."

Tod followed her, and they sat down before the kitchen table, spread Tod's new atlas out before them and drank thirstily. Tod was awed and delighted by his new possession. Perina leaned across and began to show him how to use the atlas, pinpointing their own position as a guide. She also produced a print of a Greek vase on which was the head of one of the "fair-maned" horses of the times although on the vase the mane was a deep purple. Perina explained that the "fair-maned" horses of Greece were believed to have been Palominos and then she found Greece in the atlas for him.

Maps puzzled Tod. He could not really translate flat colours and sprawling outlines into countries, but the pictures sandwiched between the maps helped him. Perina turned to a map of the Middle East.

"Look, Tod. There . . . and here . . ." she said, pointing to North Africa. "These are where our Thoroughbreds got their Arab blood. In Morocco and in Algeria, Palominos are greatly valued. They're not allowed to be exported, and no Christian— that's what I am, Tod—is allowed to own one. Over here on the map, in Arabia, they are just as precious, and they call them the 'Ashgar Muharrak' which means 'the fiery chestnuts'.

"There have been lots of famous Quarter Horses. I told you about their grandfather, Old Sorrell, and there was one called 'Marion's Girl' who, thirty years ago, was so wonderful at cutting out cattle that one man said she was the 'cow-pony with a master's degree', which meant she knew everything about the job. Another horse was famous for his speed: his name was 'Rukin String'. And I think uncle told you about the stallion 'Pronto Mio', who sold for over eleven thousand dollars and came to Australia as recently as 1966. Do you believe that little Goldy can compete with these horses, Tod?"

Tod's answer was a withering look and Perina smiled. Reluctantly Tod closed his atlas, and they both went about their various jobs.

The side veranda of the homestead was set out with rows of stretcher beds like a hospital ward, and the bedrooms all had several beds in them. Great stacks of food had been prepared; a bullock had been slaughtered and the meat dressed ready for the oven.

The other stablemen took over the Thoroughbreds while Tod, with Perina's help, saw to his precious Quarter Horses and Kelly supervised everywhere. Nakimer and Frank Howells saw the landing ground was cleared. A couple of miles from this strip they prepared a ring, a measured course, and their workmen made a broad, flat track, two hundred and twenty feet in length, with a runway both ends for the car. This was the track on which Goldy would challenge a Holden.

Everyone was keyed up. Sheds with leafy roofs had been erected; barrels of beer had been rolled down the hill and set up ready, and there was plenty of room under the shady trees for the expected guests. The men from the weir—Mackenzie's foreman, Casey, and the others—had been a great help, and had postponed their departure so as to be present on the great day.

LITTLE GOLDY

The plane came in about 9 A.M. like a dark bird against the pale morning sky. It touched down on the new runway and the passengers spilled out. Nakimer and Frank Howells led them back to the house for a light snack before they all went down to the training ground with its sheds and tracks.

The far-off "neighbours" were arriving, met by Miss Cora and Perina. The women were a little nervous of Miss Greer, who did her best to be gracious, but was glad to find she could leave things to Perina who managed the strangers perfectly. Soon the women were following the men to the ground. Tod and Alf had already taken the horses down, Alf acting as Tod's right-hand man for the day.

Stockmen had brought two hundred head of Booramby cattle into the half-moon that was the cattle-camp. This was the raw material that was to be worked on by the Quarter Horses. The cattle were quiet enough; no cattleman lets his stock run themselves tough, and the Booramby cattle were handled by experts. All the same, they would not submit tamely to being twisted and turned by horses. The people, although there were probably no more than fifty of them, moved about and looked a larger crowd than they were against the background of space, and the dry, pale-golden grass.

The events began. A few of the well-handled Thoroughbreds were paraded and admired, but everyone was really waiting to see the Quarter Horses. The first to appear were the three original brood mares, Bronze Star, Stormcloud and Fools' Gold, their young foals following behind. So these were the horses that were fast enough to race, brainy enough for polo, smooth as hacks and, most of all, brilliant as stockhorses. The beauty of Fools' Gold was loudly acclaimed, and the other Quarter Horses followed her as though she were a bell-wether.

Tod stopped his horses in front of the crowd. Several men ducked under the fence and came to run their hands over the horses, and they were surprised at the calm way the Quarter Horses, and even the foals, endured their handling. At a word from Nakimer Tod led them away and left them under a nearby clump of trees.

Nakimer moved among his guests, his face red and beaming. He climbed on a stump and shouted for silence.

"Tod's going to ride Golden Perina, the Palomino Quarter Horse. He'll show her the steer he wants her to cut out of the mob, and at the same time two of my stockmen'll try to stop Goldy gettin' the steer out. We'll see who wins."

He got down off the stump and watched Tod saddle Goldy while the two mounted stockmen waited for him. Perina held her breath. Nothing must go wrong. This was Tod's day and it must be perfect. But he was only fifteen—a genius with horses perhaps, but he had never done exhibition riding. She wished it were over.

Tod rode quietly into the herd and the two stockmen waited. The cattle moved a little, mooing restlessly as they parted before Goldy. Tod selected a small, lively steer and Goldy nuzzled it gently. Tod sat slack-reined and easily balanced, leaving the tactics entirely to Goldy.

Nakimer took out his stopwatch. Just eighteen seconds elapsed from the time when Goldy first nuzzled the steer until it was out of the herd. Then the two stockmen closed in on the steer, shouting and waving their hats. It was alarmed and it tried desperately to charge back into the herd but Goldy was between the agile, frightened animal and the mob and it became a battle of wits and fast reflexes.

Light on her hooves as a ballerina, Goldy moved nimbly before the steer. Tod swayed to her movements, but not by pressure of knees or touch on the reins did he suggest to her what she should do. The steer rushed; Goldy headed him off. The steer tried to circle Goldy; but she, agile as a cat, would not let him pass. Perina watched with her heart in her mouth while, for two minutes by Nakimer's stopwatch, the steer dodged and Goldy blocked its path. Suddenly the steer gave up. The shouting stockmen and the waving hats could not be harder to pass than this shimmering mare. For a moment the steer and Goldy stood nose to nose. Then, as the steer turned and broke through the shouting stockmen, Goldy closed up on it from behind and, quite undeterred by the hats and the loud voices, gently guided the steer to where she wanted to leave it under a tree.

The crowd shouted themselves hoarse, and the two stockmen rode back with wide grins on their dark faces. Then Tod came back and the crowd, who knew a horseman when they saw one, shouted anew. Filled with pride in his horse, Tod rode over to Nakimer.

"Well done, boy. Take her out now while she's warmed up. Take the saddle off and let her cut out a beast by herself."

Not for anything would Tod have refused, but he felt a thrill of nervousness for Goldy as she had only done this particular thing three times. He jumped down, undid the girths, and handed his saddle to Kelly. Then he sprang onto Goldy's back and rode her quietly towards the mob. He rode her through the moving cattle and chose another wiry-looking steer. Then he let Goldy shoulder it a couple of times before he slipped off her back into the dust of the herd, leaving the reins on her neck. He went quietly through the post and rails fence, and waited.

Goldy, with veteran calm, followed the steer, nudging it, working it always towards the perimeter of the milling cattle. Nakimer, timing the event, glowed with pride when, in twenty seconds from the time Tod left her, Goldy had the steer out of the mob and trotting, head high, towards where its fellows were held beneath a tree.

Tod whistled to Goldy and she came to him. He rode her back to the noisiest welcome a small crowd could make. Perina came running out and patted Goldy, her eyes shining.

"Tod, let Goldy find something. Here—take my scarf."

Tod showed the scarf to Goldy as he slipped to the ground. "Go and shut your eyes!" he said, and Goldy moved a few paces away with her rump to Tod while he tucked the scarf into Nakimer's pocket.

Someone shouted, "She's peekin'."

Tod walked away from Nakimer and called to Goldy. "Find it!"

Goldy turned, tossing her lovely head so that the movement of the wind rippled the shining paleness of her mane. She trotted to Nakimer, put out her head and sniffed at him. Then she pushed her nose into his pocket and came up with Perina's scarf between her teeth. She trotted back to Tod with it, shaking her head delightedly at the applause. Someone shouted, "Why, she's a real old ham!"

Two breeders wanted to ride Quarter Horses themselves and Tod suggested Jet and Missy as he wanted to spell Goldy before her timed gallop. The two men, Summers and Masters, knew exactly what to expect of a good stockhorse and they were not disappointed.

For the quarter mile race, on which the men

were wanting to bet, Kelly rode Jet and Alf rode Missy, while Tod was on Goldy. Jet improved on his early times, making a run of 22.1; Missy did well with 22.3; and Goldy beat them both with a gallop that shook the experts at 21.8!

Nakimer had waited all day for his favourite event, horse against car. At about four o'clock Tod lined the rested Goldly up against a fairly new Holden car. Its driver was confident he would win his race over 220 yards; but he didn't win. Goldy's strong haunches, coupled with the rather short legs of the Quarter Horse, gave her a low centre of gravity that made her getaway speed greater than the experts had ever seen. She shot ahead of the car from the standing start, and won all the way.

Tod had arranged Goldy's events so well that she was never overstrained. She was as fresh at the end of the day as she had been at the beginning, and she and Missy gave one final exhibition. They "fought" as Tod had taught them to do, as the young Abo boy imagined the Sybarite horses had fought, and Perina, leaning on the rails beside her uncle, felt her eyes filled with emotional tears at the beauty and delicate grace of the pair as they reared high, boxing each other with their elegant hooves, stretching shining necks to get in a nip, turning and prancing with the grace and power of ballet dancers, until Tod gave the word to stop. Their hooves came down on the trampled earth, and they both trotted over to Tod to be petted and given carrots.

It was over: time for the spectators to leave. Nakimer was like a schoolboy, scoffing when the men told Tod that he could have a job in their stables any time. Tod grinned, and Nakimer looked smug. He could not imagine Tod ever leaving *his* stables.

Those who had come by car went away and the plane passengers went back to the homestead to await dinner. Perina walked up to the stables with Tod and the Quarter Horses, telling him again how wonderfully everything had gone, and Tod looked at his treasures, his heart big with love and pride.

It had been his day.

Tod never thought of his food, his bed on stable-straw, as being anything for which he was in debt to Nakimer. If he had, he would have known that the debt had been repaid a thousandfold. No-one could estimate what the trained performances of *his* horses, the perfection of *his* riding would mean to Booramby in terms of money. But Perina thought about it. She would talk to her uncle about Tod's future, and make no bones about how much the old man owed to the boy.

She left the stables and hurried up to the house to help her aunt with the dinner. The verandas swarmed with men discussing the day's events. Tod and his Quarter Horses were being talked about by everyone.

That night Perina lay on a narrow stretcher in a tiny room separated from the dining-room by only a thin pinewood wall. She was too tired to sleep, which was just as well, because now, with dinner cleared away and the makeshift trestle tables dismantled, her uncle and some of his guests had settled down to a game of poker that would probably go on all night.

While the hands were being played it was quiet enough. Often Perina was on the edge of sleep when some triumphant player slapped down his hand with a shout of, "Gotcher!" Then there was laughter and the ring of voices; the sound of glasses being banged down on the wood; the riffling of card-packs; then a tense silence broken only by the bidders or by requests for cards. Someone won or someone lost. The voices broke out again.

It was impossible to sleep. Perina sighed and rose. She might drag her mattress farther away. She picked up her brightly-patterned dressing-gown, then threw it down again. She would trample on it if she wore it to drag her mattress outside. So she slipped into shirt and slacks and twisted her hair back from her face. She felt cooler and went out to reconnoitre.

Perina moved along the veranda in her soundless crepe-soled shoes to where a yellow wedge of light spilled out from the doorway. It lay on the veranda boards like sunlight, but the air above it was a blue haze from drifting smoke. Perina moved to the edge of the light so that she could look into the room without being seen herself.

Nakimer sat at the end of the table with a pile of winning chips beside him. His face was red and excited. He had not dreamed the day would be so successful when he thought up the idea of showing off his horses. He loved gambling, and now the game of poker just rounded off what the tough old man considered was a winner of a day.

Unseen herself, Perina watched the play for a time. She saw piles of chips dwindle and grow again, heard the roars of laughter when some bluff paid off. Bill Morgan, a sportswriter from a Brisbane daily, appeared to be winning. Snowy Trent, a fellow breeder, was losing to Nakimer. Frank Howells won or lost with an equally impassive face. Nakimer played recklessly, bluffing on two pairs and sometimes bringing it off.

In spite of her weariness Perina was so wide awake that she became interested in the game. No warning voice told her of the sudden cataclysm she was about to witness. There was a lull while glasses were filled. Snowy Trent's back was to her, and as he turned his head and the light flashed on his face Perina realized that he hated losing. He spoke quite casually, as if speaking to no-one in particular.

"They say Jim'll bet on anything. I'm not sure."

Nakimer fixed him with a belligerent, bloodshot eye, demanding, "What d'you mean by that?"

"Oh, I dunno. It's easy to lose money when you have it. I reckon a good gambler's a man who risks more than money. Now if that kid, Tod, was a gambler then 'e might take a chance on that Golden Perina. Jim 'ere might—if 'e was a gambler."

Through the silence someone said tersely, "Come on, deal up."

The game continued. Perina looked fearfully at Nakimer's morose face. He disliked the inference in what Snowy Trent said, and he was an old man, tired from the day's excitement. Although he played poker automatically, to a certain extent the circumstances put him off his guard.

Card-taking and card-bidding went on as usual. Perina moved a little closer. She saw three kings in Snowy's hand, but she couldn't see what Nakimer held. The bidding rose; the others dropped out. Now Nakimer and Snowy were facing each other, their right hands pushing their chips into the centre. Snowy bought more chips, then Nakimer, his last chip gone, challenged him. Both men put down their hands. Nakimer had three Queens: but Snow had his three Kings. Slowly Snowy raked in his winnings. He sat back and looked round the table.

"You blokes tired of playin'?"

No-one answered, but they all sat back. Again Snowy leaned forward and said, "I'd like to 'ave a night to remember, if Jim 'ere's man enough."

Perina felt furious with Snowy for baiting the old man, but there was nothing she could do except watch helplessly.

"Meanin' what, Trent?" Nakimer's voice was icy.

"Oh, so it's 'Trent' now you're losin'? I'll tell you, Greer. I'll double my winnin's and bet the ruddy lot against that showy Quarter Horse mare,

Goldy—No, wait a minute. The mare looked good enough today, but that's all froth. 'Ow do I know she's a stayer and worth more than a few circus tricks? Come on, now. If I win I'll take Golden Perina an' I'll give back my winnin's so you'll be gettin' a damn good price for 'er. If I lose, you keep Goldy and I get nothin'. Any man who won't take that on's a piker, an' maybe you're one, Greer?"

Perina wanted to cry out. She willed her uncle to refuse the bet. None of the men spoke, and Nakimer like a cornered bull swung his head slowly looking around him. Even Frank Howells' face was blank. By their code this was a duel between Snowy and Jim and they neither could nor would interfere. Nakimer lifted his head and the light fell full on his face, the face of an old bull being gored by a young rival and determined to make one last charge. He spoke one word.

"Done!"

The pity in Perina's heart turned to sheer fury. How dare her uncle do this to Tod again? How dare he play cards for what was as much to Tod as his own life? She remembered how Lucky had been sent away so casually, and she remembered Tod's despair. She knew with a terrible realization that Tod would never trust Nakimer again, that he would leave Booramby to go—where? Tod, with his genius for horses, his love that asked no more than to care for them, would end up thrown away, living in some sleezy town, broken by the vanity of a foolish old man who did not know what true pride meant, and was not man enough to refuse a dare.

She watched. No-one spoke. In the uncanny stillness the riffling of the pack, the sound of card sliding on card, was almost noisy. Nakimer dealt. Each man bought two cards. Perina's heart jumped. Snowy had three tens in his hand and had bought two sevens. She could not see Nakimer's hand. The two men put their hands on the table at the same time. Nakimer had three aces, but Snowy had a full hand.

Perina did not wait. She turned and ran blindly along the veranda and across the landing to the kitchen. The darkness seemed to make her knowledge of what had happened even more terrible. She switched on the light, flung herself into a chair before the table, put her head down on her arms and sobbed.

Aunt Cora was also sleepless. When the light sprang up in the kitchen a beam entered her window, and she rose, put on her austere dressing-gown, and found Perina. Aunt Cora's anger and distress frightened the girl. The old woman had not admitted even to herself how much Tod had come to mean to her, for affection that she could not control annoyed her. And now her brother, of whom she had always disapproved, had done this. And who was to tell Tod? Who was to break his heart all over again? She trembled with anger, wanting to comfort Perina, but shaking with the intensity of her rage.

Aunt Cora turned away and made a cup of tea

and persuaded Perina to go back to bed. She glanced at the clock. It was just before four. In a little over an hour it would be daylight, and Tod would have to be told. She suffered waves of fury against herself that she should be so vulnerable to another's pain. Her deepest rage was against Nakimer, but she felt a kind of anger against Perina, and Tod too, for making her suffer when all her life had been dedicated to avoiding the grief that human contacts bring. She sat gripping her thin hands together, her bony, grey-clad back to the open door. A slight sound made her look around. Tod was standing there. He nodded and gave her a grave little smile as he walked towards the veranda door. Miss Cora knew that he was going to the safe for food. All her pent-up rage at everyone, including herself, broke out like a coiled snake from too cramping a box.

"Nakimer lost Golden Perina in a poker game," she burst out.

The moment the words were out, she became filled with a dreadful panic. She had not meant to say it to Tod, standing there before her, slim and young and so easy to hurt. The colour drained from his face, noticeable despite his dusky skin. The missus thrust her hands against her throat as if to strangle the already-spoken words, and looked at Tod with fearful eyes.

He stood quite still for a minute, his face a mask, and then, without a word he went out again and the darkness swallowed him up. Aunt Cora could bear no more. She sat down and put her hands over her ears as if the secret she had spoken was shrieking back at her, and its voice was the voice of her agony.

Tod, cat-footed in the darkness, went into the stable. He knew what he must do, though the full bitterness of his betrayal had not really sunk in. Goldy stirred and whickered at him in the sweet-smelling darkness. He was not the Tod she knew; he was an automaton, going about what had to be done with a mechanical swiftness. Once he paused and put his face against the velvet of her nose.

A grass halter Tod had plaited for her hung from a peg. In a corner were the two spears and the boomerang he and Alf had made together, and with which they had sometimes hunted when the horses had been bedded down and the moon was full. The old dictionary was on a beam beside the door. He took it down, found a rag among those he used to polish the horses, and made a kind of bag, looping the string about his neck so that the book hung down onto his chest. He stripped off his shirt and shorts and stood naked in the darkness. Then he lifted his spears and the boomerang, whistled softly to Goldy, and left the stable.

Kelly, who slept above the next stable, heard movement below and came down and called to Tod. Tod stood before Kelly slim and young and disillusioned, naked as a myall. Very simply he told Kelly what Miss Cora had told him. He did not say what he meant to do, but Kelly knew. Years of civilization melted away from his old heart. The boy had been betrayed a second time, and for the meanest of motives. He put out his old hand and touched Tod's shoulder in a gesture of understanding, and went back to his loft, leaving Tod with the knowledge that he had one friend who would not betray him.

He whistled softly to Goldy and sprang on her back. He took nothing but this infinitely dear mare, leaving as naked as he had come into the world, save for the one incongruous package against his chest. The book was his, as were the halter, spears and boomerang.

Soon light would suffuse the world but now Goldy's pale body, her gleaming mane and tail, gave out an effulgence against the night as Tod rode down the hill, crossed the creek and merged into the shadowy plain beyond.

The plane took off at 7.30. In it were all the visitors except Frank Howells and Snowy Trent. Opinions were split over Snowy's wager with Jim Greer. Most of the men thought it a lousy trick to play on the old man and Snowy was disgruntled by their attitude. Only Frank Howells kept his poker face and refused to join in. But when breakfast was over and the visitors were on their way home, Frank Howells sat on the veranda and waited. He did not have to wait long. Snowy leaned on the veranda rail near him and asked in an injured voice, "What was eatin' those fellers? I won the mare fair and square, didn't I?"

"Did you?"

"Yeah, and you know it."

"I don't know it. You take a man's hospitality, you know he's had quite a day for an old feller, you know 'e's been drinkin', and so you do your stuff. Then you wonder why decent men think you're a bit of a bastard."

"Hey! You watch out what you're callin' me!"

"Oh, here comes Miss Perina. Ask her what she thinks."

Snowy was very taken with Perina and he wanted to look well in her eyes. He had sensed a cool, cutting contempt earlier on which riled him. Well, all or nothing, he'd ask her.

"Miss Perina, Howells reckons I took advantage of your uncle, playin' 'im poker for Golden Perina, and I say I won fair and square. What do you say?"

Nakimer stepped out onto the veranda. Now he was ashamed of what he had done and dreaded telling Tod. He was stricken by Perina's icy attitude. She turned and her blue eyes blazed with fury in her pale face as she answered.

"Now that my uncle's here, Mr Trent, I'll be glad to tell you what I think of you both." She turned and faced Nakimer. "Once I thought you were a man, now I know you're a shallow show-off, a Judas who has betrayed Tod a second time. You've destroyed Tod with your silly vanity." The words choked her and Nakimer looked as astonished as if a pretty little possum had turned into a death-adder. Perina whirled on Snowy Trent.

"As for you, taking advantage of a stupid old man, you're no more of a man than he is. Goldy doesn't belong to either of you. By every moral right she's Tod's. You—you disgusting thieves! I hate you!"

She forced herself to walk away, and when she turned the corner of the veranda she ran blindly, until her aunt caught her in her arms and held her as she shook with fury and tried to tell her what had happened.

"Pull yourself together, girl," said Aunt Cora sharply. "You must get that mare back for Tod. You've only struck the first blow; now come back with me and finish the job!"

They could hear Frank's voice as they walked back.

"Perina's right, neither of you own that mare. Tod made her everything she is. If you're half a man, Jim, you'll forget this 'sportsman' stuff, give Snowy a fair price, and see if he's man enough to return the mare. Oh, not to you—you don't know how to keep what's yours, Jim. Today you've lost a niece, a mare, and the best boy you ever had." He paused and fixed Snowy with a cold eye. "Snowy, you've won the mare, and if you take her you'll lose the respect of every decent man in Queensland. I'll make it my business to see that every sportswriter in Australia gets the real story."

Snowy threw up his hands helplessly. "Damn it! I don't want the mare. Take her back, she's not worth it."

Perina spoke in a disgusted voice. "As if we could trust either of you! Uncle Jim, get your cheque book and pay Mr Trent back. Mr Howells, please write out a bill of sale, if that's what you call it, and make it change-of-mind proof, making Golden Perina over to Tod."

So finally Perina stood with a slip of paper in her hand. "I don't know how the paper would stand up in a court of law," said Frank, "but apart from the interested parties, we have three witnesses to the sale, and that should do."

"Is it enough to put 'Tod'?" Perina asked anxiously. "You see, he hasn't another name."

"It would be better if he had a surname, but again, we're the witnesses."

Suddenly the gloom cleared. Perina glanced at her aunt and saw her face flushing a little, and thought, "Strange, how tough she tries to be". She looked at Nakimer and her anger faded. He looked so old and tired. He was usually spoiling for a fight, but now he had scarcely begun to put up any opposition. He seemed weary and bewildered. Age had taken the fire from him, and she saw just a tired old man before her. A faint touch of his usual self made him say, "We'd better send for the boy and tell him that Goldy is his." He stood up and looked towards the stable, adding, "Kelly's on his way up now. He can send him here when he returns."

Kelly walked slowly up the steps. He, too, was tired after the excitement of the day before. He nodded briefly to the others and stood, a thin crow of a man, looking coldly into the frosty blue eyes of the man who had been his boss for fifty years. There was no apology in his voice when he said, "Tod left—ridin' Goldy."

"Please let me talk to Kelly, uncle," said Perina.

Nakimer nodded but before the girl could ask Kelly about Tod, Aunt Cora forced herself to speak.

"It's my fault he's gone. He came into the kitchen early this morning and I told him what Jim had done. He just went back to the stables."

Then Kelly told of his last encounter with Tod and Goldy, and of how they had gone away into the night.

"You let him go, taking the mare?"

Kelly nodded. "She was Tod's mare; he had made her what she was, and he had Nakimer's promise never to sell her. Nakimer broke his word. If I had been Tod, I would have gone too."

Perina told Kelly how Goldy was now legally Tod's. "So you see," she finished gently, "he need not have taken her away if he had only waited."

Frank spoke. "Who can get him back now? Unless he wants to return, no-one'll find him, riding a mare like Goldy and knowing the country as he does."

So the great Booramby horse-show ended in a sadness and loss that was quite unnecessary. In the weeks that followed the newspapers played up the Booramby horses, both Thoroughbreds and Quarter Horses—and Tod looked out from every page. Prices of the sales were phenomenal, but Nakimer had never seemed less interested in the money angle. He wanted Tod to come home.

He had other worries, too. In the North, properties were so enormous that fencing was not always adequate, and from time to time there was trouble from cattle duffers. In the wild hills and deep gullies these men on their fast, stolen horses, made off with cattle and horses, hiding them in the hills and collecting herds that assumed large proportions, before moving them over the borders into the other states where they could be sold.

Now the thieves were becoming bolder. The Booramby muster showed definite losses of cattle, and it was the same with the other properties. But when a couple of Thoroughbreds disappeared, Nakimer became really worried. Both Quarter Horses and Thoroughbreds were always kept under close watch, and yet the Thoroughbreds had gone.

Of course the story of Tod's dramatic getaway was all around the district. Sometimes someone would claim to have seen a pale golden mare with a startlingly silver mane and tail, ridden by a slim boy. Sometimes the Booramby men saw the imprint of neat hooves in the dried mud around the bores. When the horse thieves became bolder, naturally outsiders wondered if Tod was having a hand in the stealing, but Tod's friends knew better. They knew he would never help strange men to take loved horses from the stable he had served so well.

Perina went for long rides, always hoping to see Tod. She wrote to him and left the letter in the long cave, but she never saw any trace of him. She rode to the cliff-top overlooking the narrow path down which she and Tod used to lead their horses in single file but the grass on the creek-dividing island was an undisturbed, feathery green. She rode up the high peak on the edge of the chasm from where she could see the horizon all around her but there was no gleam of gold or silver, no glimpse of the boy who would be riding Goldy.

The workmen from the finished weir had dispersed, and Mackenzie had said goodbye to the silent Nakimer, who had aged greatly. Aunt Cora blamed herself for Tod's disappearance, despite Perina's assurances that Tod would come back to Booramby, the only home he had ever known. Once, when Kelly had spoken of the package Tod had worn suspended from his neck, and said it looked like the book Tod was always reading, Aunt Cora had bent her head to hide her eyes: Tod and his treasure, the old, torn dictionary, hurt her unbearably.

"Let me send away for a new dictionary," Perina had said in an effort to comfort her, "then you'll have it to give to Tod when he comes home."

Aunt Cora had agreed forlornly and in due time a splendid, red dictionary with pictures in it had arrived for Miss Greer.

Alf, who had taken over the Quarter Horses with Kelly, kept them well cared for, but he was not

Tod; he was only a boy who liked horses well enough, doing work he had been taught. It was not for him a labour of love.

One noon Kelly heard whinnying and thudding hooves coming from the far paddock in which some of the Thoroughbreds were grazing, and he rode down to the corner of the paddock, hidden by the trees growing along the creek. Excited Thoroughbreds were moving about. One of them was missing and another was trailing a snapped rope around her neck. Kelly galloped to the far fence and, in the distance, caught sight of the missing horse, cantering between two strangers who rode big rangy horses Kelly had never seen. The outer gate was closed. The thieves had clearly hoped to operate and leave no signs, but the second horse had fought them and escaped, and they had had to move away quickly.

Kelly immediately reported back to Nakimer who phoned his neighbours—a long-distance business when the nearest was forty miles away. Word went among them until the whole district was alerted. Owners checked their horses and made startling discoveries of losses that had so far passed unnoticed amongst stockhorses that were not regularly handled.

Two mounted policemen called to check on Nakimer's losses and they told him the settlers were thoroughly roused and anxious to nip in the bud the horse-stealing and cattle-duffing. Police reinforcements were spread throughout the district, a fact they were trying to keep from the thieves.

All this was an added worry to Perina. To see Goldy would be to covet her, although it would be difficult to sell such a spectacular mare. If the horse thieves wanted Goldy, what might they not do to Tod?

Perina's holiday would be over in a week. She wanted to stay until Tod came home, not simply for his sake, but also because her aunt and uncle had become old and troubled since Tod's disappearance and needed her. Every day she rode among the horses, watching them play in the creek or graze in the big paddocks. Then one day she was surprised to find that there was not a horse in the water, and she rode up the far bank with a puzzled, uneasy feeling. She looked across the far paddock and saw only old Jake and five other horses, and the gate on the far side swinging loosely on its hinges. She calculated that eighteen horses were missing: Thoroughbreds, six Quarter Horses, and three foals—her uncle's entire stock, except for Goldy.

Perina cantered over to the gate. In the dusty ground were the marks of many hooves. She closed the gate, and turned and rode back swiftly, stopping to tell Kelly what she had seen and then riding on to the homestead. She slid to the ground, pulled the reins over her horse's head so that it would stay there in the manner of bush horses, and ran up the steps to wake Nakimer from his doze. Nakimer opened his eyes and smiled at her, and she had a sudden stab of dread that this news would break the old man.

It did nothing of the sort. His conscience was not troubled this time, and he suddenly became his old fighting self.

"By God, we'll get them for this!" he shouted. "Perina, get Kelly and the boys. I'll ring the emergency number that alerts the police. This is a job for everyone. We'll get those swine."

He made for his office at top speed and Perina smiled with relief as she rushed off to tell Kelly to get the men. Kelly was able to muster five men immediately, mounted on strong horses, and Nakimer, who seemed to have shed twenty years, showed them the police map and told them the plan.

"Get the boys going, Kelly. We've got half-a-dozen police and ourselves to man the inner ring, and if those so-and-so's break through us, then the outer ring'll be in place in four hours, and they'll get 'em. I want *us* to have the fun." He patted the coiled stockwhip that hung on his shoulder. He had been a famous man with a whip in his day. "We cover the ground from Tenby's Rock and the North Bore. I'd like to ride with you, but I can't, so Miss Perina and I'll take the station wagon."

Perina pointed to a small gadget hanging down onto his chest and asked, "What's that for?"

The old man grinned. He was enjoying himself like any schoolboy. "That's a piece of radio non-sense—sends and receives. They say you can keep in touch over distances of up to a hundred miles. The police left it with me," he added offhandedly, trying to pretend he did not care. "Lot of rot. I can cooee further than this thing'll sound!"

"You're showing off, you know you love it!" remarked Perina severely.

He smiled at her. "We'll take the guns in the car, but I don't think we'll 'ave to use them. Ready? This is what we've been waitin' for. Off you go. We've got about another hour's daylight. Kelly, I want you with us."

The men went off to get their horses, and Nakimer, Kelly and Perina got in the car. Rather to Aunt Cora's horror, a gunshot sounded faintly in the distance.

"Police," Nakimer told them, "signalling they're in position. They've been at the three mile boundary for a week. You didn't know, but I did," he added boastfully. He was in his element now, and tried the little radio-transmitter. To his great surprise, it worked. He was told that in half an hour everyone would be ready to move forward and close the circle.

The station wagon was to command a larger share of the circle than did the mounted men. Perina drove up a hill which gave a view of Red Rocks. Before them was the new weir, the dam behind it holding fifteen feet of water. Nakimer watched through his field glasses, and told Perina and Kelly as the men took up their positions. Perina looked sadly at Red Rocks and thought of the happy days she had spent there with Tod. Where was he now?

Her heart missed a beat.

She saw a streak like pale light move from behind one rock to behind another. She rubbed her eyes. In her heart Perina was sure that shimmering streak was Goldy moving fast. She felt terribly uneasy.

Eventually Perina felt she must have imagined what she had seen. But she had not imagined it. Tod was back from beyond Booramby's borders, back from living by his spear, and still dressed only in his wild man's naga that hung from his waist by a grass-woven string. His road had been chosen with one end in view; that Goldy should have plenty, and she was in superb condition.

Tod was thinner. The wild life had hardened him and his only desire was to stay away from the man who had betrayed him. Then a kind of homesickness had crept over him. At Booramby was the only family he had ever known. So he returned to Red Rocks. No-one could find him there for he knew the terrain better than anyone else, and Perina just might come to the rocks some day.

Sleeping beside Goldy one night he had felt the ground thudding under his head. He took Goldy and hid her in the secret place amongst the rocks. Then he left her and climbed a rock to look below where three men were driving several horses before them. They were not Booramby horses, but Tod knew that honest men did not muster horses at night.

Next day he followed their hoof-prints. In a cleft in the hills he saw below him at least thirty horses, and among those was one Booramby Thoroughbred. For two days he watched the men. The drowsy morning breeze brought the acrid smell of burning flesh, and then he was certain that he was looking at the hide-out of horse stealers, and that the men were busy changing brands.

Tod watched and saw the men come out of the cleft and cover the entrance with boughs and rocks before riding off. Tod did not believe they would do their thieving in daylight, so he and Goldy went into the long cave for the heat of the day, and slept. At nightfall he decided to watch for the men, and if they were heading for Booramby he and Goldy, with her speed, would go there and give the alarm.

Tod, followed by Goldy, left the long cave one evening, not noticing Perina's letter which had fallen and been covered by rubble long ago. He heard the movement of horses, then men's voices, and he stopped. A gun-shot came from somewhere. At first he thought the men must be out shooting, then other shots followed from different directions. The men's voices came to him in loud excitement and sent him running to peer over a boulder.

He saw the three horse-thieves pointing at a hill on which they could see a station wagon and men on horses—Booramby men, spaced out to make part of a circle. He put his hand on Goldy's soft muzzle to keep her quiet while he listened.

"Of all the flamin' luck! They're on to us an' we've the finest lot of 'orses we ever 'ad—"

Tod edged to the right and looked below him, feeling fury rising in him. Down there were *his* Quarter Horses, *his* foals, stolen while he slept! Quickly he counted eighteen of the finest horses of the Booramby stud. The men were shouting now and Tod moved back to his first position. One man, who seemed to be in command, had a face that was dark with rage.

" 'Ow can we keep 'em out of sight? By God, before I'll give 'em up I'll slaughter the lot!"

Tod shivered. He must hear what they meant to do.

"Git 'em movin'," the big man went on. "Git 'em down to where we saw that island. You, Gib, take the battery and dynamite sticks. Put the battery in the centre of the weir an' run the wires back to one side. 'Ave the switch there so you can run like hell! If we 'ave to, we'll breach the weir. The water'll do the rest. If we can't ave 'em, then no-one else will. When the balloon goes up that damned lot out there'll be too busy to follow us! Come on, git the 'orses down, git goin', Gib."

Tod was so appalled at what he had heard that for the first time in his life he nearly fainted, but there was no time for that, no time to wait for help. He'd just have to do his best. Gib cantered off to set the charge that would smash the weir gates and drown the horses. In an instant the other two men would be gone. Like a small thunderbolt Tod leaped to the top of the rock and threw himself down on the big man's shoulders, knocking him to the ground. Instantly the other was on him, and though he fought like a wildcat, they were too much for him. Even in the desperation of the fight he saw Goldy's nose poking round a rock, and he yelled at her to go back. Then Tod was pinioned, his arms and legs tied clumsily with a length of rope. The big man looked down and snarled.

"I oughta smash ya, ya young dingo! When that weir goes you'll go right inter the water. Now we got other things ter think about. Come on, Skid, we'll git the 'orses down. Leave the kid, 'e'll keep. I reckon we've got exactly twelve minutes ter git the 'orses on the island an' git back ourselves. Git goin'."

They mounted and Tod watched them ride away, driving his Quarter Horses before them, sending them to their death. He shuddered as he saw in his mind the thundering wall of water engulfing them. He twisted and turned, but the ropes were thick and stiff. He stopped and whistled. Thank goodness Goldy was free! She trotted anxiously to him, shaking her pretty head, and Tod held up his roped-together hands and gave her an order. She bent her head and tugged at the rope. If only she'd hurry! He praised her as soon as she realized what he wanted, and she fastened her strong teeth in the rope, pulling it this way and that. It loosened and suddenly he was free. He bent and tore the rope from his ankles. All the time his inborn tribal sense of timing told him how seconds and minutes had ticked away.

There was a quarter of a mile to go—Goldy's distance—and he had possibly a minute to get there, a minute before the explosion went off. He must get there, must disconnect the fuse somehow before it was too late. Tod hurled himself onto Goldy's back and bent low over the dry, wind-blown spume of her mane. It whipped his face as he drove her as he had never driven her before. She must do the distance in 21 seconds flat—or else. If only she understood what was at stake! Goldy flew like a bird, her sure hooves never faltering, sure as if they had been on the smooth track of her practice gallops. But this was no track: it was a rocky hill-side. And every second counted.

Faintly, on the wind, came Nakimer's great shout. They had seen the horse-thief making for the weir and now they saw Tod and guessed why he was here. Orders flew around the circle of men, keen as hunting wolves. No-one could reach the boy in time to help him, but they could close in on the thieves who would not escape, whatever happened.

The mare and the boy scrambled up the earthen side of the dam. Gib was kneeling on the walk at the back of the weir, holding the battery box necessary for the explosion. From it two wires ran back in Tod's direction. He knew the wires led to the switch behind him that would trigger off the explosion.

Gib saw him as he came over the earthen wall. Gib was a big man, and Tod knew he had little chance of holding him, yet if Gib reached that switch. For an instant Tod felt sick at what he must do, but Goldy must help to save the horses. As Gib jumped onto the flat patch of earth where Goldy and Tod stood, Tod gave the signal to Goldy to fight.

"Fight! Fight!" he said savagely, praying she would know that this must not be a polite bout such as he and she indulged in. This was life or death, and Goldy seemed to understand. As Tod sprang towards the wires he saw Goldy rear up, teeth bared, dancing towards the man.

To say that Goldy's opponent was astonished would be an understatement. He realized that the lovely mare meant business, and that she was between him and Tod. He stooped to pick up a rock, but Goldy's hoof struck his shoulder and the rock went wide. Then he was in a flurry of beating hooves and snaking neck, wild eyes and gleaming teeth that caught and nipped, hooves that struck and danced away.

Tod tugged and tore at the wires until one came away in his hand. He turned for a moment and saw Gib on his knees, terrified of the exquisite creature that was bruising and pommelling him. Here was his opportunity. He ran along the walk to the all-important battery, tore it from the concrete pavement and hurled it into the dam.

But now fresh danger threatened. The man on

the floor had an ugly knife in his hand and was reaching up and stabbing at the belly of the mare.

Tod kicked at the hand that held the knife as Goldy reared above them both, then he turned swiftly under her body and leaped onto her back. She lowered her hooves to gallop away, and as she turned the man beneath her brought the knife up again and an ugly red line scored her shimmering flank. The man had not been able to put much power into his strike, but to Tod it was as though his own heart had been cut out.

He rode down the bank to the sound of shouting, the grinding of gears, the humming of the car engine—but he heard and saw nothing. He flung himself off the mare's back and stood by her flank touching her gently, sick with anxiety, unconscious of everything but Goldy herself. She flinched and whickered, but now Tod could see that it was only a flesh wound. There would be a scar, but the muscles were undamaged. In his relief he put his arms around her neck and she nuzzled and snuffled and whickered at him, and that was how Perina found them; the almost naked boy, burnt to a tribal darkness by the sun, and the beautiful golden Palomino Quarter Horse.

Tod looked at Perina wonderingly when she told him of her letter which must still be in the long cave, and even more so when she told him that Goldy was really and legally his, and that it had been Nakimer's doing. He turned his face against

Goldy's neck and stood trying to let the fact sink in that she was his for always, and as he stood there the last drops of bitterness in his heart against Nakimer dissolved for ever.

On Kelly's advice Tod rode Goldy home, and Perina took Gib's deserted horse and rode with him. He and Perina stood beside the trail and watched the eighteen Booramby horses come up one by one, and Tod went to Missy and Jet, and big Goldy and their foals, and patted and made much of them.

Gib, who had tried to swim across the dam to safety, had been caught by the police, together with one of his companions. The third thief had tried to break the police cordon and had nearly succeeded, but Nakimer, longing to be in the excitement, had charged across the plain in the station wagon. Holding the wheel with one hand and his stockwhip in the other he had sent the long plaited leather lash curling around the man's neck, and he had jerked him neatly and painfully from the saddle.

Back at the stable Tod, with Perina's and Kelly's help, was attending to Goldy's honourable wound.

"Come with me to see Aunt Cora," said Perina when they had finished, and Kelly produced a shirt and shorts of Tod's that he had been keeping just for this moment. The homestead veranda was full of excited men discussing the capture and Tod's part in saving the horses as the boy followed Perina into the kitchen. Aunt Cora rose. She was as tall and as gaunt as ever, and Tod was glad because that was the way he knew her best. She put her hand on his shoulder.

"I'm so glad you're back, Tod."

Nakimer wanted to see Tod too, but Tod would not go among the crowd of men around him, so finally the old man too came down to the kitchen.

"Don't go away again boy," he said. "I need you, and so do the horses. Perina's told you that Goldy's yours. We'll have a real bill of sale made out."

That night Tod ate his first civilized food for a very long time, and understood what it meant to come home. As he was sitting there in the kitchen Aunt Cora came in carrying a parcel for him. Tod opened it to find a splendid new illustrated dictionary, bound in red. He did not know how to thank her, but she knew how pleased he was. She took it from him, sat down and opened the book at the fly-leaf. Then she put it on the table and wrote,

"Tod Greer, from Aunt Cora."

If you have enjoyed this book you may also like these

THE CHILDREN OF TOTEM TOWN
by Kaj Himmelstrup 25p
552 52001 2 Carousel Fiction

A carved totem pole stood sentry over their wooden village, Tonacatecutli, the Mexican god of creation. But the children's hut village was to be turned into a council car park. Could the god's influence be called upon to stop the bulldozers, even now edging forward to demolish Totem Town?

JASON *by Joyce Stranger* 20p
552 52004 7 Carousel Fiction

The pup wasn't wanted, born of a golden Labrador bitch and a giant mastiff. Then Duncan found him, a lonely young boy who needed a friend just as much as Jason needed a loving owner. The closeness between them was only strengthened when Duncan was sent away to school, and then his father had an accident. Jason had to do something.

THE BLACK PEARL *by Scott O'Dell* 20p
552 52008 X Carousel Fiction

The Black Pearl belonged to the old men, with legends and stories to tell to pass the time – or so Ramon Salazar had thought, until he came face to face with the devilfish and the struggle for the pearl began. But Ramon had more than the dangers of the sea to conquer. Others wanted the Great Pearl of Heaven, including the evil Pearler from Seville.

OPERATION SIPPACIK *by Rumer Godden* 20p

552 52009 8 Carousel Fiction

It took a war to prove the heroism of Sippacik, when she was sent out on a vital mission for the 27th Battery, Royal Artillery, stationed in Cyprus. "Seytan" – devil – was the name Arif Ali had given her, but to her owner Sippacik was the cleverest donkey in Cyprus. She had to be, she was about to face the enemy. This is her true story.

ARCHIE—YOUNG DETECTIVE *by Robert Bateman* 25p

552 52006 3 Carousel Fiction

Something suddenly moves in the club-house, a shadow that shouldn't be there. Archie stops to listen. He doesn't look much like a detective, but when his best friend is accused of stealing money from the club Henry Archibald McGillicuddy gets his chance to play at being policeman.

THE PET SHOP *by Martha Robinson* 20p

552 52002 0 Carousel Fiction

The monkey was familiar all right; it was Tony; but what was he doing in the garden? He was supposed to be locked away safely in a new cage at the Pet shop Mr. Petravic had just opened next door. Cliff and Miranda decided to try to catch him, but Tony was too clever for them. He had escaped once, and he wanted to stay free.

THE STORY OF BRITAIN *by R. J. Unstead* 30p each
552 54001 3
552 54002 1
552 54003 X
552 54004 8
Carousel Non-Fiction

A country is forged by its history, the battles and intrigues of by-gone ages laying the foundation of today. From its beginning as an island to the end of the Second World War, this series is the record of the men and women who played a role in shaping the character of England now. It traces the emergence of England as a nation.

LOOKING AND FINDING *by Geoffrey Grigson* 25p
552 54007 2
Carousel Non-Fiction

You can find sunken treasure hidden away in some long-forgotten shipwreck, or discover the past through scattered fossils and ancient inscriptions. It depends what you are looking for, how you go about finding it. It depends where you are looking, how you go about getting there. But once the search begins there's no knowing what you might stumble across.

THE WHITE BADGER *by Gordon Burness* 25p
552 54008 0
Carousel Non-Fiction

A badger was born just outside London, in fact only eighteen miles from the city centre. He was discovered by eleven year old Gary and his older brother Phil, who had arrived one day at the author's doorstep with a request to be taken badger hunting. Their first find was unusual, for it wasn't an ordinary badger, it was an all-white, an albino badger. Gary called him Snowball, and this is his story.

TRUE MYSTERIES *by Bob Hoare* 25p

552 54009 9 Carousel Non-Fiction

Tales of the unknown, stories of people who suddenly appear and disappear without explanation, and strange events which present no logical answer, sometimes turning legend into fact, or fact into legend. And always leaving a question mark.

EVERYDAY LIFE IN PREHISTORIC TIMES
by Marjorie and C. H. B. Quennell 25p each

552 54005 6
552 54006 4 Carousel Non-Fiction

This series presents a picture in words of how our forefathers lived in their prehistoric world, moving out of their caves into the earliest settlements; discovering metals; making fires; building and constructing the first organized villages. The EVERYDAY LIFE series follows them, detailing their development into civilization as we know it.

THE HOW AND WHY WONDER BOOK OF TIME 25p

552 86538 9

Do you know how men first learned to tell the time, or how an atomic clock works? This book tells you all about these and hundreds of other interesting facts on the measurement of time. Learn how to make your own waterclock or sandglass, too. This *How and Why Wonder Book* is packed with informative diagrams and illustrations.

TH
OF

The speed in
stop and as the
speed, his ears
pressure. The ... firing as they fell from the sky, every burst making him crouch lower in the illusory safety of the fabric covered cockpit. His brain working in a whirl of fear, he let his head loll over the dashboard to feign death and slid further down out of sight as the wires screamed. The whole machine began to shake like a lorry on a bad road and, his heart stuck in his throat, he waited in cringing tension for a bracing wire to snap and send the wings folding back so that he would dig his own grave with the speed of his fall.

Also in Arrow by John Harris

Covenant With Death
A Kind of Courage
The Mercenaries
The Sea Shall Not Have Them

John Harris

THE MUSTERING OF THE HAWKS

ARROW BOOKS

ARROW BOOKS LTD
3 Fitzroy Square, London W1

An imprint of the Hutchinson Publishing Group

London Melbourne Sydney Auckland
Wellington Johannesburg and agencies
throughout the world

First published by Hutchinson & Co (Publishers) Ltd 1972
Arrow edition 1976

Made and printed in Great Britain
by The Anchor Press Ltd
Tiptree, Essex

ISBN 0 09 913000 9

Contents

Part One The Journeyman

I

As the hand touched his arm, Ira Penaluna, crouched on his kit against the wooden cabin in the back of the lorry, jerked to consciousness and looked round him, dry-mouthed, stiff and cold. It required a moment to appreciate where he was, and, seeing the hunched figure further towards the tailboard peering at him, puzzled, he realised he must have been muttering in his sleep.

'Dreaming,' he said shortly.

The other man jerked a thumb and, framed by the rippling canvas curtain that jerked and snatched at its cords under the wind, he saw that the night sky was ablaze with cold fire, the clouds like a field of ploughed pearl in the moonrise.

They had been heading south against the traffic when he had fallen asleep and he realised they had come to a stop.

'Where are we?' he asked.

'Montbrohain.'

Then he heard arguing in front and became aware of the droning overhead that seemed to fill the air with its iron throbbing, rising and falling as though swept back and forth by the bustling wind.

The other man moved his hand once more against the light. 'Ours,' he said.

As the heavy machine passed above them, the lorry seemed to rattle with the vibration and the noise.

'Bomber,' the driver was saying. He was the usual stolid type who knew every road and by-lane along the front. 'After the railway at Cambrai.'

There was a smell of burning in the air and the gutted houses on either side gave the place an air of desolation. The church had been hit by a shell the previous year and the steeple had slid into the street in a cascade of bricks and slates that had become weed-festooned after a winter's rain and a summer's sun. Where the soldiers thronged round a moss-covered well in the village centre the traffic was a tangle of horses and limbers, and a large notice declaring the water fouled was just visible beyond them in the dim light.

Ira lifted his head to watch the ugly shape like a huge black 'T' heading east against the bright sky, its navigation lights burning.

'They pick up the canal when the moon's out and follow it north,' the driver pointed out.

'I wouldn't like his job,' his mate said. 'Too much like being a bus driver.'

The man in the French uniform who had stopped the lorry gazed upwards. 'They're the guys who'll win the war,' he observed solemnly. 'Big bombers. With big bombs. Scare the daylight outa the Kaiser. Do some damage.'

The bulky figure near Ira in the back of the lorry grunted contemptuously. 'Couple of chickens killed in Cambrai,' he said to no one in particular. 'Cat scared from 'ome in Le Cateau.'

The bomber droned away east and there was a pause as they all seemed to grope in their minds for the threads of the argument it had interrupted. The man in the French uniform turned again to the driver. 'Look,' he said briskly. 'I'm going south. You're going south. Why can't I go south *with* you?'

The driver's voice came, heavy and portentous. 'Because we ain't supposed to pick up passengers. That's why.'

While they argued, Ira studied his surroundings with the dull disinterest of tiredness. Nearby there was a pond which before the war had swept across it had probably been covered with ducks and brushed by willows. Now the trees had gone and it was fouled with slime, and a dead horse lay in the mud along its edge, probably hit while drinking, by a splinter from the same shell that had taken the windows out of every house on the opposite side of the road. On the wall alongside it were the words, '*1917. C'en est fait de nous*', a relic of the mutinous restlessness that had troubled the French armies in the spring.

There had been a gale a few days before, and the scattered telegraph wires festooned the chaos of fallen trees at the side of the road like creepers of honeysuckle. Men were tramping by in the darkness, phantom figures which loomed up for a moment and then vanished, and incessantly in the ears was the jingle of harness and the clatter of hoofs. Muttered curses came over the rattle of lampless lorries and the crunch of boots on the road, and soft encouragement to tired horses and men stumbling from an even greater weariness. Everything in the darkness around the lorry seemed to be surging northwards.

'Roye,' the man at the front of the lorry said. 'Just to Roye. How's about that?'

He had clearly been drinking. But he wasn't drunk. His uniform was a not unfamiliar sight on that southern part of the front, because the blue often overlapped the khaki, and French artillerymen trying to force their guns through the crowd often exchanged curses, greetings or mock resignation with their British comrades-in-arms.

'All right then,' the driver was saying. 'As far as Roye.'

The problem of the lift seemed to have been settled at last and a half-empty bottle changed hands. 'Have yourself a drink,' the driver was told. 'Share it with your sidekick. I've got another one.'

A kit-bag hurtled over the tail of the lorry, followed by a valise, and a man began to climb in after them. For a moment he pawed around in the semi-darkness, putting his hand on Ira's face as he stumbled about.

'Say, how about that?' he chuckled. 'I thought it was empty. You guys British or French, or what the hell? I'm American. One of the Lafayette boys. I just joined 'em. You heard of the Lafayette Escadrille?'

The big man with Ira in the back of the lorry said, yes, 'e'd 'eard of 'em, and the American made himself comfortable, spreading his equipment so he could sit on it and borrowing one of their sacks to put over his knees against the cold. The lorry had picked up Ira at St Omer, and his companion in increasing darkness at a hospital near Doullens, and they were now heading down the long straight road that ran from Albert to Péronne and Compiègne.

The American shuffled himself to comfort and offered cigarettes. Ira shook his head and the American seemed surprised that there was still someone in France in 1917 who didn't smoke. 'What's your outfit?' he demanded.

'Flying Corps. Both same squadron.' As he spoke, Ira realised he'd hardly seen the man from the hospital yet. Though they'd travelled all the way from Doullens together they were still like strangers to each other.

The American seemed delighted to have found fellow-pilots to travel with. 'First time out?' he asked.

'Do you mind?' The man from the hospital sounded heavily indignant. 'I came out in 1914. I've just come from dock. Suspected food poisoning. Turned out to be something else. Probably I'm on 'eat.'

The American was striking a match now and he held it up so they could all see each other. It wasn't entirely successful, but it was enough to see a vast bulk in one corner of the lorry and Ira's new coat in the other.

'How about you?' he asked Ira. 'Are *you* out from England?'

Ira nodded silently. He was hungry and tired and not disposed to talk. He had been travelling, it seemed, for ever. The crossing from Dover had been rough and the ferry had been full of men in mud-stained uniforms returning from leave and seasick drafts out for the first time. It had been crowded and freezing cold, and the train to the railhead had had half its windows out.

The American was laughing. 'Say, how about that?' he said gaily. 'It's a great war, son.' He seemed to be bursting with good humour. 'We ought to celebrate. I've got a bottle somewhere.' He began to dig into his valise, talking all the time. 'The name's Courtney. Felton Keith Courtney.'

'Forde,' the man from the hospital said. 'Toby Forde.'

'I'm Penaluna,' Ira said. 'Ira Penaluna.'

The American looked up. 'Sure sounds a proud old label.'

'Cornish, I dessay,' Forde said.

'Ira *Abel* Penaluna,' Ira went on doggedly, deciding he might as well get it over and done with quickly. He'd suffered a great deal in the course of his young life, since his family had left the West Country and settled in London. 'In fact,' he went on, 'my mother was a Bohenna, so, if you want to push it to its limit, that makes me Ira Abel Bohenna Penaluna.'

The American was suitably impressed. Swaying from side to side as the lorry rattled along, he thrust the bottle forward. 'Take a drink. It's cognac.'

Forde drank solemnly, but Ira's mother was a good Methodist from the farming country of the Devon border and her disapproval was still strong enough in his make-up to deter him.

'You not a drinking man?' Courtney asked.

'Not much.'

Courtney shuffled himself to comfort again and lit his cigarette. 'We've been having a rough time out here lately,' he said, his voice heavy with concern. 'Especially round Arras. Richthofen's been clawing those old BE2s down two or three at a time up there. There's a curse on those old crates. They make it easy for him to run up a score.'

Like Montbrohain, Langéac, the next village, was full of men, all of them tramping stolidly northwards, heavy boots crunching on the pavé as they stumbled past in the darkness, and the cobbled main street was full of carts belonging to non-combatant postal and railway formations. The lorry became an island in a sea of helmets, and as they edged slowly forward in low gear they could hear the driver's muttered curses. Half an hour later, not unexpectedly, the engine started to boil and he hauled off the road and said he was going in search of water.

Courtney indicated a café and suggested they wait inside. The estaminet was packed with men—most of them, it seemed, arguing angrily with each other about who was doing the most damage to the Germans—and, as they stood at the bar, a girl with a black fuzz of moustache and a large bust bursting out of a skin-tight blouse brought them wine. Ira joined in unwillingly and the girl sidled up to him so that he was aware at once of the aggressive thrust of her bust and the animal smell of woman and garlic overlaid by cheap perfume. She winked at Courtney and Forde.

'Your frien' would like me perhaps?' She indicated Ira, who flushed and pretended to be drinking.

Courtney chuckled.

'She wants to know if you'd like to go upstairs with her, son,' he explained.

'I know what she wants.' Ira was still flushing awkwardly.

The girl laughed and looked at Courtney. ''E becomes red,' she said. ''E is very young, *ce petit anglais*. 'E needs to grow up.'

Edging closer, she slipped her hand into Ira's trouser pocket and he jumped away hurriedly as though it were red-hot. Courtney seemed about to choke with merriment.

The girl was studying Ira again now, one eyebrow raised. 'What is your name, soldier?' she asked, and Courtney gave a hoot of laughter.

'Sister,' he said, 'that sure will be a mouthful for *you*.'

He told her and she gazed at Ira as though he were deformed. 'You must be very big boy to 'ave a name like that.'

Her hand moved towards his groin again and Ira jumped like a startled goat, spilling his wine. She laughed and began to finger his overcoat.

'New,' she observed. 'You are new officer, yes? Perhaps you don' know about war.'

Forde took pity on him and suggested that they find somewhere they could eat. The driver, still outside with his head in the bonnet of the lorry, directed them to a farm where he said they could get a good meal and, moving out of the ruck under the blackness of a clump of trees, they stumbled in and out of the deep ruts of a high-hedged lane.

Eventually, they saw the solid shape of farm buildings, like a castle in the darkness, and the softer outline of trees. The ground smelled damp and evil and, overlaying its sourness, there was the smell of a midden. In the east they could see flickering lights along the front and, occasionally, as the air around them seemed to expand and contract, they heard a dull thudding noise.

Ira stared towards the sound, the flickering light in the sky picking up the barely-formed lines on his face as flash after flash shone red-gold on the surly clouds. Everything around them seemed to be drumming and rattling from the continual murmur, and occasionally a long faint burst of machine-gun fire came to them on some trick of the wind.

'Front line,' Courtney said helpfully, jerking a thumb.

'Yes.'

As Courtney vanished, Ira stood for a moment longer gazing towards the horizon. The noise was one of infinite suggestion and immense menace. Beyond the farmhouse's bulk, he could see a row of poplars leaning away from the wind like a line of priests going to late mass, and uncovered rafters stark as the empty bones of a dead monster.

A door slammed and Courtney reappeared. 'It's O.K.,' he said. 'They'll feed us.'

Ira allowed himself to be shepherded inside the farmhouse. Muttered French came to him in a female voice and he found himself in a dark room that was bitterly cold and smelled of damp. Courtney's gaiety was undiminished.

'It's a great place,' he said.

His enthusiasm seemed a little misplaced, because when the farmer's wife appeared with an oil lamp the room turned out to be furnished only with a table and four chairs. On the walls were portraits of dead soldier sons and a painting of Napoleon, smothered in gloom, after his defeat at Waterloo. The dictator's scowl seemed to set the mood of the place, which was heavy, oppressive and, above all, horrifyingly cold. It didn't seem possible after the hot summer they'd been having in England, and Forde, who had shrugged himself out of a British warm as big as a tent, hurriedly put it back on again.

Courtney ordered eggs and chips and the Frenchwoman brought a dusty bottle which she clapped on the table with three glasses that looked as though they'd been in use for centuries.

Courtney sloshed the wine into them cheerfully. It tasted tart and had vague overtones of iron filings.

'That's great,' he said.

His enthusiasm was still running away with him and he seemed game to make a night of it. He wore the flat-topped French képi on the back of his head, and his uniform was pulled out of shape with books and papers that were stuffed anyhow into his pockets.

'It's a great war,' he said again, and Forde smiled. He was a big, quiet-faced, quiet-eyed man with red countryman's cheeks, Ira saw, now that the light was on his face for the first time—ordinary, nondescript, like thousands of other young men, unheroic, belonging in quiet fields or busy offices, typical of the whole mass of the British Empire caught up by the fighting.

They sat round the table in the tomb of a dining room, trying to rouse a little cheerfulness in themselves with the tart thin wine, then the Frenchwoman appeared with the food. She seemed eager to talk and as she chattered Courtney sat staring at Ira. Despite his obvious youth, there was something about him that suggested he was made of enduring fibre. He was squarely built, with a thatch of jet-black hair above a straight well-shaped nose and eyes of a vivid blue which glowed back at Courtney as he hunched over his plate.

'Been flying long?' Courtney asked them.

Forde was occupied with filling his glass. 'Long enough to 'ear it's dangerous,' he said.

Courtney turned to Ira. 'It's different from what they tell you at home,' he informed him earnestly. 'You think you're hot stuff when you're training. You get a different picture out here. All the same, you're lucky you're going south. It's quiet down here. What field are you guys going to?'

'Huyzes,' Forde said, and Courtney crowed with delight.

'Right on the south end of the line where the British join the French. We're near Chauny on the north end of the French. We often bump across the boys from Huyzes. You're flying Pups.'

Forde nodded and Ira found himself wondering how he

managed to squeeze his colossal frame into the cockpit of the tiny scout.

Courtney was still talking. 'I heard Pups were being cut up by the Boche,' he said.

'You're all right so long as you stay 'igh,' Forde observed.

'Yeah. Maybe.' Courtney leaned towards Ira. 'Look out for these new Albatros DIIIs, son,' he advised. 'They sure are fast as hell and a whole lot better than a Pup.'

'Pups are all right,' Ira said unexpectedly. 'Better than a pusher, anyway.'

Courtney was reaching out for more wine. 'Average life of a scout pilot out here's about three weeks,' he said.

Forde looked up. 'I've 'eard different,' he said shortly.

'They got Albert Ball, all the same.'

Ira caught the glimpse of pity in the older man's expression as he glanced at him, then, as their eyes met, Courtney looked away.

'There's talk of another push,' he said, and Forde nodded.

'Yes, I 'eard.'

'Maybe your crowd want to snatch all the kudos before the Yanks get across to win the war for 'em.' Courtney grinned. 'Or maybe'—he dropped his voice to a conspiratorial undertone—'maybe they're worried about the French. The story goes that you guys are pushing in the north because they can't be relied on any more. There was talk of mutiny down here in the south.'

Forde seemed unimpressed. 'There'll probably be talk of mutiny up there in the north if they go on much longer,' he said.

Courtney nodded. 'You begin to wonder when it'll finish,' he agreed, suddenly gloomy. 'Sure, we're in, but now the Russians are out, so we're all square again, aren't we?'

They all felt better with the food inside them and, hearing the lorry outside, they paid their bill and set off again towards the traffic. The noise of the guns had died away by this time and the flickering lights had vanished from the sky. The moon had driven clear of cloud, too, now; and the road ahead shone with a crisp cold silver that picked out groups of shuffling men, horses and lorries.

They dropped Courtney at Roye and as he humped his kit over the tailboard he paused and turned to Ira. 'You'll be O.K. down this way, son,' he said. 'Just watch your tail, that's all. Keep those eyes of yours going round that old sky. There sure is a lot of it and you'd be surprised how many corners it's got where the Hun can hide.'

He stopped, as though embarrassed by his concern, and turned to Forde. He jerked a hand at Ira. 'Take care of him,' he said.

Forde nodded. 'I'll take care of him,' he promised.

'Us older guys have gotta look out for these kids,' Courtney went on seriously. 'They're the pioneers of the future, the generals of the next war. We've gotta make sure they're around to do the job.'

He waved and grinned at Ira. 'We'll have to get together,' he ended enthusiastically. 'We'd make a great team. We fly ships with an Indian head insignia. Look out for us. Mine's Number Five. If I see a V-strutter on your tail, I'll chase him off.'

As the lorry started again, there was silence in the back for a while, then Forde lit a cigarette. Despite the darkness, Ira was aware that he was studying him.

'You've been out before, 'aven't you?' he said unexpectedly.

Ira's head jerked up. 'How did you know?'

There was a flash of teeth in the faint light. 'You can tell. Old 'and's depression on returning to the scene of the crime.' Forde made it sound ponderous and melodramatic. 'We all feel it. And though you got a lot of answers, I noticed you weren't askin' no questions.' He settled himself to doze, a shapeless untidy hulk half-seen in the shadows. 'Everybody asks questions first time out,' he ended drowsily. '"Where's the front?" "What's it like?" "Oo's Richthofen?" ' His teeth flashed again in another smile. '*You* didn't,' he ended.

2

Huyzes. Typical of its almost unpronounceable name, the village was an anonymous cluster of one-storey houses, built round a church, a Mairie and the inevitable Place de Paris. There were two farms, both constructed round middens; and the village well, surrounded by the curdled grey water of the village washerwomen, centred a group of orchards fringed with summer flowers. With the rusting iron crucifix which had leaned at an angle ever since it had been scraped by a German gun limber in 1914, it looked as worn and old as the rooks that hovered on ragged wings above the trees.

The aerodrome was on higher ground above the sloping area of ridges and folds, alongside a thinly planted wood with a line of flapping Bessoneau hangars heavy in the grey light that came from a lowering sky. A grass-covered hump-backed bridge of red brick crossed a sunken farm road and, on the other side, among the sparse trees, there were groups of tents, stores, parked lorries and a few wooden huts with oiled-silk windows. Along the far edge of the field were older buildings occupied by a regiment of French pioneers working on a new road towards Soissons and the French front.

Outside one of the wooden buildings in the cheerless early light a Le Rhône cylinder, hanging from a little gibbet as a gas alarm, moved slightly in the cold breeze.

'C.O.'s office,' Forde said, but he didn't suggest that the lorry should stop and directed it instead towards the trees, and they stopped outside one of the living huts which some wag had labelled nostalgically The Olde Bull and Bush. A batman, a middle-aged man with the lugubrious countenance of a family retainer, who was cleaning shoes outside, looked up.

'Mr Forde, sir! Nice to see you back!'

'Nice to see *you*, Warburton. Here's your new charge. He's Mr York's relief.'

'Thank you, sir. Sad about Mr York disappearing like that.'

Warburton paused, then jerked his head. 'There's another new young gentleman just arrived for the hut, sir. A Mr Colyer. In place of Mr Bassett.'

Forde's eyes narrowed. 'What 'appened to Bassett?'

'Picked a Blighty out of the raffle, sir. Went home yesterday.'

'Did 'e, by God?' Forde gestured at one of the bunks in a corner of the hut. 'What about Pottinger?'

'He's flying now, sir. The new gentleman's on his way to the office to report.'

Forde threw his kit down. Above his bed Ira noticed a vast number of books among which the *Farmers' and Stockbreeders' Annual* was strikingly prominent. He was jerking a hand now at the bunk in the opposite corner. 'You'd better have that one,' he said. 'Then you'd better nip along and report.'

Colyer, a pale-faced boy with a new uniform and a nervous look on his face, was nearing the squadron office when Ira caught him up. He seemed grateful that his initiation into a new way of life was to be shared by someone else.

'You got much flying time?' he asked anxiously as they fell into step.

Ira nodded. 'A bit,' he said.

Colyer looked uneasy. 'So've I. But not much. I thought I was hot stuff at home, but I got a different picture at the Pilots' Pool.'

He turned and stared at the rolling field and the damp grass scored with skid marks and flattened by wheels. It was L-shaped, with the hangars on the base leg. Beyond the trees a balloon hung in the air, obscene and graceless against the cloud.

'Not very big, is it?' he commented uneasily. His head jerked at a line of poplars at the end of the field. 'And those trees down there—smack in your way when you're trying to get in.' His landings were clearly still not sufficiently practised for him to feel confident.

'I expect we'll manage,' Ira reassured him.

Colyer's mood changed from depression to bewilderment.

Apart from a few moving figures near the distant hangars, the place seemed deserted. He gazed bleakly at a partly dismembered aeroplane in the distance.

'Where are they all?' he demanded.

A hammer was clanging on metal somewhere and they saw a puff of blue exhaust smoke that came with a crackling roar from an unseen aeroplane behind the corner of one of the Bessoneaux. The slow clack-clack of a gun being fired on a range beyond the trees drifted to them on the breeze, then a tall dog with a wall eye and sparse grey fur appeared and wagged its tail doubtfully at them. It looked like a threadbare doormat.

Colyer patted it uncertainly, but it immediately lost interest and cantered away loose-limbed to join several other dogs—all strays, by the look of them—which seemed to have attached themselves to the aerodrome. Colyer stared at them with a worried frown.

'Bit different from Filton,' he commented.

As they stood watching, they became aware of the sky filling with the low buzz of engines, and men appeared miraculously in ones and twos from the hangars and huts, to gaze intently towards the east. The sun, coming through the broken cloud at last, was low over the horizon and it was difficult to spot the machines as they came out of the glare. Then Ira saw them beyond the trees that so troubled Colyer—two double lines of wings that grew rapidly until they could be identified as Sopwith Pups.

A thin-featured man with a long nose appeared in the doorway of the hut near the gas alarm. He seemed incredibly tall and his thinness was accentuated by jodhpurs and the tight stock round his neck. He wore a jersey but no hat or jacket, and the grey wall-eyed dog, which was playing now with a spaniel, broke off the game and took up a position behind him, staring at the sky with him.

'Both back,' the man in the jersey said sharply to someone inside the hut, then he disappeared again, and they saw mechanics running. The first of the approaching aeroplanes was now beginning to drop to earth, its motor poppling, its exhausts sending out puffs of blue smoke. Its wings rocked as its wheels touched the uneven surface of the field, and the mechanics swung it round towards the hangars, where the pilot cut his engine and jumped out immediately to stare anxiously at the sky where the second machine was turning now, its bank flat and cautious.

His face was grimy with grease and a coating of grey powder, and Colyer nudged Ira with his elbow. 'Had a brush with the Germans,' he said in an awed whisper. 'That grey stuff on his chin. It's from his gun.'

The mechanics were crowding round now, questioning and gazing at the sky. One of them called sharply into the hangar and more men joined them, also staring upwards, and a buzz of conversation broke out. Even Colyer became aware of an atmosphere of anticipation.

'Something wrong?' he asked.

No one answered him. The second Pup was dropping to the ground now, its descent still cautious, and Ira watched it with a bleak face and narrow eyes.

'That chap's taking it easy,' Colyer remarked.

As he spoke, a flat sound like a paper bag bursting came to them and they saw the upper wing of the Pup had snapped back.

'Oh, my God,' Colyer said.

The nose of the Pup had dropped at once and before they could realise what had happened it had dived in a twisting movement round the broken wing to crash on to a ruined cottage at the far side of the field. There was a moment's absolute silence as the puff of dust rose into the air, then Ira was aware of a lark singing and Colyer gaping, his eyes shocked, as everyone started to run.

Outside the office, the pilot of the first Pup was talking loudly to a middle-aged officer wearing a cavalry tunic with the ribbons of the D.S.O. and the M.C. beneath a frayed observer's wing.

'He must have had a bullet through his main spar,' he was saying. 'And he must have known it—*all the way home*! You could tell by the way he was flying.' He was a pale-faced boy wearing a stricken look that was a mixture of strain, barely subsided fear and shocked outrage, and he turned bitterly, one arm swinging in a wild gesture as though appealing against the injustice of what they'd just seen. 'We haven't a chance against those bloody DIIIs in Pups!'

The older man's face tightened and, putting a hand on his shoulder, he turned him quickly and firmly. 'That's a stupid way to talk, Stonehouse,' he said. 'We can handle the Hun all right.'

As they vanished into the office, the group broke up and the door slammed. Colyer turned with shocked eyes towards the cottage where the mechanics were already at work with shovels among the debris, then he swung towards Ira.

'What a rotten way to start,' he said.

After a while the door of the office opened again and the pale-faced boy reappeared, smoking, his face taut, his flying clothing unfastened, his fur-lined boots hanging loosely so that he had to walk with ungainly steps, his helmet, scarf and gloves hanging from his hand. He pushed past Colyer as though he didn't exist.

As Ira stepped forward, the door slammed in his face again, then it immediately reopened and the middle-aged officer stared at him.

'Sorry,' he said shortly. 'Come in.'

He held the door open for them and vanished. Inside, the man with the jersey was sitting in front of a typewriter, a pipe stuck in his mouth, a heavy frown on his brows. The grey dog lay at his feet, looking more than ever like a worn-out rug. There was an atmosphere of tension and anger in the office that could have been cut with a knife.

The man behind the typewriter seemed not to notice them and Colyer hesitantly leaned over the desk.

'I say, old son,' he said nervously. 'Where's the C.O.?'

The man with the pipe looked up at once, his head jerking with the movement. His eyes glinted frostily.

'Here,' he said. '*I*'m the C.O.'

Colyer's jaw dropped and he leapt to attention, his face crimson. 'Colyer, sir,' he blurted out. 'Second Lieutenant Colyer! This is Second Lieutenant Penaluna!'

The man at the typewriter eyed him bitterly, as though the accident they'd just seen was entirely his fault. Then the disapproving stare moved to Ira's face and finally swung back to Colyer. The door opened and the middle-aged officer reappeared, and the man behind the desk, moving from the typewriter to allow him to sit down, reached for a major's tunic hanging on the wall and began to put it on. Buttoning it up in silence, he picked up a cap and stick from the desk and stared again at Colyer.

'I'm Sillito,' he said. He nodded at the older man. 'That's Captain Stoke, the Recording Officer. How much flying have you done?'

Colyer swallowed dryly. 'Twenty hours, sir.'

Ira noticed the angry glance that Sillito gave the older man. 'That all?'

'Yes, sir.'

'Not much, is it?'

'No, sir.'

'How much on Pups?'

'Five, sir.'

Sillito took the pipe from his mouth, seeming to make an effort to control his anger. 'Well, we'd better have all the usual nonsense: Religion. Next of kin. How old are you, by the way?'

'Nineteen, sir.'

'Well, you're young enough to learn. You'll be in B Flight. Captain Campbell.' The chilly glance flickered over Ira's new overcoat. 'How old are *you*?'

'Twenty, sir.'

Sillito's eyes narrowed. 'You sure?'

Ira swallowed. In fact, he was one year older than the century. 'Yes, sir.'

Sillito stared at him for a moment, then he nodded. 'How *about you*? You qualified on Pups?'

'Yes, sir.'

'Hope you've got a few more hours than Colyer.'

'Yes, sir. I . . .'

But Sillito was obviously unprepared to listen and Ira's mouth clamped shut. He felt neglected and unwanted and he became rigid with a determination to offer nothing that wasn't asked for.

Sillito pulled on his cap and headed for the door. 'You'll be C Flight,' he said. 'Captain Wyatt. You'll find him at the hangar. I'm busy just now. You'll have seen why. I'll have a talk with you later.'

Wyatt was a short angry-looking man with a Canadian accent whom they found in one of the Bessoneaux talking to a flight-sergeant as they peered together into the cockpit of an oil-stained Pup. Colyer stared in awe at the gun over the engine and the mechanics patching a series of bullet holes in the tail. Wyatt studied their new uniforms with distaste. Like everyone else he seemed unsettled by the accident and resentful of their presence.

'Like the last lot,' he commented bitterly. 'Still wet behind the ears. Which one of you's C Flight?'

'I am,' Ira said.

Wyatt nodded, frowning. 'I'll get Kelly,' he said. 'He'll take you up and see what you can do.'

'Does he have to?' Ira asked.

Wyatt's frown deepened. 'Yes, he does have to!'

While Ira was still flushing angrily, Kelly appeared. He was a tall man in an oil-stained infantryman's uniform with leather patches on the sleeves.

'Which one of you's C Flight?' he demanded sharply, like Wyatt, like Sillito, like all of them, in no mood to be friendly.

Ira stepped forward and Kelly stared at him for a moment, then he jerked his head. 'Go and get your helmet and let's see what you can do.' He nodded at a patched and battered Pup outside the hangar. 'That'll be your machine.'

When Ira returned a few moments later he was wearing an oil-stained yellow leather coat that looked several sizes too big for him. Wyatt stared narrowly at it and turned to the flight-sergeant.

'Wonder if the little blighter bought it second-hand?' he said loudly.

Ira heard him and frowned, his resentment growing, then Kelly jerked a hand at the sky.

'We'll climb to five thousand,' he said. 'Then we'll separate. I'll just vanish, you'll find. Just keep circling and I'll try to jump you. Know what I mean?'

Ira stared at him coldly. 'Yes,' he said. 'I know.'

He moved to the battered Pup, and Wyatt, the wind flapping the skirt of his coat, watched as he walked round it, glancing at elevators, ailerons, wheels, struts and wires. He had been joined by two or three other officers now and, though he knew they were all watching, Ira carefully remained unflustered by Kelly's agitated waving. He was in no hurry to leave and, moving the controls, he sat for a moment in the cockpit, pumping up pressure and kicking the rudder bar while the mechanic turned the engine back to suck in petrol. Then he gave his goggles a slow deliberate rub with a not very clean handkerchief and, as the engine roared, eased the throttle back and adjusted the petrol. As the chocks were pulled away, he turned the machine quickly, revving the engine to swing it round with the rudder and send the dew flying in a spray from the grass.

It was a bright day now, all gold and cream, with clouds starting at about four thousand feet and rising in separate masses that drifted before a westerly wind. The two Pups climbed alongside an ivory tower whose walls threatened to fall in on them, then, as Kelly disappeared, Ira circled slowly, his head moving from side to side. He knew exactly what Kelly intended to do. He had dived away steeply, and Ira had seen him moving across the pattern of the earth towards the patch of cloud.

He began to notice small things about him—the doped fabric above the spars rippling with the passage of air over it, the sparkle of light through the propeller. The thought that he was sitting on a wickerwork seat a mile above the earth, suspended only by the pull of a motor and the spread of the wings, entranced him and, huddled in his fragile cockpit, he looked down on the blue-tinted earth below, dazzled by the light of the sky and conscious of a sense of superiority over other human beings.

Below him, the field looked like a postage stamp with the Bessoneaux mere square dots along the brown-green patch of the wood. Near them he could see a line of small pale crosses which he knew were Pups and, as he watched, he saw two of them begin to move along the edge of the L-shaped patch of green and pass over the thin shadow of the wood heading east.

He was still staring about him, aware of the drumming of the fabric along the fuselage, when he spotted Kelly just behind him in the eye of the sun. It was nothing more than a momentary glimpse against the glare, but he turned slightly so that Kelly's approach would have to be made more steeply.

Kelly was drawing closer now, and Ira waited patiently, pretending not to have seen, then as Kelly slipped into place behind him, he swung the Pup into a roll and, laying the machine flat against the air in a vertical bank, dropped with immense satisfaction into place behind the other machine as it shot past.

Kelly's head whipped round in a startled glance as he saw Ira sitting where he'd been sitting himself a moment before, then he flung his Pup into a tight turn like a startled starling, Ira following him closely, and for ten minutes flung his machine about the sky in an attempt to throw him off, diving, turning, rolling, trying everything he could think of. Ira sat confidently behind him, clinging maliciously like a limpet to his tail, until Kelly finally throttled back and began to descend. Ira escorted him down, just above his tail as he dropped towards the field, and as Kelly put his machine down, he landed behind him in a perfect three-point touch-down, and taxied up to the hangars. The grey wall-eyed dog and a couple of terriers trailed, barking wildly, behind the mechanics as they ran to meet him and swung him into line and, as he cut the engine and climbed out, they approached, panting heavily like a reception committee. He noticed now that there were men standing in groups watching.

Kelly stared at him for a second, frowning. Ira's face was blank and devoid of triumph.

'Where did you learn to fly like that?' Kelly asked.

'Joyce Green.'

'They're bucking up since I was there.'

As Kelly turned to where Wyatt was standing, Ira waited quietly longside the Pup, his hands in the pockets of his vast yellow coat.

'What's the idea sending me up with *him*?' he heard Kelly say. 'He can fly rings round me. Who is he? Bishop or somebody?'

They talked together angrily for a moment or two, then Wyatt turned towards Ira, his eyes hot, his frown deeper than ever. Clearly he felt someone had made a fool of him. He watched Ira pull off his helmet and begin to unfasten the oil-smelling leather coat.

'That's a bloody gorblimey rig you've got there,' he observed sourly.

'It was my father's,' Ira said shortly.

As he struggled with the buckles and opened the coat, Wyatt leaned forward abruptly.

'Is that a ribbon you're wearing?' he asked sharply.

Ira looked up. 'Yes.'

'You've been out before?'

'Yes.'

'It's the M.M., isn't it?'

'Yes.'

'What did you get that for?'

Ira fought down the blush he felt rushing to his cheeks. 'My pilot was hit . . .'

'Your pilot! You've done a tour as an observer?'

'Yes.'

Wyatt gaped at him.

Ira had the vast leather coat off now and was standing with it over his arm, clad in an R.F.C. maternity jacket that was brand new but equally huge and ill-fitting.

'For Christ's sake, man,' Wyatt said disgustedly, 'you've got a Croix de Guerre there, too! You've got more medals than anybody else on the squadron except George Stoke who got his in South Africa in 1900. Why the hell didn't you say so?'

Ira stared back at him unforgivingly. 'You didn't ask,' he pointed out.

3

Sillito was sitting at his desk when Ira reappeared in his office. Stoke was leaning on the typewriter alongside him, watching quietly out of the corner of his eye. Ira saluted warily.

Trying to recover a little face, Wyatt had dispensed with formalities and had sent him up at once to memorise the pattern of the earth and it had been strange to look down again on the zigzag curve the trenches made in the chalky soil as they swung east round La Fère, and the faint brown haze in front of them where the barbed wire lay. There had been balloons below him as he had climbed for height, fat as maggots, one group to the west, one to the east, their observers watching the opposite sides of the lines. High cirro-cumulus had spread like a fan above him, giving the day a curious other-world look so that he had found himself caught unexpectedly by memory.

His first trips over the lines in 1915 had been in an assortment of appallingly inflammable aeroplanes which had been flown by his pilot in a mixture of high spirits, mock resignation and a curious belief in the superiority of the R.F.C. Despite his nonchalance, however, the young man behind the stick had gained experience from a hundred trips over the lines and Ira's mistakes had been quickly corrected. On his first meeting with a German he'd hardly dared to fire in case the approaching aeroplane had proved to be friendly, and he had jumped at the shouted instruction from the rear cockpit—'Let the bastard have it, you stupid sod!' After that he'd begun to take the view that 'thrice blest is he who gets his blow in fust', and not only had he not killed any of his friends, but he'd also frightened away a great many Germans before they'd approached close enough to be dangerous.

Sillito gestured to a chair. 'Make yourself comfortable,' he said gruffly. 'I hear you're quite an aviator.'

The grey dog licked Ira's hand and Sillito indicated it in a stiff effort to appear friendly that was obviously out of character. 'Known as Monkey Brand,' he said. 'Looks a bit like the soap advert.' He gazed at Ira again and went on quietly: 'You've been out before, I gather.'

'Yes, sir.'

Sillito frowned. 'How old were you?'

Ira paused, thinking quickly. 'Nineteen then, sir.'

'You sure?'

'Quite sure, sir.'

Sillito's cold yellow eyes blinked, then his mouth opened slowly and closed again. He glanced at Stoke, then back at Ira. 'What did you get the Croix de Guerre for?' he asked.

'We shot down a Halberstadt that was bothering a French Caudron. The Caudron had a general in it. I think he was very relieved. It was a long time ago now.'

Sillito's expression didn't change. 'Are you a good shot?'

'Always did shoot, sir. Partridges in Cornwall. They're fast-fliers. It's a bit like deflection-shooting from an aeroplane.'

Sillito glanced at Stoke again, then he turned once more to Ira. He spread his hands on the table. 'You'd better come clean,' he said. 'Where did you learn to fly like that?'

Ira blushed. 'I could always fly, sir.'

Sillito's beaked nose jerked up. He seemed to think his leg was being pulled. 'What do you mean, you could *always* fly?'

'My father was Jack Penaluna, sir. You've probably heard of him.'

Sillito stared at him again. '*The* Jack Penaluna?'

'Yes, sir. I helped him build his machines.'

'I saw him fly at Farnborough in 1911. Cody was there. And De Havilland.'

'So was I, sir. Holding their coats.'

Sillito's reaction didn't encourage humour. He leaned forward, his eyes narrow. 'With all this experience, what were you doing as an observer?'

Ira looked embarrassed. 'I don't think they believed me, sir, when I enlisted. They'd only take me as a mechanic.'

'I doubt if *I*'d have believed you. What about squadron experience?'

'3 Squadron, sir. Then BE2cs with 16 Squadron as an observer. Then home for a pilot's course.'

'I thought you could always fly.'

'I could, sir. But I never held a ticket. They sent me solo after an hour. I think they hoped I'd break my neck. I came out again on FEs with 11 Squadron. We were just converting to Bristols when they sent me home again for a commission and single-seaters.'

'And where did you learn to handle a Pup like that?'

'Joyce Green, sir. They sent me there for a few weeks on Home Defence.'

Sillito leaned forward. 'Chap I knew was there,' he said. 'Came out to France with me in 1914 as a mechanic. McCudden. Ever meet him?'

'Yes, sir.'

Sillito gave him a sidelong glance. 'We seem to have picked you up ready-made,' he observed. 'And that fancy roll Wyatt told me about?'

'Captain McCudden taught me.'

'Hm.' Sillito's beak nose lifted. 'I think you'd better teach Wyatt,' he said. '*And* a few others, too, including me. We've only just gone on to Pups from One-and-a-half-strutters. You can probably fly 'em better than we can. As you're probably aware, today's little bit of trouble isn't the first we've had and we could do with someone like you.' He paused, then began to reach for a sheaf of documents on his desk to indicate the interview was over.

'By the way,' he said coldly, as Ira turned to the door, 'you'll be doing pallbearer duties at the funeral tomorrow. New arrivals always get them.'

The funeral brought back to Ira the small sensation of anger that had just begun to vanish—as though it were a chilly reminder to him that he belonged to a lost generation that dared not look too far into the future—and he had a feeling that until he'd been on the squadron a little while he was going to draw a few other onerous duties the old hands preferred to dodge, too.

When he returned, Pottinger's kit had already been packed and Forde was sorting out his letters, vast and calm as he lay stretched on his bunk.

'Just going through 'is stuff before we send it home,' he said. 'He'd been out quite a while and I'd got used to him. It makes you feel bloody old sometimes. Like Wyatt. Like Stone'ouse. '*E*'s overdue for 'ome, too. Pottinger was a special pal of his.'

His words didn't help to disperse the persistent chilly feeling and Ira sat down heavily on his bunk, faintly oppressed by the unfamiliarity of everything. Even death seemed sharper and less dignified than it had the previous year.

Colyer was eyeing the two small strips of ribbon on his breast. He'd hardly taken his eyes off them from the moment he'd first seen them and all through the funeral Ira had known he'd been itching to ask about them, but wasn't sure whether it was polite. His concern with them suited Ira, because it kept him from noticing his tunic, which, he knew, was a size too large for him. His mother had insisted on going to the tailor's with him when he'd been measured for it and making sure it was big enough.

'You'll grow into it, dear,' she'd said, and Ira had been regretting ever since that he hadn't had the courage to resist her.

Colyer could hold back no longer. 'What did you get them for?' he demanded abruptly.

Ira told him, without looking up. 'It was different in 1915,' he explained.

Even the sky had been different in 1915, he thought—lonelier, emptier, clearer somehow—and meeting another aeroplane had been a little like two ships passing on a vast ocean. Their machines had been as wide-winged as dragonflies and as incredibly flimsy, and approaches had been made warily while the observers struggled to heave the solitary gun into position. It hadn't been long since they'd been potting at each other with rifles.

They had none of them known any rules in those days, and there had been no such things as fighters, so that the job had usually been given to the crew who were least successful at photography or artillery-spotting and they had managed as best they could, flopping round the sky at fifty miles an hour. The aeroplanes had been awful, with everything in the wrong place because they'd still been finding out about warfare, and there'd been no formation flying because they'd all flown different types that moved at different speeds.

'They gave you a medal just for getting off the ground,' he explained. 'And the pilots liked to have me with them because the engines weren't very hot stuff either and they felt if we had to force-land I could get the clockwork going again.'

Forde was staring at him silently from where he was glancing now through Pottinger's diary for anything that might offend his relatives. 'I once went to see your dad give a demonstration at Shoreham,' he said gravely. ''Is engine wouldn't start. 'E never got off the ground.'

Ira smiled. 'It sounds like him.'

'Did *'e* teach you to fly?'

'No. But it wasn't hard to learn in those days. If you got up, you could almost float down. So long as you'd got a good sense of balance, because it was a bit like sliding down the banisters holding a blancmange. You put your cap on backwards, switched on, counted four, and heaved her off.'

Forde carefully marked his place in Pottinger's diary with a scrap of cardboard torn from a Gold Flake packet and put it aside, rather like a father prepared to have a heart-to-heart with a difficult son.

''Ow old were you? You musta still been in nappies.'

Ira smiled again. 'Nearly. I built a man-carrying glider and I'd just got it up to the roof when my father decided it was best to let me try the real thing. They had a Gnome-Caudron. It did thirty-five flat out and stalled at thirty-four.'

Forde frowned. 'You ought to be all right 'ere,' he said. 'We could do with a star turn. 56 Squadron had Ball. 60's got this madman, Bishop. All we've got's *me.*'

Colyer was staring shining-eyed at Ira. 'They'll probably make you a flight commander,' he said.

A look of alarm came to Ira's face. 'Bossing other chaps about? Some of 'em are old—married, with kids. They wouldn't go for that. I'm not Richthofen.'

'Well, at least, if you met him, you'd know what to do.' Colyer glanced at Forde. 'Have you ever seen him?' he asked.

Forde shook his head. ' 'Appily, no,' he said.

Colyer eyed him eagerly. 'What's the best thing to do if you do?'

'Do a bunk, quick as poss.'

'You mean cut and run?'

'Not 'alf.'

'Isn't that a bit lily-livered?'

Forde gazed at him for a moment before replying, then he jerked a thumb at Ira. 'Despite the example of our gallant young friend 'ere, lad,' he pointed out heavily, 'aviators out here sometimes get summarily done to death. I don't fancy being one of 'em.'

'Yes, but I mean . . .'

Forde interrupted sadly. 'This is *real*, lad,' he said. 'Not death or glory or a fate worse than death, or the stuff Kipling wrote about without ever experiencing it. Not like that junk they tell you about God's wisdom and Heaven and believing in Father Christmas. Being dead's different. There's nothing there. It's like going into a dark house and finding you've left your matches behind, standing there trying not to breathe—black, empty, nothing—never again—ever! *That*'s being dead.'

The outburst seemed to remove all thoughts of nobility from Colyer's mind. He glanced at Ira, then back at Forde. 'Have you been out long?' he asked.

Forde pushed Pottinger's effects aside and swung his feet to the ground. 'I came out first with the Yeomanry.' His slow speech and broad accents and the occasional lost aitch had all along suggested long acquaintance with farmers. 'I got a commission in 1915. Then I got sick of living in conditions that would 'ave depressed a poacher's lurcher and transferred. It broke my 'eart what they were doing to all that farmland. I wanted to be a farmer meself, y'see, but all I managed was assistant to a corn merchant. I worked for me uncle and it was a good job they called me up. We were going bust. Sometimes, now, it feels I've been out a lifetime. Especially with Richthofen and Voss making things difficult for us all.'

'Are they really hot stuff?'

Forde grinned suddenly. 'So they say. And to 'elp your ease of mind, I 'eard in 'ospital that they'd moved down 'ere for a short rest as a bonus for being so bloody unpleasant to 'em up at Arras in April. Just another of those things they introduce to make flying complicated. Like rotary engines and bad weather.'

Ira caught the brief frightened but undaunted look that crossed Colyer's face. It sprang from the unexpected discovery that came to everyone eventually—that they were vulnerable, after all, and that immortality was subject to a great deal more than skill.

'It isn't much of a prospect, is it?' Colyer said.

Forde grinned again and went on with cheerful indifference. 'You get used to it,' he pointed out. 'Like wooden legs. The object's to get through the first few weeks.'

The question that had been trembling on Colyer's lips burst out at last. He was badly in need of reassurance.

'What's it really like out here?'

Forde shrugged. 'Food's awful.'

'I meant the flying.'

Forde shrugged. 'Comes and goes,' he said. 'Pretty 'orrible in the last week or two. I don't think we've ever caught up after the slaughter in April. They say we lost a 'ell of a lot of good fellers then, and they've never been properly replaced, so you can bet these days if you 'ear shooting, the target's you.' He smiled, his eyes disappearing into thick folds of flesh. 'It's proper dangerous when you come to think of it, isn't it?'

'Can't we do anything about it?' Colyer's words came in a bleat of indignation.

Forde shrugged. 'If we can catch the Albatroses at the right 'eight we can. Unfortunately, the 'Un's clever enough to make sure we don't.'

Colyer's eyes flickered to Ira. 'Will it get worse?' he asked.

Forde's big shoulders moved again. 'Well, it won't get better,' he admitted.

'They said at the Pilots' Pool I'd be just in time for the offensive here.'

Forde spoke with apocalyptic weightiness. 'Well, certainly, there 'asn't been one round this quarter for a long time, so some bloke with red on 'is 'at's bound to think of it sooner or later.' He smiled reassuringly. 'War's made up of personal sorrows and individual miseries, lad, so just make sure you don't cause none for your friends. Don't try 'eroics. Take your time. Find your way about and concentrate on staying alive. The 'Un's got the advantage of speed and armament just now and the wind's always blowing from *our* end of the pitch. So stick close to the chap who's leading and keep one eye over your shoulder.'

Colyer gave a nervous laugh. 'You make it sound dangerous,' he said.

Forde paused, thinking, then he looked up, his eyes frank. 'Well,' he said, 'when you consider that practically every aviator in the world's been mustered together in France in a strip of territory some three hundred miles long by ten miles wide, it's no bloody wonder that there's a lot o' pigeons among 'em and that there's a pretty picking for them that are 'awks.'

4

The stars were still shining as they finished their hard-boiled eggs, but Forde remained irritatingly cheerful.

'I can never understand,' he said in loud puzzled tones as he lit a cigarette, 'why they can't make these bloody eggs soft. I wake up 'ungry enough to eat a mangy pup and I reckon a 'ard-boiled egg's about the most indigestible thing there is in the world to go to war on.'

No one answered him because no one else felt like chatter at that hour, and they trudged silently to the hangar, wrapping huge scarves round their necks and fastening belts and buckles and buttons in the faint steely light that was beginning to show trees and huts and farm buildings. Colyer had got up to see them leave and stood nervously alongside Ira's Pup as he strapped himself in, his coat flapping in the wind.

'I wish I were coming with you,' he said.

As the mechanic swung his leg and leaned on the blade of the propeller, the engine started with a burst of blue castor oil smoke and cold air was slapped into Ira's face. The other two engines burst into life and Ira saw Forde, bulging out of a machine with a large J on the side, then, as Wyatt gave the signal, he opened the throttle and lifted the Pup's tail. It was just light enough to follow Wyatt as he climbed, but the sun was already catching the peaks of a patch of cumulus to the west, and beginning to lay an orange stain over the River Oise, so that it wound below them in glittering curves that were hidden here and there by patches of mist.

The countryside seemed dead and remote, with just an occasional lifting column of smoke, but as they climbed they met the light coming from the east, a pale tinting of the earth which turned gradually to bronze. Then the first rays of the sun pushing into the heavens took the steeliness from it and changed it to blue.

Ira felt no tremors of nervousness, only a desire to acquit himself well. He knew he could fly and he knew he was experienced in the air, and in this quiet sector he felt that with luck he had a chance to survive because he had long since passed through the first stage of trepidation and the second of foolhardiness to the final one of realising that it was safer to take no risks. Yet he was still virtually untouched by the war. He'd been lucky enough to have had few narrow escapes and had rarely found himself in situations that were difficult to get out of, so that his store of courage had not been drawn on often enough to wither and die.

Chauny, Guiscard, St Simon and St Quentin passed beneath him, all a little shabby-looking in the bright summer sunshine, and he felt a sense of committal. Just to the north he could see the Amiens–Albert–Cambrai road, misty in the pale light, driving straight as an arrow beneath the patchy cloud towards the east. There were already other aeroplanes about, alight with the rising sun. Beyond the kite balloons, a lonely BE2c, as outdated as a Dodo, crept sheepishly towards the line for an artillery shoot, and further east two FEs, looking like birdcages with their openwork tail structure, dared fate with a patrol beyond the German lines.

As they crossed the trenches, the sun was in their eyes, throwing the contours of the ground into marked shadows, so that the battle line crawled like an ugly grey snake in and out of the mist on either side of them. The trenches, almost unchanged since the war began, interlocked like a jigsaw, and the whole countryside around, torn by explosives through three years of fighting, looked like the surface of a pond in a heavy rainstorm.

He had just turned his attention to the sky again when he heard a sharp 'crack' that made him jump, and felt a blast of air that flung his machine violently upward. He was flying through a puff of acrid-smelling smoke and the sky about him was abruptly dotted with other black puffs. Wyatt promptly changed course and started to climb, and the next lot of explosions was below them, dark cotton-wool balls directly on the spot where they'd have been flying without their change of direction.

His heart thudding, Ira's eyes flickered about the sky. Anti-aircraft fire always made him jump, and he knew from experience that although it was only occasionally dangerous, it could serve to give a pinpoint to enemies unseen against the sun. It was all part of the pattern of knowledge a pilot built up from flying over the lines.

Another series of black puffs appeared, but they were almost out of range now and he cleared his gun with a short burst. He was flying just behind and to the right of Wyatt, his head moving backwards and forwards, his eyes sweeping the sky, staring down into the dazzling yellow eye of the sun for any early-flying German who might be coming up to meet them.

In the distance now were groups of clouds, like cotton wool touched with gold where the rays of the rising sun caught them. Behind them brighter banks of cumulus loomed, slab-sided and solid-looking, lighting the heavens with a reflected glow. As Wyatt changed course again, losing height, another BE drifted past below them, fragile, wide-winged and almost stationary as it faced the wind. They were at nineteen thousand feet, with Ira numb with cold and breathing through his mouth in great gasps to get the thin air into his lungs, when Wyatt rocked his wings and pointed below to his right.

Staring down, Ira caught a glimpse of the sun on the leading edge of a tilted wing and was able to identify the machine as yet another slow-flying BE, then astern of it he caught another flash and picked out a flight of three Albatros DIIIs climbing up from German territory. Instinctively he glanced around him and above, but there was nothing there and he followed Wyatt down in a long dive at two-thirds throttle, aware of the sudden pounding of his pulses.

It was like performing in a vast sunlit amphitheatre with the Germans below, new spade-tailed machines with swept-back wings, moving like exotic butterflies with their red fuselages and vari-coloured rudders and ailerons. As he edged out from Wyatt's slipstream to give himself elbow room he saw that they were intent on the BE and seemed to be unaware of their presence.

Wyatt's dive was becoming steeper now and the Germans were growing larger and larger. Far from being unaware of their presence, however, the Albatroses were expecting them and swung away in wild vertical banks like startled birds above the sad stricken shape of the BE which was fluttering down now towards the east. Wyatt began to fire too soon and Ira hurriedly fixed his sights on the tail-end machine, an Albatros with a green rudder; but the Pup swerved unexpectedly as he flew through the German's slipstream and by the time he had corrected it the Albatros had vanished. His head flicking from side to side, he found it again to his right and fastened on its tail but, when he pressed the trigger, his gun refused to work and, apoplectic with rage, he grabbed for the hammer and tried to knock the cocking handle down. It remained immovable and with the green-tailed Albatros whirling in a tight bank now, trying to pull round behind him, he hurriedly abandoned his efforts to get the gun going and gave his whole attention to flying.

They had lost a lot of height with the dive and with the advantage of their lighter wing-loading lost, the three Albatroses seemed to swing in on them like a pack of sharks closing round a group of swimmers. Stuck in a tight turn, flat against the sky, the blood draining from his face, Ira was choked by the thudding of his heart and staggered at the easy superiority of the green-tailed machine opposite. It was gaining on him all the time, its turns growing tighter and tighter so that he could see directly into the cockpit across the intervening space.

Dry-mouthed, he was shocked to realise how much things had changed since he had last flown in France, and, remembering how they'd driven the Germans from the sky over the Somme the previous year, he found something vaguely obscene in the way the Albatros seemed to be waiting its opportunity to kill him. Glancing back, his chest hollow with fear, he saw that the German was close enough now for the pilot's head to be almost behind the sights of his guns, and as his eyes flickered backwards again, he glimpsed orange flashes over the snout of the machine. Tracers shot past his wing tip, and he tried to pull out of the turn. Immediately, there was a crash in the cockpit that made his heart stop as a bullet shattered his height indicator and he flung his machine back into the bank again, realising he had done exactly what the German was trying to make him do.

Talking loudly to himself in a fret of terror that was as nauseating as it was unexpected, he watched himself in a detached way kicking at the rudder bar, stunned by his own helplessness. Whenever he tried to fly straight the German was waiting for him and the heavy crackling noise behind his tail came like the tearing of canvas, and he saw the thin streamers of tracer flashing past—close enough for him to smell it—to form a pale geometric pattern across the area of the fighting.

Swinging wildly across the stained sky, stupefied at his helplessness, he still remembered not to drive the revs too high for fear of seizing the engine up. The noise behind him seemed nearer even than before and, glancing round, he realised the German was close enough now to see the oil smears on his engine. But then, unexpectedly, it soared out of sight in an easy lifting climb and, breathless, still cold with fear, Ira saw that the other two Pups had vanished and that the German was swinging away. There seemed to be no explanation for the abrupt end to the fight and in a nervous flurry of activity he set to work again with the hammer on the cocking handle.

Then, suddenly aware of his loneliness and vulnerability in the empty sky, he glanced upwards and immediately saw the reason for the green-tailed Albatros's loss of interest. Three more DIIIs were dropping down on him, growing visibly larger as they approached and, jamming the hammer into its socket once more, he jerked the stick forward so abruptly he was almost flung from the cockpit as the Pup dropped towards the earth, its engine full on, his only thought that of getting to safety.

His speed indicator went across to the stop and as the controls grew stiff with the speed, his ears crackled with the changing pressure. The Germans were firing as they fell from the sky, every burst making him crouch lower in the illusory safety of the fabric-covered cockpit. His brain working in a whirl of fear, he let his head loll over the dashboard to feign death and slid further down out of sight as the wires screamed. The whole machine began to shake like a lorry on a bad road and, his heart stuck in his throat, he waited in cringing tension for a bracing wire to snap and send the wings folding back so that he would dig his own grave with the speed of his fall.

He realised the shooting had died away at last and carefully pulled the throttle back to ease out of the dive. His head ached abominably after the change of altitude and sharp pains dug at his ears, but he couldn't believe his luck. The Germans had vanished and, lifting himself in the seat, he drew a deep shuddering breath, sweating and emotionally spent.

His engine started to splutter after the dive and he began to pump up pressure, his confidence sadly shattered. Air fighting was as different now from the previous year as the slow waltzes they'd performed in 1916 were from the inexperienced exchanges they'd had in 1915, and he had made mistake after mistake.

The sun was catching the roofs of Huyzes-le-Grand as he returned. Wyatt and Forde had already landed and were talking loudly together.

He caught the word 'Richthofen' and, as he disarmed his gun, Forde appeared alongside him. He looked shaken.

'Makes you realise why they pay you an extra eight bob a day flying pay, doesn't it?' he said. 'Nobody with the intelligence of a wart-'og would do what we do for less—especially with the Richthofen mob in the area.'

Colyer, complete with orderly officer's armband and Sam Browne, was listening intently. '*Have* they come down here?' he asked.

Forde shrugged. 'Judging by the warpaint and the amount of spite! God knows 'ow they 'ear these things in a 'ospital at Doullens.'

Ira was climbing from his cockpit now, still a little dazed, and Colyer moved round the machine, staring at the holes in it, not yet quite one with the grimy-faced young men who chattered noisily from the explosive excitement of the fight and the intoxicating effect of high altitude.

'What were they like, Ira?' he asked.

Still shaken, Ira was unfastening his yellow coat, wooden-featured beneath the dirt. He hadn't fired his gun once, yet there was torn fabric in his rudder and wing-tips and he was still stiff and cold with fright.

'Go on!' Colyer was still staring at him. 'What were they like?'

As he pulled off his helmet and ran his fingers through his flattened hair, Ira became aware of him at last, his face reproachful, smooth-cheeked and clean in front of his own grime, and he smiled raggedly, beginning to feel a little like one of the Light Brigade back from Balaclava.

'A bit rough,' he said, with a curiously adolescent look.

'Did you shoot any down?' Colyer asked.

'Give us a chance.'

Colyer frowned. 'I wish they'd let me go,' he said. 'The Old Man had me firing at the ground target again.'

'Did you hit it?'

Colyer smiled. 'I frightened a flight-sergeant on a bicycle in the next field but I bet I was nowhere near the square.' His smile faded and he looked depressed. 'My God, if it's as difficult as all that to hit a stationary target, what must it be like trying to hit a moving one?'

As they pushed their way into the Bull and Bush, a fresh-faced boy, with fair hair and pink schoolboy cheeks that matched his breeches, leapt to his feet. Sensing at once that the newcomer had less experience than he had himself, Colyer began to put on the airs of someone who'd been flying at the front for months. The new arrival listened to him with the same breathless awe with which Colyer himself had listened to Forde, then as Ira tossed his leather coat down, he caught sight of the ribbons on his breast.

'I say,' he said eagerly, 'isn't that the M.M.?'

'*And* the Croix de Guerre,' Colyer said proudly, as though they were his own. 'He's been out before.'

Ira threw a boot at him and they fell wrestling across his bed just as Forde arrived. His face was as blandly disapproving as an elder brother's.

''Ere,' he said sternly. 'This is no way to behave in front of new boys.'

He turned to the fair-haired youngster. 'Make yourself at 'ome,' he said. 'We don't 'ave no rules, except the usual ones of nice manners, kindliness, brotherly love and good be'aviour. I try to keep this establishment respectable.' He sounded a little like a landlord admonishing a youthful drunk, and McCabe clearly didn't know whether to take him seriously or not.

'I need comfort, see,' Forde went on stolidly. He began to struggle out of his coat and take off layers of scarves and sweaters and toss them down, then he sat on the edge of the bed and began to drag off his thick stockings and trousers. 'I'm an old 'and, see,' he said. 'Him'—he jerked a thumb at Ira—' 'e is also an old 'and. Despite the chubby cheeks and the bloom on 'is skin—and, I suspect, the marbles in 'is pocket and the toffee covered with fluff—'e flew when aeroplanes were so like box kites small boys were in the 'abit of tying strings to them and trying to get 'em into the air.'

He heaved himself to his feet and, standing in vest and long pants, began to wash himself in the tin basin at the end of the hut.

'Actually,' he said, 'you couldn't 'ave arrived at a better time. There's a mess do tonight. Stone'ouse 'as at last qualified for 'ome. Two other fellers are goin', too.' He thrust his head down then stared round, dripping water, his face severe. 'It oughta be a good opportunity to introduce you to the dangers of life out 'ere.'

The celebrations came entirely up to Forde's satisfaction—noisy but never ill-tempered, so that they appealed to his sense of rightness and respectability. Over the coffee, Sillito tried to make a witty speech about the posted men being the finest ever let out of prison to win the war, but it came out stiff and quite humourless, and Stonehouse, surprised and grateful that he had survived his tour of duty, was already too far beyond intelligibility to reply. Instead Atwater, a member of B Flight, who clearly fancied himself as an operatic tenor, moved to the piano and, with his hands together and his eyes on the ceiling, proceeded to worry the life out of *Come Into the Garden, Maud*.

Forde turned out to be the mess pianist and, with great gusto and not a little skill, played all the songs from the London musicals till he had the whole squadron shouting, even amiably allowing four of the strongest men to hold his vast bulk upside down while he continued to find the keys. English, of A Flight, who was in fact an American who had joined up in Canada, began to throw bread and gruesome jokes about death began to shove through the chinks in the din with dirge-like songs like *The Young Aviator Lay Dying* and *The Ballad of R. Suppards*. Colyer was removed to his bed early in the proceedings, green about the gills and anxious only to sleep, then the front was taken off the piano for the final uproarious spasm, and rioting broke out.

After it was all over, Forde, dry and loquacious, sat with Ira and McCabe round Colyer's snoring figure as though they were holding a wake round a corpse.

'Stone'ouse's lucky,' he said solemnly. ''E's goin' 'ome before the offensive starts.' He paused, puzzled. 'Funny to think of it, isn't it? 'E's been out six months now and, fortified by 'is patriotism, he's shot down one 'Un and shared two others. Two altogether, say. But 'e's been shot down twice himself and smashed up two other buses in crashes. When you think of it, we need the Balls and the Bishops 'oo run up these big scores to make up for all the normal people like 'im and me who just get in the way and come to messy ends.'

His expression changed and beyond the façade of calm cynicism Ira caught a brief glimpse of anxiety, then it was gone as quickly as it had come and he was cheerful again, as though the enemy aircraft he had to meet almost every day of his life could inflict no more pain than wasps.

'*I*'ve decided,' he announced gravely, 'that we're not fighting to win the war at all. We're just fighting to save our skins, and when you come to think of it, I'm not at all sure even that we're winning.'

McCabe looked shocked. 'We certainly won't if we think that way,' he said with the unbending firmness of a school prefect.

Forde looked at him pityingly with the condescension of his extra years. 'Son,' he said, 'when I first came out here that was my idea, too, but 'aving realised that at some point in my career I might easily kick the bucket, my views have undergone a considerable change. Like Stone'ouse I'm fighting now to go 'ome. I imagine the 'Uns feel the same, too, because they know, like we do, that the war's just a conspiracy between the generals and the munitions-makers to kill us all off so there'll be plenty of money and jobs for them to share among their pals after it's all over.'

He reached for a cigarette and looked at Ira. ''Ow about you?' he demanded. 'You're obviously a young feller who's had a lot of experience of the old sword-in-'and stuff. What are *you* fighting for?'

'A better world,' Ira said with pious solemnity.

Forde looked cynical. 'And what do you expect for *yourself* outa this wonderful new world we're going to 'ave?'

Ira considered, then he grinned. 'Money,' he said.

Forde put on a great show of being shocked. 'You rotten little 'ypocrite! What do you want that for?'

'I expect I'll want to get married eventually.'

Forde stared at him solemnly. 'You in love?'

Ira stared back at him. His idea of love had been formed from novels and books of poetry and was nearer to friendship than anything else, warm, secret, chaste, with a kiss almost a betrothal, and his experience of girls had been largely confined to demure young ladies who spent the evening blushing as much as he did himself.

'No,' he said. 'Not at the moment.'

He threw the words out casually, unwilling to disclose that most of his encounters with the opposite sex had left him sweating, scarlet and stonily shy.

'And this money you're after? How're you going to get it?'

'Perhaps I'll go into farming.'

'Know anything about it?'

'I can soon learn.'

Forde sighed heavily, his vast bulk heaving on the bunk. 'I've 'eard,' he said in his portentous way, 'that it takes farmers a lifetime to learn their trade, sweet'eart.'

Ira frowned. 'Oh! Well, something else then. Something that'll let me go on flying. I wouldn't like to give that up.'

Forde drew a deep breath. 'I'd give it up tomorrow,' he said fervently. 'But, then, I'm just a normal, 'am-fisted feller, not someone who flies as though he came out of an egg. Why not go back to the job you were doing before the war started?'

Ira was shocked. '*I* don't want to spend the rest of my life doing a nine-to-five job. I was articled to a solicitor.'

Forde looked up slowly. Outside, the guns in the east were banging away, rattling the hut and all its fittings and making the stovepipe clink in its socket on the stove. From time to time they heard distant crashes towards Amiens, as though bombing were taking place. His eyes were suddenly faraway.

'When I was doing a nine-to-fiver,' he said longingly, 'I didn't know 'ow wonderful it was. I fancied art or travel or something like that. Then I discovered that that kind of feller spent most of his time broke, and I was just beginning to grow interested in young women.' His face broke into an unexpected full-moon grin. 'I think when the war's over,' he ended, 'I'll just be a womaniser.'

The idea of the vast Forde as a ladies' man made Ira smile and Forde stared indignantly at him.

'Womanising's part of a soldier's pay,' he explained firmly. 'There's nothing like the worn bosoms of 'ores for jaded military men to rest their 'eads on. Come to think of it, I've 'eard there are young women beautiful beyond all comprehension near *'ere*. At Le Ponet, twenty miles away. The 'Un's never been there and they've never refugeed. There are even more, so I'm told, at Butte-Jourdain further on—the sort that loop the loop for you without even being asked, because they've forgotten what it's like to 'ave a man around the 'ouse. I go weak with lust just at the thought of 'em.'

McCabe glanced quickly at Ira. 'How do you get there?' he asked.

'Scrounge a lift.'

'Sounds a bit uncertain.'

'It is uncertain. So uncertain, in fact, I've been thinking of buying Stone'ouse's motor bike. It's a French one 'e acquired when 'e first came out. He 'it a tree when he was stewed and it did it a lot of no good.'

'I'd go halves with you,' Ira said.

McCabe leaned forward. 'Can you ride three on a motor bike?' he asked.

'It's been done.'

'What about Colyer?'

'Well, we can't ride four aboard, that's certain.'

Forde became brisk and businesslike. ' 'Ow about us pooling our resources?' he said. 'We shan't all be off duty at the same time.'

It seemed a sensible arrangement and Forde stuck out his great fist. They shook three-handed, then Forde solemnly picked up the unconscious Colyer's limp fingers and held them on top.

'I 'ope 'e's not as frightened of motor bikes as I am,' he said.

5

Stonehouses's motor cycle was a two-cylinder three-speed Moto-Rêve of doubtful vintage with a buckled front wheel, twisted handlebars and a great deal of rust.

'Even to my atrophied intellect it looks more *rêve* than *moto*,' Forde commented dryly.

Ira thought differently. 'It'll be all right,' he said confidently, 'when I've had a go at it.'

Forde eyed him curiously, as though he'd discovered there were unexpected depths in him that required careful plumbing. 'Know anything about 'em?' he asked.

'Yes.' Ira nodded. 'Used to have one of my own. I've been riding 'em ever since I was a kid.'

'Some'ow I thought you might 'ave,' Forde observed. 'Is there anything you *'aven't* been doing ever since you were a kid?'

Since the gaily painted Albatroses which had so frightened them all had vanished again as abruptly as they had appeared and air activity had lapsed once more into nothing worse than undangerous skirmishes, there was sufficient free time to strip the old machine to its component parts and examine the damage. Wyatt's patrols made little demand on them. He was a nervous leader, unskilful at using the sun or cloud cover, and tended to make his attacks too soon or too late, so that the few German two-seaters Ira saw always escaped to the east; and with flying reduced to a boring business at height, his face daubed with whale grease, he occupied himself chiefly with keeping his circulation going and deciding what to do about the motor cycle.

Forde lit a candle with mock solemnity on his locker like a Catholic novitiate.

'A week nearer autumn,' he said. 'When flying's a bit more intermittent and life 'as a chance of being more prolonged,' and they were just beginning to look forward to enjoying life when the Germans opposite came to life once more.

It was a bright morning and, apart from the occasional flash of a propeller in the vast blue emptiness burned pale by the sun, there was nothing to indicate they were even moving. The aeroplanes hung stiffly above an earth that seemed to revolve slowly beneath them like an endless magic lantern film from childhood and the patrol was uneventful. On the way back to Huyzes, however, Wyatt went far too late to the rescue of an ancient BE fighting its way home past a pair of Albatros DIIIs, and they had to look on helplessly from their escorting position above as it struggled to safety, its flight growing more erratic and laboured until it finally fell to pieces from the hammering it had taken.

Feeling old and depressed, Ira watched with narrow eyes as it spiralled down to smash into the trenches near St Simon, and began to wonder angrily if it was friendship that caused Sillito to fail to recognise Wyatt's lack of skill. The idea worried him and he made up his mind smugly that if ever he were in the same position he would never hesitate, even at the cost of friendship, where lives were at stake.

Deciding that his chances of ever being in that happy position were so slender as to be negligible, he forced himself out of his musing again and gloomily recommenced his slow quartering of the sky behind him. As his head turned, his heart stopped and he jerked to the present at once. A group of tiny specks hung above them, transparent against the blue and, frightened out of his wits and shocked at his own negligence, he pushed up his goggles to stare again, and the flight broke up just in time.

The clatter of fast-firing Spandaus, like the sound of tearing canvas, filled his ears as four Albatroses led by a grey machine with a three-wing design hurtled past him in a shallow dive. It was the first triplane he'd seen and, though it didn't seem to be particularly fast, it was very manœuvrable and when he fired at it, it soared upwards in front of him like a lift. His stomach hollow with apprehension, he was just clawing for height after it when he saw Forde diving westwards with his propeller stopped, and as the grey triplane swung after him, he rolled into a steep dive and drove it off his tail.

The other Pups had vanished by this time and as they struggled westwards they saw the faces of men in the trenches turned up towards them and a few arms waving, then Forde was skimming roof-tops to put his machine down in a field near Vermand. He was just climbing from it as Ira landed alongside, and he came towards him, his beefy face wearing an unsteady grin.

'If I'd 'ad a parachute,' he said shakily, 'I'd 'ave jumped. What was that thing like a Venetian blind? It was enough to put the wind up you just to look at it.'

He took out a handkerchief to wipe his face and Ira saw he was sweating. 'If they can 'ave parachutes in balloons'—he was persevering with his theme as though it bothered him a little—'I'm 'anged if I can see why *we* can't 'ave 'em, too. Surely it wouldn't be asking too much for some feller to invent one you could strap to the fuselage.'

As they recovered a little, Ira fished in his pocket for the tools he always carried and while he loosened the cowling of the Pup, Forde walked slowly round the machine, fingering the torn fabric and listening to the ticks and creaks as the hot engine cooled.

'Twangs on the old nerve-strings a bit, that sort of thing,' he observed uneasily. 'With the 'Un getting all 'ostile again, it don't pay to sing and play the piano much.'

As they peered into the engine, soldiers appeared from nowhere and began to crowd round, watching them as they worked.

'I think you got one, sir,' one of them offered eagerly.

'Don't kid yourself, lad,' Forde said. 'It took us all our time to stop them getting *us*.'

A small man whose narrow face was obscured by a colossal steel helmet pushed forward. He wore spectacles and had the busybody look of a barrack-room lawyer.

'What do you feel like when you see 'em coming, mate?' he demanded.

'Frightened,' Forde said shortly, obviously disliking him.

'I mean, what do you *think*?'

Forde stared at him coldly. 'I think what lucky buggers they are to 'ave better machines than we've got,' he said. 'And now unless you're an expert on Le Rhône engines stand back a bit and let the dog see the rabbit.'

The man in the big helmet stood his ground, and indicated a group of Nissen huts in the distance.

'There's a transport unit over there,' he said. '*They*'ve got mechanics if you want one. I'd go for you and ask, only there's a lot of spare parts off lorries and motor bikes and things, and somebody's been selling 'em to the French, and they won't let you in without a pass.'

Forde glanced at Ira who had withdrawn his head from the engine space of Forde's machine and had paused with the screwdriver still in his hand.

Forde grinned. 'Don't worry, lad,' he said to the soldier. 'We'll go ourselves. Just mind you don't get killed in the rush.'

During the afternoon, they persuaded the driver of a squadron tender going to Peronne to go out of his way a little and take them to Vermand, and they returned with a load of spare parts. Forde pulled up a box to watch as Ira and Colyer bent over the Moto-Rêve. The piano was going in the mess and they could hear Atwater working over an aria from *Carmen*.

'Sounds as though it's getting noisy,' Forde said. 'P'raps we ought to join 'em.'

Colyer shook his head. 'Not me,' he announced. 'I'm down for the early-morning show.'

Forde stared at him expressionlessly for a moment, as though assessing his chances of survival. 'You don't 'ave to go into training, lad,' he pointed out. 'So long as you can see, it's enough.'

Colyer wasn't so sure. 'I'd like to be as alert as possible,' he pointed out earnestly.

'Your sense of duty becomes you,' Forde said solemnly. 'Just don't let it ruin your life.'

Colyer woke them at four o'clock the following morning. He was fully dressed, shaved to the bone and already swathed in scarves, gloves and coat. He looked white, tense and nervous.

'Goodbye,' he said. 'I'm off.'

'You're coming back, aren't you?' Forde asked.

Colyer seemed doubtful—and a little hurt that they couldn't be bothered to get out of bed to watch him fly off to his death.

As they sat in the mess over breakfast, Colyer reappeared, looking gloomy.

'Tell Papa, darling,' Forde urged.

Colyer had never seen a thing and, unwilling to return home in case he was considered a coward, had flown the whole patrol with a gun that had jammed as soon as he'd cleared it with his first trial burst.

Forde was exploring the depths of his egg and didn't bother to look up. 'What 'appened?' he asked.

Colyer looked worried. 'All of a sudden everybody started banking away, then I heard some guns going and found I was on my own.'

'You're enough to demoralise a 'ole army corps,' Forde said amiably. 'You were being pounced on by nasty evil-minded 'Uns, lad.'

Colyer shrugged and poked despondently into his egg. 'I was still wondering what to do when I saw everybody below,' he said. 'They were heading home, so I joined 'em. I even got through those bloody trees all right for once.'

'And duly received congratulations from all concerned on landin'?' Forde asked.

Colyer sighed. 'Until I mentioned that my gun had been out of action the whole time. Then they promptly jumped on me.'

'Said you were a fool?'

'Yes.'

'Disgrace to the flight?'

'Yes.'

'Put everyone's life in danger?'

'Yes. How did you know?'

'It 'appened to me.'

The afternoon haze lay in thick patches, particularly near the line where it mingled with the smoke, and Wyatt seemed more nervous than normal, as though he were afraid of losing his bearings. There was a group of DIIIs to the east, but they vanished at once and the ground mist began to increase until they were flying over a limitless expanse of brilliant white haze that made Wyatt more uncertain than ever. Fortunately a gap came up just when they needed it and they went through it to find themselves over Moy where they were able to find their way to Huyzes by following the road to La Fère at tree-top height.

Forde hadn't enjoyed the flight home. 'I don't like manœuvring in wet grass at a 'eight of fourteen inches,' he said sourly.

After tea, Ira began to put the Moto-Rêve together. The result was rather a botched-up job because the wheel they'd acquired proved smaller than the original and it gave the machine a nose-down appearance.

'Ought to be good in a dive,' Forde commented.

The days were growing perceptibly shorter now and the indifferent weather had several times brought mist which had made flying difficult, and the following day they were awakened by the roar of rain on the roof of the hut. Knowing there could be no flying, Ira pushed the motor cycle inside and, setting McCabe and Colyer to work with sheets of emery paper scrounged from the hangar, he was rubbing away at rust with them when Forde arrived. He'd been to look at a litter of pigs on the neighbouring farm and he had to climb over the machine to get to his bunk. He stood on his blankets with the mud still on his boots and a look of disgust on his face.

'I didn't expect the bloody 'ut to be turned by a set of mechanically minded infants into a workshop,' he said with a neigh of horror. 'Won't it go without all this nonsense?'

'No,' Ira said. 'At least, not very fast.'

'We don't want a racing bike! The slower the better as far as I'm concerned, in fact. I tend to be of a nervous disposition.'

There were three whole days with the rain lashing down out of a leaden sky and the water running down the chimney to sizzle on top of a red-hot stove. The hut was full of draughts and the area outside became a quagmire of mud that they tramped across the wooden floor. Everything was slimy with mistiness, and the wind roared in the stove-pipe so that the blaze consumed coke and coal at an alarming rate.

In the north the new offensive in front of Ypres had come to a halt once more in the Flanders mud and the front all the way to the south had become stagnant again.

Between patrols, blank again for the most part and boring to people like Kelly and Atwater, who were itching to write their names in glory, Ira tried out the Moto-Rêve, riding it at full speed round the field, gleefully bouncing it over the bumps and through the puddles and revving its engine to screaming point until he was pelted with a hail of hairbrushes and boots from neighbouring huts. Driven away by the abuse, he wheeled the machine to where Forde, Colyer and McCabe were standing—triumphant but red in the face at the insults, and spattered with mud and oil thrown out by a faulty rocker gear.

'You only need a lump of toffee stuck in your cheek,' Forde said with cold disapproval, 'and you'd look like an urchin from an infants' school.'

He eyed the strange-looking machine critically. 'Looks bloody queer,' he went on. 'Is it dangerous?'

Ira grinned. 'Not unless you make it angry.'

'Will it get us to Le Ponet?'

'Of course it will.'

'Good. Tomorrow's the day. Who goes first?'

'I do,' Ira announced firmly. 'Me and Colyer. We did most of the work.'

With the weather clearing, everyone began to emerge from their holes, flapping damp clothes in the wind. C Flight flew the afternoon patrol but they were again disappointed. There was a lot of murk up to three thousand feet where the mist ended in a few angry rags of cloud and, as usual, Wyatt attacked too soon from a poor position so that their quarry, an antiquated two-seater, simply flopped into the mist and escaped.

Forde was irritated by their continuing lack of success and in no mood to be enthusiastic as Ira and Colyer brushed up their best uniforms. 'I want a full report on the girls,' he said sourly. 'C Flight are off tomorrow and I shall 'ave to know where to look.'

The mist had cleared completely as they straddled the Moto-Rêve outside the hut. Through the trees and over the field the curtain of the storms that had stopped flying on and off for several days had lifted a little and beyond it the sky was full of liquid light, pale gold and luminous green, set with small islands of brilliant red where the late sun struck the clouds. Towards the front line a pile of thick grey cumulus was turning purple so that the reflected light touched the countryside with colour.

A farewell committee had turned out to see them leave and stood in a half-circle, grinning.

'Can anyone buy into this company?' Kelly asked.

'It's a family concern,' Forde pointed out coldly. 'We 'ave no shares for offer.'

'Let's know if you find anything,' Kelly suggested. 'So we can borrow a tender and *all* go.'

'You keep out of this,' Forde said indignantly. 'Or blood'll run in the gutters. I don't expect much competition from three war babies and I'm not 'aving none from you.'

Ira put the machine into gear and began to push. When he was beginning to grow red in the face and everyone had started to jeer, the engine exploded into a roar and he had to fight to straddle the saddle before the Moto-Rêve leapt out of his hands. Colyer hurriedly cocked a leg over the roll of felt they'd tied to the luggage carrier for a seat, moving warily as he settled himself. 'Try to miss the bumps,' he said, 'or I'll do myself some mischief.'

As Ira let in the clutch with a jerk, Colyer grabbed hurriedly for his neck to avoid disappearing backwards over the rear wheel, and catcalls broke from the watching men as they roared in an uncertain and undignified circle.

'What's she like in a loop?'

'Bit more right rudder, old boy!'

Ira fought off Colyer's grip, red-faced with shame at their unpromising start, then, with the tyres throwing out a spray of mud, he headed at full speed for the shouting men and, as they dived for the rain-wet hedge, he roared out of the camp, laughing.

'For God's sake'—Colyer's breath came in jerky pants as they shot over the hump-backed bridge and banged to earth again—'don't—do—that! I nearly took off!'

They rattled towards Le Ponet over the rough French roads, wriggling in and out of the army traffic that filled the pavé, and whenever the road was clear, Ira, caught by the sensation of speed, opened the throttle to its limit. As they clattered into Le Ponet and stopped in the main square, Colyer jumped off the carrier and backed away at speed.

'For God's sake,' he said furiously. 'I thought you were going to kill me!'

His indignation was so marked it was some time before they could make a start on the search for the girls Forde had heard about. Neither of them was very experienced and they weren't sure how to set about the task. In the strained and dangerous life they lived, women had a special importance, twice as tender as normal, twice as gentle, twice as beautiful, and they were faintly sentimental about them, despite the dirty stories and the pretence of heavy lust, and anxious not to put a foot wrong.

Eventually, their eyes were caught by a girl driving a pony and trap. She was more an adolescent than a young woman and she was wearing the inevitable black, but in their all-male world she looked exciting.

'I say!' Colyer breathed enthusiastically.

Ira grinned. 'You've gone sprat-eyed,' he said.

'Well, follow her, man!' Colyer came to life with a jerk, and they followed the trap eagerly, arguing as to who should be responsible for the first move.

'Go on!' Colyer said. 'Speak to her.'

'Me?' Ira looked indignant. 'It was your idea.'

In the end, hungrily watching the pony and trap, they drummed up their courage and decided that they'd drive alongside and that Colyer should strike up a conversation from the carrier as they passed.

'Suppose the horse takes fright and bolts at the noise of the bike?' he asked uneasily.

They chugged along slowly behind the pony and trap for a while. It had long since dawned on the driver that she was being followed and, as she kept glancing over her shoulder at them, Ira found himself longing for sufficient experience to be able to tell whether her expression was one of alarm or encouragement. So far in his life he had never managed to do anything much more daring than walk side by side with a girl down a lane, suffering from an agony of embarrassment as he fought for something to say.

When they had finally opened conversation with their quarry, he decided, he would adopt a careless detached manner which would suggest he was indifferent to the company of young women. It seemed a safe yet mature attitude and left plenty of room to manœuvre.

'Go on,' Colyer hissed from behind. 'Get on with it. Rev her up!'

The girl gave them another glance over her shoulder which, by this time, Ira was convinced was one of alarm, then, just as he accelerated to draw alongside, he found himself staring at a high-tonneaued De Dion just coming round the corner, driven by an elderly chauffeur and containing a girl wearing blue-braided serge. Her face was pale, with thick dark brows over huge eyes, and he was suddenly aware of being able to muster no attitudes whatsoever, mature or otherwise.

He knew he'd never seen anything so lovely in his life. It was as though the world had emptied at the sight of her and all the millions of other men and women had vanished. His heart cried out in worship and an intoxicated conviction that somehow she was bound to him.

He had stopped the motor cycle abruptly as the car vanished behind them, and he became aware of Colyer pounding his shoulder in fury.

'You've missed her, you fool! What did you stop for?'

Ira stared at him in a daze. 'Didn't you see her?' he asked. He felt he had been hit between the eyes. 'The one in the car.'

Colyer stared at him. 'Girls in motor cars don't speak to chaps like us,' he said.

Realising the truth of what he said, Ira started the Moto-Rêve again just in time to find that the pony, cart and driver had vanished into a farm opening. As they slid to a halt, they saw it reining in outside a house.

'Well,' Colyer said disgustedly, 'you made a fine mess of that!'

Back at Huyzes, Forde was ponderously contemptuous of their efforts. 'I've never 'eard of such inefficiency,' he said.

'There was this one I saw,' Ira offered.

'Some old 'ag with feet like buckets and breasts like clock-weights, I suppose. And what did you do? Let her slip through your grasp, meek as Moses.'

'We never had her in our grasp,' Ira said heavily, eyeing Colyer, shamefaced and inadequate.

'You don't 'ave to suffer from epic masculinity to pick up with a young woman,' Forde pointed out firmly. 'You want to remember that every Frenchman who's old enough and strong enough to carry a rifle went away three years ago and most of the poor buggers won't ever come back.' He gestured at McCabe. 'Tomorrow,' he said, 'the lad there's goin' to war. Atwater's gone down with tonsillitis—all that bloody singin', I expect—and he's to spend the morning practising and go out in the afternoon in the full flush of what 'e's learned.'

He stared round at them severely. 'When 'e comes back,' he ended, 'I'll show you what courtin's all about.'

6

Forde was knotting his tie by the cracked mirror over his bed.

'Picking girls up's not difficult or dangerous, lad,' he was saying.

'It is for me,' Ira observed. He lay on his bunk, watching Forde enviously, remembering the few attempts he'd made in his life which had all been ordeals not far from torture. He longed to be a cynical old roué as Forde was, but in all his dealings so far with the opposite sex he had found it impossible to be light-hearted, and even the girl in the De Dion had remained in his mind as a cherished image to be hugged to himself like a secret.

He had already started to address letters to her that were passionate, poetic and noble, to let her know exactly what he felt about her. They were not set down on paper because he didn't know where to send them and the very strength of his feelings would have embarrassed him too much.

Unaware of the lost expression on his face, Forde was still holding forth to the mirror. 'You 'ave to pretend not to be interested,' he advised. 'Keep 'em at a distance. Be aloof. That's the best thing. It's what's known as technique. It's no good advancing backwards, is it? Women like a feller to be bold.'

As they talked, the drone of engines sounded over the day-time noises of the field and they cocked their heads, counting.

B Flight had disappeared east on an offensive patrol to stir the Germans to action, and six machines had taken off in a grey afternoon that was as thick as clotted cream.

'I don't like these big patrols,' Forde had said as they had left. 'I reckon they're winding the war up to make it more dangerous.'

McCabe had been pink with excitement and pleasure and full of a nervous anxiety to do his bit, and Forde had watched him vanish beyond the trees with an expression that was unexpectedly sad.

' 'E makes me feel old and tired,' he had said.

His eyes fixed on the mirror still, he was listening now to the 'whooshing' sound as the planes passed over the hut. 'Four,' he counted. 'Five. Six.' He grinned and began to brush his hair. 'All back. And that's as it should be. While I admire 'eroes, I've noticed you 'ave to strain a bit to pick up the taint of glory.'

Ira swung his feet from the bed and walked to the door. Warburton, the batman, was standing outside the hut with a pair of boots in his hand, staring towards the hangars, and as Ira appeared he put the boots down and squinted into the greyness.

'Something's happened, sir,' he announced. 'The ambulance's gone across.'

Concerned, Ira hurried across the field to where the ambulance had drawn up outside B Flight hangar. Mechanics and medical orderlies were lifting someone from one of the Pups and the flight-sergeant had taken off his jacket and laid it on the ground as a pillow. As the crowd opened Ira saw one of the medical orderlies beginning to unfasten a stained leather coat.

Colyer was standing with his helmet in his hand, his chin grimy with gunsmoke, his face tense and nervous-looking.

'Who is it?' Ira asked.

'McCabe.' Colyer spoke with a bleak irritation, and he was so tense and white-faced Ira found he couldn't look him in the eye. Sillito was frowning heavily and Monkey Brand, standing nearby, surrounded by the rest of the dogs, stared nervously into the group, his tail drooping.

Ira turned again to Colyer who moved his hand with a puzzled angry gesture.

'We trailed our coats near the aerodrome at Cambrai.' He sounded edgy, as though reaction was just beginning to set in. 'The Hun came up in swarms. We had a bit of a dust-up.' He spoke in short abrupt sentences, devoid of feeling or heroics. 'We splitarsed about a bit and sent two of them down. Nobody seemed to be hurt, though we all got a few holes. On the way back I noticed him wandering out of formation. Dropping down occasionally and then levelling off again. But I didn't think it was anything more than engine trouble.'

He stared at Ira, his eyes a little wild, like a frightened animal that had scented blood. 'What a bloody awful business!' he burst out. 'What a rotten thing to happen to him!'

Forde was just putting on his jacket when Ira reappeared in the Bull and Bush and he noticed his expression at once.

'I thought they were all back,' he said.

'They are. It's McCabe. They're working over him now.'

'Is he bad?'

Ira nodded and Forde sat down slowly and reached for a cigarette. 'He didn't last long, did 'e?' he said. 'There's a jinx on this bloody 'ut. Bassett. Yorke. Pottinger. McCabe. I reckon somebody's got it in for us.'

Ira frowned. It was hard to accept death and mutilation when they lived like country gentlemen with no immediate signs of battle about them. Going to war and returning to tea and toast and drinks and the piano gave them all an extra awareness of the astonishing opposites with which they lived and McCabe's bunk already looked as cold and cheerless as a coffin. His disappearance was too personal to ignore and it was hard not to see his bed sagging under his weight or his clothes hanging on the wall shaped to his figure.

Colyer appeared, throwing himself heavily on to his bed. For a while he was silent then he spoke harshly. 'Sillito's got wind of a new Allied offensive before the winter sets in,' he said.

'P'r'aps the 'Un'll get wind of it, too,' Forde observed gloomily. 'And think it a good idea.'

C Flight flew the patrol the following morning, but there had been an epidemic of engine trouble, and Wales, one of the older hands, a quick, nervous man with ears set so low on his skull he was known as the Low-Wing Monoplane, had to turn back so that they went out only three strong. It was a bright morning but there appeared to be a promise of rain with a lot of heavy grey clouds about that Ira didn't like. An artillery battle was going on near St Quentin and the ground was dotted with the grey wool of shell bursts streaming eastwards in the wind.

There seemed to be a lot of German aircraft about and he saw what looked like a bright spark trailing a thin column of smoke drop out of the clouds in the distance—an aeroplane falling in flames from some fight out of sight above them.

His engine was firing unevenly and he wished Wyatt would climb higher, then ten minutes later the Le Rhône started to splutter and he began to use the hand pump, wondering if he ought to go home. Wyatt appeared to be content to keep the ground in sight, however, and didn't go far over the lines so he decided to stay with the flight.

They exchanged greetings with a couple of RE8s artillery-spotting near Moy and kept them in sight for a while because German aircraft in the distance seemed to be looking for a chance to rush them. Eventually the RE8s disappeared westwards and Wyatt turned north, his manner still indecisive, as though he weren't sure whether he could afford to be aggressive with only three out-of-date machines or not. By this time, nimbus was being driven across the sky by a south-westerly wind and it became harder to guess what was lurking above, and the patrol ended with a desperate scuffling fight over Moy where Wyatt allowed himself to be caught by a group of DIIIs that dropped like stones on them through a gap in the clouds.

Forde's machine was badly shot up and he was frightened and heavily indignant, and the few drops of rain that began to fall as they walked back to the Bull and Bush seemed to set the seal on his annoyance.

'Wyatt's a mess,' he growled. ' 'E's got no idea. I think someone ought to protest.'

'He's got two Huns,' Ira said.

'Two 'Uns don't make 'im a warrior,' Forde snorted. 'Even *I* could find myself behind a 'Un in a fight. I might even hit 'im, too, if he didn't see me. C Flight's had too many casualties lately. No wonder Stone'ouse went 'ome gibbering.'

Ira didn't reply and Forde went on earnestly. 'I get the wind up just *being* with Wyatt,' he said. 'I've always believed in being kind to these 'airy types from the colonies, but I just don't think he's got the knack. I know we've only got Pups, but so 'ave A and B, and *they* seem to get a few 'Uns and lose less men. 'E's just a good bus driver, that's all. 'E doesn't have the dash for scouts.'

During the afternoon they flew another patrol towards Cambrai. The day was brighter by this time and the shifting wind had dropped to a light breeze that drove the dispersed clouds like sheep before it. Above, the sky was clear except for a patch of cirrus towards the east and it looked empty and blank and blue.

Ira didn't trust it and kept putting his thumb against the sun and twisting his head to study the area behind him. The rumour that another offensive was brewing up might prove right and aeroplanes appeared too quickly from nowhere to be incautious. Towards the south, the sun was shining along the edges of the cirrus that hung in the sky, splendid, motionless and dangerous, but Wyatt somehow didn't seem to regard the bright islands and isthmuses of cloud as hiding places or as refuges where they could shelter if they were in trouble.

There were several British two-seaters below them, which seemed to bear out the growing rumours of battle, and a group of DIIIs near St Gobain Wood which were well placed for attack. But Wyatt dived too soon as usual and the Germans seemed to show more aggression than normal, and they circled furiously, trying to get each other in their sights, until the Germans simply dropped away from them towards Cambrai, their shark-noses down, their greater speed carrying them to safety. There seemed no reason for their disappearance until another group came down from among the scattered cirrus that had so worried Ira and they had a difficult three minutes before they were able to escape.

'Wyatt frightens me to death,' Forde grumbled as they struggled out of their leather coats. 'The way 'e 'angs about like a wet week-end'll get us all killed. 'E probably even needs specs.'

McCabe's replacement was in the Bull and Bush when they arrived, already sorting out his belongings, his presence depressing in the way it drew attention to the fact that McCabe had vanished. He was a tall handsome man, about as old as Forde, with a neat narrow head and a small moustache. His tunic and breeches were immaculate, his buttons denoted the Guards, and there was a small gold stripe on his sleeve which drew Forde's eye like a magnet.

'A wound stripe!' he said. 'Did you get that flying?'

The newcomer glanced down at his sleeve with a bored expression. 'Not really,' he said in brisk no-nonsense accents that sounded as though they came from Eton or Harrow. 'Only just started, actually.'

'Where did you get it?'

'Arse, matter of fact.'

Ira grinned and Forde persisted. 'Not what portion of the anatomy,' he said, coldly pompous. 'What section of the front?'

The other gave him a cool stare. 'Up at Ypres. Bit of a frost, really. Scrap of shrapnel nicked my rear end when I was trying to keep my head down. Makes me sit with a bit of a list.'

'Why did you join this mob?'

The other man gave a fastidious little smile. 'Didn't like the dirt,' he said. 'Decided there must be a cleaner way of fighting a war. Transferred. Uncle of mine pulled a few strings. Didn't approve, of course. Thought the Flying Corps very *infra dig*. "Get oil on your clothes," he said.'

Forde extended a hand. 'My name's Toby Forde. I expect you've got a very cup-of-tea name.'

'Avallon actually. Basil Avallon.'

Forde began to strip to his long underpants to wash the grease from his face. 'Landed gentry?' he said.

Avallon considered. 'I suppose you'd call us that.'

Forde stared at his well-cut breeches and field boots, very marked among the motley assortment of slacks, golf stockings and puttees about the field. 'I'm a socialist myself,' he said with a grin. 'But I'm also a right old snob. It wouldn't 'alf add tone to the 'ut if by any chance you 'ad a title. You wouldn't 'ave, would you?'

'Not me.' Avallon had a very firmly built-in ennui. 'My Old Man. It'll go to my elder brother Francis. In the Guards at Ypres. Believes in horses. Looks a bit like one, actually.'

The sky clouded over during the afternoon and as rain began to fall, Forde sat on a box just inside the hut, smoking while Ira worked over the Moto-Rêve. A damp breeze carried flurries of rain and brought with it the faint sounds from the hangars.

'You seem 'ellish keen to make that thing go faster,' he observed.

'Why not?' Ira asked. 'It only wants tuning.'

'You're always tuning the bloody thing! One of these days you'll kill yourself.'

Ira said nothing. He had ridden at lunatic speed to Le Ponet more than once already in the hope of seeing the girl in the De Dion again, coasting hopelessly round the town on the off-chance of meeting her face-to-face. He'd never stopped to think what he'd do if he did, and he knew his infatuation was entirely make-believe so that he never told anyone where he'd been.

Forde was staring at him with a puzzled frown. 'You're a stand-offish little buster, Sunny Jim,' he said. 'A right dark 'orse. If we 'adn't got Granny Sillito for a C.O. you'd 'ave been a flight-commander already. But you don't seem a bit big-'eaded about it—a very difficult thing not many people manage. I can smell 'ot air at once and there's none round you. If *I* could tinker up engines and 'ad a couple of medals . . .'

'They're only little ones,' Ira pointed out.

'They're medals, all the same. If I 'ad that lot, it'd cost you tuppence to talk to me. You've got a funny way . . .'

'I have?' Ira looked startled.

'Sort of quiet. With a 'abit of hiding be'ind your own face. Sort of sure of yourself. *Are* you sure of yourself?'

Ira considered. There had been many times when he had felt anything else but. 'I suppose so,' he said.

'Don't you get nervous?'

'Often.'

'What about?'

Ira grinned. 'Dying.'

'Who doesn't? But not about aeroplanes?'

'I suppose not.'

'What then?'

Ira paused. 'Girls,' he said. 'I never know what to say or where to put my hands. I tried smoking but I don't like it very much.'

Forde stared at him for so long he blushed. 'You ever been with a girl?' he asked.

'Of course I've been out with a girl.'

'I didn't say "out with". I said "with" 'Ave you?'

Ira bent quickly over the engine of the Moto-Rêve. 'Of course I have,' he muttered.

'I don't believe you, lad. Try again.'

Ira lifted his head. 'No,' he admitted. He sat back on his heels, still thinking of the girl he'd seen in Le Ponet. 'I've often considered it, though,' he ended with a rush.

'You 'ave? *What* did you consider?'

Ira blushed again, aware of his inexperience.

'Suppose I got knocked out?' he said. 'I've often thought what a pity it would be if I did. I mean—without—well, you know.'

'Yes, I do.' Forde's tones were sympathetic. 'It troubles a lot o' fellers out here. I've felt the same thing.'

'*You* have? I thought . . .'

'Oh, I have, I have.' Forde waved his hand. 'More'n once. With me, it's different. *I* think what a right old waste it'd be to be knocked out without being married and havin' kids.' He stopped and was silent for a while as he lit a cigarette, then he looked at Ira again.

'Do you feel strongly about it?' he asked.

Ira shrugged. 'It wouldn't matter so much if there weren't a war on,' he said earnestly. 'It seems to make it a bit more important to hurry these days, though.'

' 'Avin' a girl's not everything in the world, lad.'

'It is when you haven't got one.'

' 'Ow about havin' another go at Le Ponet, then?' Forde suggested. 'With me as a passenger.'

Ira flushed and stared at the spanner in his hand.

'I used to be a proper lad back 'ome,' Forde said. 'A right one for the girls in a blazer and straw 'at.'

Ira tried to imagine Forde in a striped jacket and white flannels making advances to a girl and he found he was a little afraid of being guided by someone with as much experience and confidence as Forde appeared to have.

' 'Ow about it?' Forde urged. 'Riding up bold as brass and seeing what there is.'

Ira considered. 'Soon,' he promised.

But when it came to the pinch he found the very fact that Forde was predicting something dangerous and embarrassing was enough to put him off and preferred to go alone, pursuing his hopeless quest in Le Ponet. Two emotions had warred within him for a long time—the desire to prove he was a man and a terror of making a fool of himself. The few clumsy embraces in the dark he had so far experienced in his life had seemed very daring to him, but they'd been unrewarding and frustrating because they were only the brink of a deeper abyss.

He made excuses. The rain. Lack of funds. The Moto-Rêve. Forde told him that rain was nothing to worry about—he wasn't flying to Butte-Jourdain—and even offered to lend him money. But he dodged the issue still, slipping off alone and lonely, hopeful and despairing at the same time.

Then a Bristol Fighter squadron just out from England began to operate from the other side of the field, living in tents in utter discomfort in the damp weather and sharing the mess, and there was a series of near-accidents that kept them busy; and a period of brilliant weather caused the whole question of Butte-Jourdain to be forgotten as they were involved in a series of high patrols where the shortage of oxygen made them sleep like hogs on their return.

Wyatt's fumbling patrols continued, though fortunately without losses. A Flight shot down a two-seater and B shared another.

'Never C, I notice,' Forde said. 'I long to be a 'ero and all I manage is train-bearer to Wyatt. I'll be glad when he goes 'ome.'

The lack of success seemed to trouble Wyatt, too, because he was always bad-tempered when they returned, as though wondering what they'd done wrong.

Rumours multiplied. Sillito had it that the coming offensive was to be in the north, but, from the number of men and guns on the road, something was going to happen in the south, too. Avallon was allowed to go on patrol earlier than Colyer had been and Ira noticed that his flying was neat and not nervous and that he took more than an average interest in his machine. He looked as though he might be good and had a lot of confidence.

'It must be something they do to 'em in the Guards,' Colyer said enviously.

He was going through another bad patch. He had been caught by a gust of wind and dropped towards the top branches of the trees at the end of the field and it had given him such a fright he'd run into the sunken road. He'd escaped injury but, two days later, his engine had cut on take-off and though he'd escaped again without a scratch it didn't help his peace of mind and caused a lot of bad temper among the mechanics and a few sharp words from Sillito.

C Flight was flying the late patrol to the north and Wyatt, obviously concerned with his non-success, took them all on one side before they left.

'We've got to go in faster,' he said. 'We're missing chances.'

He seemed worried and Ira wondered if Sillito had at last been talking to him in that icy disapproving manner of his.

The day was bright with a good deal of cumulus above four thousand feet. The sun was flaring through a red western mist and the circle of the horizon reflected its glow. To the east there was a thin line of advancing cloud and the sky had an elderly autumn look about it.

Ira's engine was again not giving full revolutions and sounded as though one cylinder wasn't firing properly, but it kept picking up and he decided to continue, then about eight or nine miles away he saw a large group of Germans barely perceptible against the dark cloud and for once they didn't turn away. With only four of them, it looked like being dangerous, but a flight of SEs arrived from nowhere, clean-looking little machines which were supposed to be very good, and the Germans decided that the odds were too loaded against them and disappeared east.

The SEs vanished after them and Wyatt, knowing they hadn't a hope of keeping up with them, turned towards St Simon again, and as he reached for height Ira saw an old LVG two-seater below them, a mere speck against the blue-grey earth, sliding sideways, it seemed, across the broken squares where the fields had been overrun by war. There were a few scattered puff balls of cloud near it and it was slipping in and out of them so incautiously he was certain it was there to draw them down.

He stared about him, fully expecting to see glittering dots against the translucent gold of the heavens, but the sky seemed to be empty and his eyes went back to Wyatt who'd taken a quick look round and was now rocking his wings and pointing downwards.

Ira glanced upwards again, not at all happy. Some instinct warned him of danger. There was something sinister about the piles of cumulus he couldn't explain. There was no reason for it, but it was a sort of extra instinct that had grown on him, a curious certainty that there were German fighters about. Then along the edge of the cloud to the east beyond the LVG he saw them clearly, seven small dots like insects across his front, and above them three more.

Wyatt had already started his attack by this time and, as the Pups approached, the LVG broke off its slow backwards and forwards patrol and went into a shallow dive. The Albatroses began to drop down just ahead of it, in a perfect position for an ambush, and lifting the Very pistol from its socket, Ira drew out a red cartridge. The flare soared ahead and fell away on Wyatt's left.

They had already lost precious height, however, and the DIIIs were dropping rapidly down on them, and in a moment the sky was full of aeroplanes whirling in a mad free-for-all. As Ira fired, one of the DIIIs reared up and vanished, then he saw Forde swinging in a frantic ring-a-roses with the same green-tailed machine he'd seen more than once before, and changed direction towards him. As his gun clattered, the Albatros swung unexpectely in front of him, only yards away, it seemed, and, petrified with fear as the two machines slid towards each other, he wrenched furiously at the control column. The German slipped past with a yard or two to spare and as he pushed the stick over to lay the Pup against the air in the opposite bank, he found himself looking into the guns of another machine. Unbelievably, the German missed and soared up above him so close he ducked instinctively, expecting to see his centre section wrenched out by the other's wheels.

As the shadow flicked across his face, he clawed for height only to realise that the sky had emptied abruptly. Looking round, he saw two Pups diving for the lines and half-rolled and dropped into position on their tails. Behind him the sky was criss-crossed with lines of tracer and by a long curving pall of smoke near Autrecourt Wood where someone had gone down.

As he landed and climbed slowly from the cockpit, the rigger cluck-clucked at the bullet holes in his tail.

'Who's missing?' Ira asked.

'Captain Wyatt, sir.'

Sillito appeared with Kelly and Wales, all talking together, their voices just a little too loud and excited, and as Ira jumped down, Forde turned to him at once, making a heavy attempt at humour. They were all jumpy and it seemed to need something to knock the bleak fury from their faces.

'Just name what you want, lad,' he said. 'My land. My castle. The hand of my only daughter. That's the third time you've knocked one off my tail when I thought I was a goner.'

It was suddenly chilly for the first time since the summer and Ira and Forde were toasting bread against the red-hot stove when Kelly appeared. He was a big ginger-haired Irishman with a face that was nothing more than an assortment of lumps; and ears, nose and chin all seemed to be last-minute additions, red-raw from the cold.

'They found Wyatt,' he said flatly. 'The C.O.'s given me the flight. Wales'll be deputy. The new chaps'll be arriving tonight and we've been promised a chance to work 'em up before the offensive starts. I'll try not to get us in a mess.'

When he'd gone, Forde stared at the closed door for a moment. 'I sometimes wonder,' he said slowly, 'what *I*'d do if they made *me* a flight-commander. Probably die of fright. What would *you* do, Sunny Jim?'

Ira began to pull a matchbox to pieces, deep in thought.

'I'd try to change the ratio,' he said firmly. 'Less holes in us and more in them.'

Forde laughed. 'That makes sense. 'Ow would you go about it?'

Ira paused. 'I'd sit upstairs till I saw my opportunity,' he said. 'Then I'd go full tilt.'

'You'd still get 'oles in you.'

Ira shrugged. 'Perhaps not,' he said. 'It always seems stupid to me getting your machine full of holes. We're not here to show how brave we are.'

'Put 'im down for a general. 'E's got the right idea. What *would* you do, then?'

'I wouldn't stop to play ring-a-roses for one thing. I'd go straight through, and before they knew what had happened we'd be half a mile away. Dog-fighting's out of date.'

'Last year there wasn't any,' Forde reminded him. 'Only two aeroplanes like box-kites floating round each other with the observers taking potshots with rifles.'

'It's still out of date,' Ira insisted. 'It became out of date the day we started to fly formations.'

Forde gave him a long sideways glance. 'Sunny Jim,' he said. 'When you get the flight I 'ope I'm right beside you.'

Ira shrugged. 'You'll get the flight before me,' he pointed out.

Forde reached out to the toasting fork he was holding and removed a forgotten piece of charred bread.

'Don't you be so sure, lad,' he said.

That evening, with the damaged ball-race that had troubled his engine replaced, Ira took up his machine to test it. The sky had cleared and seemed full of fire as the sun caught the underside of the cloud formations. Below him a river, a tributary of the Oise, was a winding golden snake where the sun caught the water.

No two days were alike, he thought. Not even any two patrols, or even any two hours. It must have been this constant change, he decided, that had attracted his forbears to the sea. He felt good and realised he was lucky to have survived so long.

He felt sure of his skill and browsed on the strange fact that while he behaved with certainty in the air, he was nervous with girls. Perhaps it would be a good idea to grow a moustache, he decided optimistically. It would make him look older and that would be a help. He could probably also stop eating the toffee his mother sent him and try instead to cultivate a pipe like Avallon.

Reaching seventeen thousand feet, he carefully put the Pup through its paces, diving and rolling and chasing its own shadow in and out of the clouds, then he climbed again until he came out into the clear blue evening light once more. As he circled, reluctant to return to earth, he caught sight of St Gobain Wood below him and realised he had drifted south. Seeking his bearings, he saw the flash of sunlight on varnished wings just to the west of him and below, and saw two aeroplanes manœuvring round each other. The hair on the back of his hands prickling with excitement, he put the nose of the Pup down and approached cautiously. A French-marked Spad was attacking a German DFW, turning in a clumsy fashion that was easily countered by the two-seater. The German crew seemed experienced and the pilot of the Spad was in danger of being shot down in his attempts to get close.

He dived more steeply, then as the Spad banked, he saw an Indian head insignia on the fuselage and the number five, and as he stared, his goggles on his forehead, it suddenly dawned on him that the pilot was Courtney, the American who'd travelled with them to the front on the day of his arrival.

As he banked steeply, close to the Spad, the pilot's head jerked round and he began to point frantically at the DFW. The sun was glinting on the two-seater's wings as it turned to pick up its direction home, and as it settled on a course to the east, Ira swung in front of it so that it had to edge once more towards Courtney. The American made another clumsy dive at it, only to receive a spray of bullets from the observer for his trouble, and the DFW again turned for the German lines. Once more Ira moved to head it off, but yet again Courtney was driven away by the gunner's expert aim. His helmeted head seemed to exude frustration.

Realising it was growing dark and that before long they'd be too late, Ira lost patience and went down on the DFW in a steep dive from astern as it turned away, and pulled up under its tail. Closing to within thirty yards, with the machine as big as a house in his sights, he pressed the trigger. The DFW reared up abruptly, then fell limply over on its side and began a long curving dive towards the darkening earth.

Sitting in the empty sky, Ira watched the stricken machine grow smaller and smaller, looking at first as though it were going to crash in St Gobain Wood. But its steep jerking fall continued to curve beneath him until it finally seemed as though it were going to end up in La Fère. Then, as the arc changed again, it moved further back towards the south, dwindling in size until it was nothing more than a moving speck against the increasing greyness that lay over the earth. It passed St Gobain Wood and was moving now almost as though it were flying straight and level, but he knew from experience it was still falling steeply, and it had passed over the edge of the wood when it suddenly vanished into the shadows just outside Coucy and a small speck of light glowed briefly and died away.

It was dark when Ira entered the Bull and Bush. Though above him the clouds had still been bright, dusk had come on him rapidly as he had fallen to earth and he had had to fly at full throttle to get in before the spreading shadows made it impossible. His fitter and rigger had been waiting for him and as he had approached Huyzes someone had started to let off flares and Very lights to give him direction.

As he pushed into the hut, squinting against the light, Forde jumped up at once.

'Was that you they were firing Very lights for?' he demanded angrily.

'Yes. It was a bit dark.'

'Where the 'ell have you been?'

'Only testing,' Ira said. 'I was a bit late getting back.'

'You're always testing some bloody thing! We thought you'd gone west. It put the wind up us.' Forde's voice was worried and faintly indignant, like a mother's when her child has been out too late.

'Had a bit of a dust-up with a Hun,' Ira said, throwing down his helmet and struggling out of his coat. He was still surprised at the ease with which he'd destroyed the DFW. It had seemed so simple, it was frightening.

Colyer was beaming. 'I say, Ira. How splendid!'

Forde had his great fists in his pockets, staring. 'You've been fighting?'

Ira grinned. 'Yes, Mummy. Helping Courtney. That Yank we met.'

'Did you get 'im?'

'I didn't see him crash but I think I did.'

Forde smiled. 'Well, I'm blessed,' he said. 'You come in 'ere with a shinin' schoolboy face looking like a kid who's been rattin' round the back of the pigsty and tell us you've knocked down a 'Un. All innocent and looking like you don't even shave. An' somewhere east of 'ere a bunch of rotten 'Uns are at this moment sharing out a supper of sausage and sauerkraut which won't now be wanted.'

Ira was standing with his coat in his hands, staring in front of him, still a little startled at what he'd done, and Forde gave him a push so that he fell across his bunk.

'For God's sake,' he said loudly, 'what the 'ell are you looking so bloody worried about? That's what you're 'ere for, isn't it?'

7

The following week another German machine, a lonely lost Albatros he found over St Quentin in the late evening light, fell before Ira's gun.

Forde was waiting for him in the hangar when he returned, and he eyed him with a puzzled frown as he stripped off the old yellow coat and began to take the cowling off the Pup.

'You're a funny feller,' he said.

Ira looked round. 'You're always saying that.'

'Well, it's true. If I'd just shot down a 'Un, I'd be in the mess celebrating. *You* just come back 'ere and start working over that bloody gun again.'

'It keeps jamming.'

'I expect it's wore out. You fire it so much at the ground target it's tired when it gets in the air. If I didn't know you better I'd say you'd got a solid block of wood between your ears. You ought to be out gettin' drunk or chasin' girls. . . .'

Ira said nothing and Forde got into his stride. 'What about that motor bike we bought?' he demanded. 'I thought we bought it for that very purpose. When are we going to 'ave a night out? At Le Ponet, for instance?'

Ira looked up. He was still keeping up his vigil in Le Ponet for the girl he'd seen in the De Dion. With all the ardour of youth, he'd never quite given up hope, though by this time it was beginning to fade a little. He gave Forde a sheepish grin.

'Later,' he said. 'We'll go later.'

The bright summer weather was only a memory now and the days were often full of drizzle, strong winds bending the trees and streaming the leaves on the branches like battle flags against the tattered clouds. There was a damp chill in the huts at night now, and Forde was just beginning to look forward to long days of rain and no casualties when A Flight was involved in an appalling accident right in the middle of the field when they were all watching a football match against the Bristol squadron and could see everything that happened.

Coming down after a patrol, two of its pilots appeared out of the mist just as one of the Bristols, loaded with bombs, was being swung on to the take-off area by its ground crew. They all heard the Bristol pilot open his throttle to move out of the way of the first Pup, only to be hit by the second one a moment later. The bombs went off with a metallic crash that wiped out the Pup and the Bristol and its ground crew, while the blast lifted the first Pup on to its wing-tip and sent it smashing into the ground to crumple up and burst into flames. The roar of the explosion seemed to tear the flesh from their nerves and, as every window in the area fell out, they flung themselves to the ground. Lifting their heads, they saw the burning Pup and a brown cloud of smoke and pulverised earth drifting away in the breeze, and the remains of six or seven men lying among the scattered wreckage of the three machines.

Lunch was a silent affair with the empty chairs, and Warburton, the batman, walking round smothered in scarves and pullovers, wore a face as gloomy as the weather.

'Such a pity about all those young gentlemen,' he said. 'All nice officers, every one of them.'

Forde directed a murderous look at the small of his back and he went on in a mourning voice that was cheerless enough to send shivers up their spines.

'I always wonder when *you* go up,' he said, 'if you're ever going to come back again.'

As Forde reached for a cigarette, Ira was frowning heavily at his boots. After a while he looked up. 'I'm going out on the bike,' he said.

Forde stared at him for a second and seemed to accept that he needed something to rid him of the rage and horror that showed in his face.

'I'm coming with you,' he said firmly.

They reached Le Ponet in record time and the sensation of speed and the effort of wrestling with the motor cycle took Ira's mind off the accident. Forde's reaction as he drew to a stop in the Place de Paris was exactly the same as Colyer's had been. He heaved his vast bulk off the machine and backed away as if it had been red-hot.

'Never in all me puff have I been driven like that before,' he said ponderously. 'I thought I was a goner 'alf a dozen times.'

'Oh, shut up,' Ira said, and Forde stared at him, his expression concerned.

'What's up, Sunny Jim?' he asked. 'Somethin' troubling you?'

'Crashes always give me the pip,' Ira said. 'Especially unnecessary ones like that one this afternoon. It's different when they're shot down.'

Forde's expression was puzzled. 'I'd 'ave thought you were used to that sort of thing,' he said quietly, probing without appearing to.

Ira shrugged. 'Perhaps it's something that's been with me for years,' he said, his mind flying back to a crash at Brooklands before the war. The machine had been a fragile edifice like a boat with wings and, as it lay crumpled on the ground, it had seemed to consist only of canvas, wood and wire, and not of twisted flesh beneath the splintered wreckage.

'When my father broke his neck,' he said slowly, 'I had to go home and tell my mother what had happened. They were so busy digging him out, they forgot I was watching, and I couldn't think of anything else to do but go and give her the news.'

Forde continued to stare at him for a moment, his eyes gentle, then he pulled his cap further over his ears with the air of a man who was prepared to suffer in a good cause.

'Le Ponet's not far enough,' he announced. 'Too many soldiers. Let's try Butte-Jourdain. And this time let 'er rip.'

Set well behind the lines, Butte-Jourdain had retained its air of prosperity. Its houses were red-brick and ugly with slate roofs, but the absence of damage gave it a look of security that was missing from the towns and villages nearer the front. Wrinkled Aisne farmers in leggings and scarves and well-fed businessmen moved about the damp streets, all in black but neat and well brushed, and there were buxom countrywomen with baskets and an occasional trim-legged girl. There were a few French staff officers about, too, in dark blue with scarlet and gold képis, and cookers parked under the trees feeding a battalion of Frenchmen passing through towards the line. A few of the men were washing under a communal pump among the horses and waggons, their bare flesh blue-white in the chilly air.

Forde's eyes flickered over the teeming hubbub of the streets. 'Let's 'ave a go at the outskirts,' he suggested. 'Too many fellers 'ere.'

Ira started the motor cycle again and they moved away from the shuffle of hoofs and feet. On the very edge of the town they passed a large De Dion standing by the roadside and, as they clattered by, Ira caught a glimpse of a chauffeur staring into the open bonnet. He recognised him at once and turned his head immediately to catch a glimpse of the girl sitting in the rear seat. She was wearing the same blue-braided outfit he'd seen her in before, with a voluminous scarf round her throat and a muff and fur cap.

He slammed on the brakes without thinking, just as Forde was leaning forward to yell instructions in his ear, and they halted so violently he rolled off the pillion into the road.

He picked himself up with lumbering slowness, cumbersome with his own size and weight, and began to brush the mud off his uniform. 'I've 'eard of 'alf-wits with more sense than you've got, lad—' he began with stoic patience, then he noticed that Ira was straddling the machine and staring back the way they'd come, his eyes shining.

'Now what's up?'

'There! By the car!'

Ira jerked his head towards the De Dion where the girl had now climbed out and joined the chauffeur.

Forde's eyes shone. 'My word,' he said, beaming, 'you do spot 'em, lad! I didn't know you had it in you!'

He jerked his coat straight and, pulling his cap over his eye, set off at once towards the De Dion.

'Where are you going?' Ira bleated, feeling he was in danger of being cheated by someone with the advantage of vaster experience.

Forde jerked a thumb. 'I'm going to see if I can 'elp,' he said.

Numb with fury, Ira watched him come to a halt by the girl and begin to gesture at her, speaking a mixture of schoolboy French and rural Sussex at the top of his voice, as though the fact that her native tongue was different from his own could be overcome by treating her as if she were deaf.

''Elpez?' he was yelling. '*Aidez-vous?* I mean—er—*vous êtes* in difficulties, *peut-être*?'

Red-faced and indignant, Ira stared at the lovely shining darkness of the girl. Ever since he'd first seen her he had been full of the irrational and indefensible belief that he had only to speak to her to claim her, and now here was Forde shouldering his clumsy way in before him. Making up his mind abruptly to do something about it, he opened the throttle of the motor cycle and whirled it in its own length to roar back down the street. He felt none of Forde's confidence, but he was bursting with rage, and with a tight feeling in his throat he heaved the Moto-Rêve on to its stand and strode forward, to stop before the girl, feeling as if made of wood, his movements ungainly, his speech jerky, his tactics incredibly clumsy.

'*Quelque-chose vous troublez, Mademoiselle?*' he asked stiffly.

The girl rounded on him at once, her face lighting up. '*Vous parlez français?*' she said delightedly.

'*Un peu.*'

The girl indicated the car. '*Mon automobile ne marche pas,*' she said. '*Peut-être vous pouvez . . .?*'

Ira blushed. *'Avec plaisir, Mademoiselle. Je croix que ce n'est pas tres difficile et je suis expert.'*

'Que de bonne chance.' The girl's face broke into a beaming smile and she leaned closer with breathtaking familiarity so that he caught a whiff of perfume, and indicated the chauffeur. *'Il est actuellement cocher,'* she whispered. *'Il est un peu fou avec l'automobile.'*

As Ira opened the bonnet, he was aware of Forde staring at him, his expression a mixture of disgust and fury.

'You've never spoke to *me* in French like that,' he said in a harsh whisper. 'Not once.'

'You can only understand pigs and cows,' Ira said smugly.

Forde glared. 'Where the 'ell did you learn it?'

'Lots of Cornishmen speak French. They pick it up from the Breton fishermen from across the Channel.'

'Well, I'm buggered. 'Ere I am with the first decent young woman I've seen for months and you sail in, your big feet flapping, and snatch 'er from under me nose. Why didn't you tell me?'

'You never asked.'

It turned out that the girl could speak a little English and they were able to converse haltingly while the ecstatic Ira disconnected a fuel lead and lifted it to blow through it.

'Sale,' he remarked sagely, still unable to believe his luck. Within five minutes the De Dion's engine was chattering away again and the girl beamed at him. He felt as though he were floating two feet off the ground.

'You are very kind,' she said slowly in precise English while he was still protesting that he didn't need thanks. 'I would like it if you will drink some wine with us. Perhaps you will follow me to my 'ouse.'

Ira had lost his nerve enough to be able only to stammer and Forde shot him a disgusted look. 'If you don't mind,' he said firmly, 'I'll *ride with you.* My young friend 'ere's only just bought 'is motor bike and he doesn't drive it very well.'

Just outside the town, the car turned though large iron gates at the entrance to a square stone house and stopped on a gravel drive outside the door. As Ira lifted the motor cycle on to its stand, Forde introduced himself.

'Tobee Forde?' The girl smiled as he essayed a clumsy bow in French fashion. 'I am Marguerite de Tassier de Lonville. And this?' She turned and beamed at Ira.

Forde gestured indifferently. 'That's Penaluna.'

'*Comment?* Penaluna?' She frowned. 'What is this name? Please to write it for me. Per'aps it is Breton.'

Blushing, Ira obliged and, as she tried to pronounce it, he noticed that Forde was frowning again. When she disappeared to fetch her mother, Forde turned furiously on him.

'Trust you to 'ave a bloody name that sets the whole 'ouse by the ears,' he growled.

The girl's mother was small and plump and dressed in black, with a pale face and the inevitable purple sacs under her eyes. She swept into the room with a beaming smile and a volume of shouted French.

'My mother says you to stay to tea,' Marguerite said slowly, addressing Ira. 'Will you please to do that?'

Ira was speechless with joy and the older woman bustled off towards the back of the house, clapping her hands. Vermouth was poured in large glasses and they were led into a lounge furnished with an overabundance of cushions, curtains and knick-knacks, prominent among them the photograph of a group of French officers.

'*Mon mari,*' the older woman said. '*Et mes braves fils.*'

They nodded awkwardly and the girl tried to make conversation. '*Vous êtes pilotes?*' she asked, indicating their wings.

'That's right,' Forde said enthusiastically, and was about to launch into a diatribe on their work when she turned to Ira and touched his ribbons.

'And you, I see, are very brave *pilote*. You 'ave our Croix de Guerre. The brave Guynemer 'as that one.'

The meal was difficult. Forde found himself saddled with the older woman who hardly spoke a word of English and they had to struggle along with signs, odd words and vast silences. The girl was absorbed with the blushing Ira, speaking in long gusts of French while he fought to find something to reply other than 'yes' or 'no'. Afterwards, when the chauffeur, who seemed to double in the rôle of butler, had cleared the table, Madame de Tassier handed Forde a large brandy and offered to show him a new form of *solitaire* she had discovered.

'C'est formidable,' she said. *'On peut jouer toute la soirée.'*

Watched by the furious Forde, Ira and the girl talked in limping spasms until it was dusk, then, rather to his surprise, Ira found himself in a chilly music room, trying to decide when to turn the sheets of music as she sang. Since he couldn't sing a note himself, it wasn't easy. Especially with the girl unsettlingly close beside him. He was awed, shy, apologetic and afraid of being considered impudent, and her direct dark gaze and soft definite voice made him feel guilty, feverish and absurd. As she stopped and dropped her hands to her lap, he stared with troubled eyes at the music. The silence became an intolerable embarrassment and the girl looked at him with amused eyes.

'Quel âge avez-vous, Eerah?' she asked.

'Twenty,' Ira said firmly.

As she lifted a hand to take the music from him, their fingers touched and the contact made him jump.

'*I* am twenty-four,' she said, looking up at him. 'I am a little older and, I think, a little more experienced in the ways of the world.' She turned on the stool and studied him, her face in shadow. 'Have you won many victories in the air?'

'One or two,' Ira said. 'Not many.'

She leaned more closely towards him. 'You have been watching me a long time, I think, haven't you?' she said.

The possibility that she'd seen him on his lonely voyages through Le Ponet horrified him and he denied it at once, crimson-faced.

'But I saw you the first time,' she chided. 'And I have seen you many times since. I have a friend I visit in Le Ponet and I can see the square from the window.'

He was almost speechless with shame, but she laughed gaily.

'It doesn't matter,' she said. 'I am very flattered. And having met me, do you intend to come again?'

'Of course,' he said eagerly, glad of the growing dusk that hid his face and fighting to sound not only eager but intelligent. 'I'll bring you some bully beef to help your rations. We get too much of it, anyway. And jam, too.'

'We do not need your bully beef.' She seemed to be laughing, so that he felt as clumsy as a farm boy. 'Though it is a delicate thought. Most soldiers I meet wish only to go to bed with me.'

Ira was faintly shocked. He'd never had a girl talk to him of bed before, and he began to wish that Forde were nearer.

'You are silent,' Marguerite said.

'I can't think of anything to say,' Ira blurted out, and she rose and stood near him in the dusk, a slim figure in a pale blue dress that seemed to glow with her own light, her face half in shadow, looking at him under her eyebrows. He stared at her, tongue-tied but unbelievably happy, wishing desperately he could respond with some bantering remark that would make him sound clever and witty. All the previous girls he'd known had demanded very little mental effort from him and provided absolutely no danger, and he found himself searching his barely formed personality for some aspect of himself he could present to this demanding young woman.

'Why did you help with the motor car?' she asked unexpectedly.

'It seemed a good way to get to know you,' Ira said, managing an insane creaking laugh.

'You *wanted* to know me?'

'That's why I kept looking for you. I thought you were the most beautiful girl I'd ever seen.'

As he ended in a breathless rush, she studied him for a moment silently, then she went on with a grave smile:

'And now you think you are a little in love with me?'

Though his thoughts had already included marriage and a family, Ira denied it, blushing furiously, and she smiled again.

'Oh, yes, you do,' she said. 'But you will meet many more, Eerah. I am just a nice-looking girl, a little older and more experienced than you, whose man has gone to war and is very lonely.'

'Are you engaged or something?' Ira asked. It seemed very important.

She shrugged. 'He disappeared a long time ago,' she said. 'I'm not sure now whether he will want to come back. So I try to find warmth and affection where I can—even among the young men of another nation.'

'How awful for you!'

She gave a low laugh. 'Not at all. We must all experiment a little before we marry.' She looked at him, her brown eyes merry. 'Do you want to kiss me, Eerah?'

He fought to stop the flush that flooded to his neck and cheeks at once, and she laughed.

'I think you are a little afraid of me, eh?'

'Good Lord, no,' Ira said stoutly.

'I do not believe you. I think it is because in England the French have a reputation for being hot-blooded, while Englishmen prefer to stand in their cold houses, chewing their pipes and only feeling at ease when they are accompanied by their dogs. You are younger than you say.'

'I'm twenty.'

She looked at him under her eyebrows. 'Of course,' she agreed gently. 'And you are a great warrior.' She put out her hand to touch the ribbons on his breast. 'You have two medals to prove it, so you should behave like one, Eerah. Once Maman is occupied with *solitaire* she doesn't know when to stop.'

Ira studied her longingly but full of anxiety. He had never before realised that females were anything else but demure and passive and he was just wondering how he was supposed to react to what seemed an invitation when, dimly and thankfully, through the pounding of his heart, he heard Forde's voice in the hall, loud and unnecessarily insistent, saying it was time to go.

Feeling ten feet tall, Ira said goodbye. Forde was silent and thoughtful and Ira caught his eye on him several times, speculative and disapproving.

As he let in the clutch of the Moto-Rêve, he saw Marguerite blowing kisses from the doorway and, in his agitation, he almost hit the gatepost. Forde had said goodbye quickly and without much interest, apparently unaware of Ira's feeling of enchantment.

'What the 'ell were you up to out there in the music room?' he yelled in his ear as they set off down the road.

'We were playing music,' Ira yelled back.

It sounded feeble even to Ira, and Forde snorted. 'That's ripe!' he said. 'You ruined my evening, lad,' he went on in sorrowful tones. 'I didn't go there to play patience with Mum, y'know.'

'No, I suppose not,' Ira said humbly.

'You came in with a face like an early Christian martyr. I 'ope you weren't making suggestions to 'er.'

Ira was on the point of admitting that he'd done nothing beyond answer—largely in monosyllables—a series of embarrassing questions, when he decided that perhaps Forde might admire him more if he made it sound less tame.

'I had to put on a show,' he shouted over his shoulder.

'You looked as though you'd been pole-axed.'

'What do you expect when a chap's been alone with a girl?'

Forde was silent for a while behind him, then his voice came again, faintly puzzled. 'Sunny Jim, you're a proper old Wee Willie Winkie, aren't you? You 'aven't gone and fallen for 'er, 'ave you?'

'Fallen for her?' Ira stared ahead at the road in the darkness, a little bewildered because it was only too true.

'She was only 'aving you on, y'know.'

Though in his heart he hadn't really been able to accept as genuine Marguerite's interest in him, Ira refused to believe him, but Forde went on remorselessly. 'She's probably got some other feller just round the corner, lad. The village chemist or some chap 'ome on leave.'

Ira said nothing and Forde went on, yelling against the wind and the noise of the machine. 'She was 'aving a bit of fun,' he was saying. 'That's all. I mean—look at you. A breathless

Anglo-Saxon infant who don't even know whether 'e's coming or going. I suppose you held her 'and in your sweaty paw and stared sprat-eyed at her, wondering what to say.'

Again, it was too near the truth to be comfortable and for a long time they roared along in the darkness in silence, until Ira's disbelieving mind began to drift into an amorous fantasy in which the brief tenderness in the music room was magnified to something else entirely, and his mind wandered from the road. Before he knew what was happening, Forde's top-heavy bulk had taken control and he was lying in the road with the Moto-Rêve alongside him, its rear wheel spinning, its exhaust clattering within a yard of his ear.

'Are you drunk?' Forde shouted furiously over the racket.

Ira stared back at the curving road. He hadn't even noticed the corner. 'It's not easy driving a bike with a chap as big as you on the back,' he hedged.

Forde climbed slowly to his feet and stopped the engine. In the silence Ira stared at him, a little dazed and stupefied. He was knocking the muddy grass and twigs from his uniform. His anger had subsided now and he seemed puzzled.

'Are you going to see 'er again?' he asked.

'Me?'

'That's what you want, isn't it?'

Ira wasn't at all certain what he wanted. 'I suppose so,' he said doubtfully.

'Next time then,' Forde said, 'I'll give you some idea what to say and 'ow to go about it.'

'It didn't do *you* much good,' Ira observed smugly.

Forde lifted his eyes. 'That was one under the belt,' he growled. 'You've got a nasty streak in you, Sunny Jim, that shows up now and again. But perhaps you're right at that. You're so bloomin' innocent, she probably wants to mother you.'

8

It was still misty the following day and, with no flying, they were sitting over a late breakfast with Colyer still holding forth about the accident. There was only a wide scorched circle now where the explosion had taken place, and a great deal of new earth.

'Cleared up in an hour or two,' Colyer said. 'Sillito got everybody on it.' He looked up at Forde and Ira, suddenly realising that they had not been present.

'You went out,' he accused.

Ira looked blank. Forde was gazing into his egg with a suspicious expression on his face. 'I think it's gone off,' he announced.

'It was my turn for the bike,' Colyer said indignantly.

Forde poked around a little with his spoon. 'Pity,' he said. ' 'Ave to wait till next time now.'

'Where did you go?'

'Just out.'

'Did you find any girls?'

Forde looked up from his egg at last and stared coldly at Ira. 'Yes,' he said shortly. 'Tall. Beautiful. Of fair proportions. Even spoke a bit of English. Sunny Jim 'ogged her for the 'ole evening.'

Colyer's expression changed and he stared admiringly, and Ira found himself saddled with a new and wholly undeserved reputation. 'I say! Did he really?'

'In the music room with 'er,' Forde went on severely. 'While yours truly was fighting to get away from 'er ma.' He looked disgusted. 'You know what?' He looked bitterly indignant. ' 'E even speaks the lingo.'

The day stayed wet and cheerless and Forde wandered away to look at a new calf he'd found in the village. Ira decided to tune his machine because he felt he needed time to set his thoughts in order. Ever since the night before he'd had romantic dreams which had persisted in taking a turn towards the erotic, and it was something he needed badly to think about.

Forde returned, heavy-faced, to announce that the calf had died and to hold forth disgustedly on French farmers, then, with Avallon at the controls, the Moto-Rêve wobbled dangerously off towards Péronne with his enormous bulk overflowing the rear wheel.

In the late afternoon, as Ira finished work, the clouds broke up and he roared across the field for a test flight. The sky was burnished gold and he was caught by the infinity of uncluttered space. Above the clouds where the debris of battle disappeared at once even the war was pure, and he flew along quite content for twenty minutes before turning for the line. The sky was the same blue as Marguerite de Tassier's dress had been the night before and it caused his mind to wander to the things he believed she'd been hinting at. For a moment or two he flew along in a daze, then he came back to the present with a start, realising how dangerous a pastime daydreaming was in the air.

As he sat up straighter, he realised there was a German two-seater over St Quentin working backwards and forwards on its own, quite unharassed, its crew obviously feeling safe. He studied it for a while, surprised he'd not noticed it before and wondering what to do about it. It had a biplane tail and looked fast and different from anything he'd seen before and he debated whether to attack it. Two-seaters were dangerous things to tackle alone and the standard practice was for two Pups to work together.

He recognised the German machine from descriptions as a Hannoverana and somehow, whatever the machine's reputation or the skill of the pilot, he realised it was his if he wanted it. Now that he had adapted to the changed conditions of 1917, he knew he had a special skill, and shooting came as naturally to him as breathing.

Making up his mind, he climbed higher, heading eastwards towards enemy territory. Keeping one eye all the time on the busy Hannoverana, he began after a while to descend in a slow glide, but the German crew saw him long before he was in range and the machine went down in a steep dive for home, fast enough to make it not worth while chasing it. In disgust he turned for home himself, then he realised he had plenty of petrol left and that there was another hour and a half of daylight, and the German had seemed confident and sure of himself. Instead of flying back to Huyzes, he started to climb again towards the east and after twenty minutes he saw the Hannoverana again, moving back into position. This time he lost height in a wide circle to come up below the German's right wing.

The Hannoverana was in position again now, flying towards the west, and Ira crept slowly nearer, still below and out of sight, and as the German turned east, with the observer looking over the other side of the fuselage, he slid below the tail.

At thirty yards he opened fire and immediately saw fragments fly from the fuselage. As he banked away he saw the observer had disappeared and that the Hannoverana was diving towards the east again, its dive growing steeper all the time, and as he sat above it, his eyes sweeping the sky for some avenging flight of Albatroses, he saw it level out and crash just behind the German lines. It flew between two shell-torn trees, came to a stop and up-ended. It had taken him nearly an hour of careful stalking.

Artillery-spotters had already reported the crash when he landed and Wing were trying to find out who was responsible. He filled out his report, then lay on his bunk to write a letter to his mother, suddenly guilty of neglecting her for too long.

He couldn't think what to tell her, so he described his fight with the Hannoverana, then he found the effect of the altitude was making him sleepy and pushed the letter aside to be finished later. He was awakened by a light in his eyes and the sight of Forde staring down at what he'd written.

'So you've been out scraggin' the 'Un again?' Forde said. 'In a Pup, too! You really are a spiteful little feller, aren't you, when you aren't let out in the evening?'

He jerked a hand at the letter. 'You're not sending that 'ome to Mum, are you?'

'Why not?'

Forde shook his head. 'I dessay I shouldn't 'ave read it,' he admitted, 'but it was there for everybody to see. It's no good,' he said sorrowfully, 'Mum won't really want to know about 'er little lad killin' people, y'know.'

Ira looked up at him and then down at the letter.

''Course she wants to know we're winning the war,' Forde went on. 'You can tell her that anywhen you like. But she don't want gory detail. She wants to 'ear that we're going to end on top, of course, but she don't want to know 'ow because, otherwise she'll get to thinkin' that before long Sunny Jim 'imself could die the same sort of messy death.'

He reached out and, tearing the letter across, handed it to Ira. 'Tell 'er about the birds and flowers and what nice friends you 'ave,' he advised. 'You've got to learn what tender 'earts these females 'ave. The girl in the café at Péronne wept tears of blood over Colyer's youth. He was stewed and we 'ad to bring him 'ome on the bike with us.'

'Three of you?'

'We managed. It was all right till 'e started to fight.'

The clouds gathered again during the following day and rain turned the roads to slush, with heavy mist to prevent flying.

As Ira took down his best tunic and began to brush it, Forde watched him carefully over the top of a book.

'You going to see that young woman?' he asked at last.

'Yes.' Ira's face was expressionless, but there was a surge of excitement flowing through his veins.

Forde said nothing, gazing at him as he washed and fought to slick down his thatch of black hair at the mirror.

'Don't kid yourself she's in love with you,' he said after a while. 'Like a lot of young women these days she probably just enjoyed 'aving a man around because all the ones she knows 'ave gone off to the war.'

Ira ignored him and began to set his cap at an exact angle over his eyes. Forde sighed.

'I suppose a lad with as much potential as you shouldn't waste 'is chances,' he went on. 'Just try to keep your 'ead, that's all. As if you were after a 'Un. Cold-blooded . . .'

'I'm not cold-blooded!' Ira swung round indignantly.

'All right, then. Lukewarm.'

Ira stared at him furiously. The thought of the meeting he had planned crucified him under his calm, but he had always believed in facing up to things and he was edgy with nerves.

Forde began sarcastically to sing *At Seventeen He Falls In Love Quite Madly*, then he stopped abruptly and clumsily pushed a bundle of notes into Ira's hand.

'Dessay she'd like some chocolates if you can find some,' he said awkwardly. He sounded tired and disappointed in Ira. 'I suppose this is the 'ole point of war, when you come to think of it, isn't it? Loot and lechery—the 'ole essence of an otherwise messy business.'

He watched as Ira tried to push the Moto-Rêve to a start. There was no sign of life from it and Ira dragged it on to its stand, panting and red-faced, his cap over one ear.

'I expect it was you lot,' he accused furiously. 'Riding three aboard! When one of' em's you it's enough to break a bloody battleship!'

Forde grinned. 'Those are terrible words from a lad from a godly 'ome,' he said.

Ira stared back at him, his face surly, and began to work with oily fingers and a scowl on his face, his hunched shoulders showing his rage. Getting the engine running at last, he began to go through his ablutions once more and was just struggling to get rid of the last of the oil when Colyer and Avallon appeared. Colyer eyed him with interest.

'Going out?' he asked.

'Yes.'

'I'll come with you.'

'Don't talk soppy,' Forde said sharply. ' 'E's off courtin'.'

Colyer glanced at Ira, then back at Forde. 'That girl?'

' 'Oo else? 'E won't want you taggin' on.'

Colyer grinned. 'Suppose some other chap's there?'

'Well, unless he's got three gongs, 'alf a dozen 'Uns and eyes like stars, 'e 'asn't a chance. Sunny Jim's quite presentable in a way, y'know. Nice straight nose. Baby-blue eyes. Pity 'e 'asn't got a uniform that fits.'

Reddening, Ira stared down at his enormous jacket. As he pulled it straight, Forde jerked a hand at it. 'You could always take a few of the things outa your pockets,' he suggested.

Sullenly Ira removed an adjustable spanner, a screwdriver, a pair of pliers, a notebook, a roll of insulating tape, some wire and three none-too-clean handkerchiefs.

'No toffee?' Forde asked.

Ira looked rebellious, then he grinned. 'Stopped eating it,' he said.

'About time. Think you could find 'er a few flowers?'

'Flowers!'

Forde rolled his eyes. 'Why is it that the young Anglo-Saxon always goes into a decline the minute flowers are mentioned?' he said. 'Lad, you're competing against the French, who know not only exactly 'ow many roses to take a young woman but also exactly what colour.'

'On one knee, remember,' Avallon urged gravely.

'Should he bow, do you think?' Colyer asked. 'And kiss her hand, like the Frogs do?'

They ignored Ira's red-faced rage and Colyer picked up his cap and began rubbing at the badge. 'No good muffing your chances,' he said. 'I bet Romeo didn't arrive with dirty buttons.'

'*Or* oil on his codpiece,' Forde added.

'Would have if he'd flown Camels,' Avallon said dryly. 'Probably even a little loose in the bowel from the castor-oil fumes.'

Ira pushed them away and snatched at his cap. Outside, he started the Moto-Rêve and sat astride it for a moment or two, listening to the clatter of the exhaust. The other three stood in the drizzling rain to watch him leave.

'What's she like for manœuvrability, Ira?' Colyer asked.

Blushing furiously, Ira let in the clutch and the motor cycle leapt away with a jerk. Glad to be alone, he drove rapidly down the wet road from Huyzes until he picked up the Route Nationale. All the traffic of war seemed to be moving north again now—lorries, caissons, guns, strings of mules and horses, and from time to time columns of marching men. Cavalry filled the fields, their lances stuck in the ground, the damp pennons at their tips slapping in the breeze.

To his annoyance, the rain became heavier and his breeches were wet and his boots spattered with mud. He was several times on the point of abandoning the whole project, but, arriving in Butte-Jourdain sooner than he expected, he decided to continue and persuaded an old woman at a cottage to sell him a bedraggled bunch of chrysanthemums from the front garden.

As he roared out of the square, his feelings were so churned up inside him in a mixture of trepidation and excitement he narrowly missed a water-cart, its driver huddled on the shafts. Stopping near the Tassier house, he went through in his mind all the things that had been said on his last visit, then, feeling like a schoolboy and desperately conscious of the limpness of his bouquet and the heavy wet-wool smell that came from his voluminous jacket, he climbed slowly from the machine. The ancient chauffeur, a green baize apron over his head to keep off the rain, was just moving round the side of the house and, feeling committed by his recognition, Ira managed a nervous smile.

'*Mademoiselle Marguerite?*' His voice came in a croak and he had to clear his throat and try again. The old man's eyes flickered up to one of the bedroom windows.

'*Et madame la Mère?*'

'*A Rennes, Monsieur. Avec son mari.*'

Ira's heart sank. He wasn't sure he had the courage to face the daughter alone. He licked his lips, jerked his vast jacket straight, more than ever conscious of the sad way it hung off his shoulders and, taking off his cap, headed uncertainly for the house.

He had stopped in the hall, eager, scared and desperately uncertain of himself, when he heard a door slam somewhere and Marguerite appeared at the top of the stairs, trying to pin up her hair. She stopped dead at the sight of him, then she gave him a twisted uncertain smile and vanished again abruptly. Still clutching the limp bunch of flowers, he became aware of a deep male voice from the room above him.

'*Quel petit anglais? Dis-lui de partir!*'

The voice was gruff and casual and Ira turned slowly to become aware of the ancient chauffeur standing in the kitchen doorway, his face expressionless. Beyond him, he saw a blue jacket hanging over a chair, wearing the bars of a major in the French Army. On the table alongside were gloves, a swagger-stick and a flat-topped képi with crimson round the brim.

The old man said nothing, then the door at the top of the stairs opened again and he saw Marguerite appear once more. To his surprise she was not so dark and shining as he'd imagined and for a moment he thought it was the grey light of the day playing on her. He had a feeling there was someone else there, not Marguerite, and that the shadows were making her look like Marguerite. Then he realised it was because she was older than he'd thought and not so beautiful and, his cheeks reddening, he turned abruptly and dived through the door, overwhelmed with humiliation.

As he reached the Moto-Rêve again, he realised he was still carrying the flowers. He stood for a second, staring at them, then he flung them angrily from him and savagely dragged the motor cycle off its stand. He could still hear the words of the Frenchman. *'Quel petit anglais? Dis-lui de partir!'* It had been a voice that was maturely adult and had belonged to a man sure of his stature and his authority, and the words rang through his head like a tolling bell. 'What little Englishman? Tell him to go away!' The contempt lay like a stone under his heart.

The rain had stopped and the weather was showing signs of improving when he reached Huyzes. The hut was empty and he huddled on his bed, shivering in his wet clothes, shaking with humiliation until he could sit still no longer and finally went down to the hangar. Despite the heavy cloud and without seeking permission from anyone, he had his machine started up. Only the fitters and the dogs saw him go and he climbed to fifteen thousand feet over Chauny where he found a DFW as adventurous as himself and promptly shot it down. It was a surgically neat operation and he felt better as he saw it roll into a trench at high speed in a shower of chalky earth.

The hut was still empty when he returned, and when the others appeared later he pretended to be asleep to avoid telling them what had happened. The following morning in clearing weather, before anyone was awake, in his need to expunge the rage from his soul, he found a solitary lost Albatros over Moy and destroyed it before the pilot was even aware he was there. Almost immediately afterwards, he found an old LVG lurking among the clouds and, without bothering to stalk it, drove in close. It was a stupid thing to do, but his heart was still full of anger, and as he fired he saw the heavy black smoke pour from the LVG's tall exhaust stacks as the pilot opened the throttle, and the observer's wind-blown mouth shouting instructions to his partner. For a moment he thought he was going to fly straight into the German's tail.

As the LVG lurched sideways, the observer was still returning his fire and a bullet shrieked over his head from the cowling, making him duck, and he heard a frightful clang in the engine. He wrenched the Pup to the right, his heart in his mouth and convinced he had set himself up as a sitting target, but as he looked round in terror, he realised that the two-seater's wings were beginning to move above the stricken machine and that there was a cloud of steam escaping from the engine.

Swinging in a flat glide to the west, he saw the German pilot, his machine as mortally hit as the Pup, trying to manœuvre into a turn towards the east, then, as he watched, the whole centre section collapsed and the wings fell away. The stripped fuselage spun down like a spent rocket stick, while the wide white wings, with their Maltese crosses, fluttered slowly after it, catching the light as they twisted and turned.

The sky was abruptly empty again, criss-crossed by the trails of tracer, but the Le Rhône was behaving queerly now and even as he peered at the gauges, trying to diagnose the trouble, it stopped dead with a strange moan. The silence hit him like a blow in the face. He could hear only the mournful humming of the wires, the muted rumble of the bombardment below, and the faint rattle of machine-gun fire.

He crossed the German lines only just above stalling speed,

terrified of being caught by some prowling Albatros, and heard a whole barrage of rifle and machine-gun fire directed at him. He was low now over the shell holes and the straggles of rusty barbed wire and, seeing what appeared to be an undamaged area of green, he aimed for it. But even as the machine touched he realised it was marsh and the Pup pitched forward so that his face bounced against the front of the cockpit. For a second, stars whirled in his head then he was hanging upside down while petrol dripped on him from the tank.

Dazed, aware of blood on his face and chin, he unfastened his harness and fell on his head. Immediately hands began dragging him to safety.

'For God's sake,' he mumbled through the blood in his nose and mouth at the soldiers who were helping, 'put those cigarettes out or I'll go up id flabes and so will you. I'b covered with betrol.'

They stood him on unsteady legs and dragged him at a shambling run to the safety of a trench, and, flopping into it, they all sat round and beamed at him as though they'd performed some feat of sleight-of-hand.

'You 'it, sir?' one of them said, indicating the blood that was pouring down his chin.

Ira snuffled. 'Dose bleed,' he said. 'Banged it.'

He was suffering from a raging thirst and his head was aching from the crack in the face. He struggled through his leather coat for the grubby handkerchief he kept to polish his goggles, but he was still shaking from the crash and couldn't find it and had to use his sleeve to wipe his face. He had forgotten to push his goggles up and the crash had embedded small splinters of glass in his cheeks, but he didn't seem to have suffered any other harm except for a little damage to his self-esteem and the knowledge that his plight was entirely his own fault.

'Expect the C.O.'ll want to see you,' one of his rescuers went on, and, still snuffling blood, still dazed and still seeing double, Ira followed him down the trench. At the door of a muddy dug-out, a young captain with an eye-patch and a wound stripe greeted him.

'Saw you get that Jerry,' he said. 'Better come in and have a drink to celebrate.'

He led the way down a flight of slimy steps to a dark hole in the earth smelling of cigarettes and sewage. There was an older officer there, sitting at a wooden table.

'This is the chap that got that Jerry,' the one-eyed captain said. 'Give him a drink. I'll bet he needs one.'

The older man passed Ira a mug and, dizzily, without thinking, Ira tossed the contents back. It was neat whisky and he promptly dissolved into a spasm of coughing.

The one-eyed captain grinned and helped him to take off his leather coat, then he shoved another mugful of whisky at him. Ira shook his head, but the captain was insistent and, because he was too dazed to argue, Ira drank it. He felt as hollow as a drum and he could feel the whisky sloshing round in his empty stomach, fiery and dangerous.

Suddenly he began to laugh.

'What's so funny?' the officer with the eye-patch asked.

Ira didn't reply, but went on laughing at the idea of going berserk across the sky and almost getting himself killed just because he'd discovered that what a girl had said to him hadn't been meant. Intrigued by the idea, he sat down on a box still laughing, wondering where the humour of it had come from so unexpectedly, indifferent to the pain in his face, and trying to stop but unable to and having to let himself go. The two infantrymen were staring at him, puzzled, waiting until the fit of laughter died away.

'You got any other Jerries?' the older officer asked eventually.

'Onc or two,' Ira said.

'Pour the lad another drink, Arthur,' the one-eyed captain said. 'He obviously deserves it.'

By this time, Ira was becoming sleepy from the whisky and the pain in his nose, and they agreed to give him a guide to the dressing station. The line was quiet and the dressing station was empty except for a doctor writing reports.

'I think I've broken my nose,' Ira said in a thick voice from the doorway.

The doctor grinned. '*I* think you have, too,' he said.

He picked the splinters of glass out of Ira's cheeks, then took hold of his nose and yanked it straight. Ira felt the grind of broken bone and gave a yelp of agony. The doctor eyed him gravely as he blinked the tears from his eyes.

'Nothing to worry about,' he said. 'People get noses like that playing football. It'll never be quite so beautiful as it was, but it shouldn't impair your breathing once the blood clears up.'

He slapped a piece of sticking plaster across Ira's face and patted his shoulder. 'Ought to be all right now we've cobbled you up,' he said. He passed over a glass. 'Here, drink this.'

Thinking it was medicine, Ira swallowed it quickly, only to find it was whisky again. He stared at it, horrified.

'Don't you like it?' the doctor asked.

'Never drunk it before today,' Ira admitted.

'Won't do you any harm,' the doctor said. 'Make you sleep. You're going to have a couple of gorgeous black eyes.'

He handed Ira his bloodstained flying coat. 'Might even appeal to the ladies in an odd sort of way,' he said critically, studying his face. 'Though they won't find you quite as attractive as before. Have you got a girl friend?'

Ira concentrated with difficulty. 'No,' he said, frowning as he shrugged himself into the coat. 'I never did have.'

Part Two The Hunter

I

'Three in two days,' Avallon said wonderingly. 'Sillito ought to arrange for us all to be slighted in love. Particularly if it could produce the same spiteful streak it produces in you. We could win the war in no time.'

'I wasn't slighted in love,' Ira protested, gently touching his swollen nose. 'I just changed my mind and came away, that's all.'

'Kelly says Sillito's put you in for another gong,' Colyer interrupted, and Forde, who had been listening silently behind a book, pulled a face.

'Lord preserve us from ribbon-'unting 'eroes,' he muttered.

'I don't hunt ribbons,' Ira said.

'Nobody could get as many as you do without trying. I reckon we ought to have you shot at dawn and stuffed and mounted on a plinth outside the squadron office. So all the new boys could drop on one knee in front of you. Like a shrine.'

'I was frightened to death,' Ira snuffled.

'That makes you at one with the rest of us. That girl at Butte-Jourdain never dreamed of the damage she'd visit on the 'Un. I expect you feel now like you'd like to blow a gasket.'

Ira hurled his leather coat at him. Forde brushed it aside, his eyes kind and devoid of sarcasm, his manner gentle in the way of many big men.

'Put it down to experience, lad,' he advised. 'You've just grown up a bit, that's all. The scar tissue'll toughen and disappear, just leaving the instinct not to play with fire. I know about lads. I've been one meself. They cherish golden memories in the mind and clutch rosy-'ued thoughts of blessed damosels to their bosoms. Eventually, 'owever, like the rest of us, they discover that blessed damosels aren't really so bloody blessed, after all, and safely grow out of it. Providing you survive, you ought to be a boodwar Casanova yet. I should 'ate you to finish your tour out 'ere and go 'ome covered with glory and medal ribbon and not know 'ow to use it to your advantage.'

Sillito was sitting on a stool outside his office, with Monkey Brand at his feet, waiting for B Flight to return. He was wearing flannel trousers, carpet slippers and a jersey and had his face turned to the cold sunshine, his beak of a nose red-tipped, his thin cheeks pale so that he looked drawn and tired. He rose, unravelling his long thin legs awkwardly as Ira appeared round the corner of the hut.

'Hello,' he said, his expression distant. 'Where did you come down?'

Ira told him and a look of disapproval flickered across his narrow features. 'Might have helped if you'd telephoned,' he said coldly. 'We were ringing up everyone we could think of to find out what had happened to you.'

Ira's face fell, shocked that Sillito should complain about his absence before he'd even asked if he'd broken any bones.

'It was a bit difficult,' he said sullenly, aware of a personal feeling of victimisation.

Sillito's expression didn't change, but his face tightened a little. 'How do you feel?' he asked glumly.

'Bit dazed still, sir.'

'Nose or whisky?'

'Both, sir,' Ira admitted, surprised that Sillito knew about his condition as everyone had taken a lot of trouble to keep him out of sight. 'Chiefly whisky. I've never drunk the stuff before.'

Sillito's gloom vanished abruptly and he gave a laugh that remained oddly mirthless. 'I heard you arrived smelling like a distillery,' he said. 'It happens to us all the first time we're friendless and far from home.' He went into the office and pushed a chair forward.

'I see you did it again,' he went on, sitting down.

'Did what again, sir?'

Sillito stared at Ira. 'Another Hun. Three in two days, in fact. You're piling up quite a score, aren't you?'

'Flukes mostly, sir.'

'Nobody gets *that* many flukes. I gather your machine's going to take some putting right, so you'd better have the new one that flew in from Candas. You ought to be all right with that. With a bit of luck you ought to add to your score. We could do with a few more Huns. I've just heard they've killed Guynemer. Up in the north in Belgium.'

Ira said nothing. Sillito always seemed to take it as a personal loss when anyone was killed, whether they belonged to the squadron or not. He sat for a moment in silence, almost as though he were holding a personal requiem for the Frenchman, then he looked up and went on:

'I hear we're the next outfit to be equipped with Camels,' he went on. 'That ought to make a difference to you. They've got two guns and bigger engines.'

It was several days before Ira's nose was better enough for him to breathe easily, but he utilised the time going over every inch of the new Pup. It had a better engine than the one he'd crashed, and he went up over the aerodrome and did joyous loops and spins for half an hour before heading north away from the sun.

Opening the throttle, he began to climb. Climbing an aeroplane gave a man moments when he picked up in spirits as he passed through an invisible barrier to emerge into a separate environment above the clouds. The transformation from dark autumn to blazing sunshine was always uplifting and it was always hard to believe that the dazzling sea of snow below could be the ragged covering that hung above the earth. He always enjoyed altitude and it was a golden morning with white castles and towers rising to tremendous heights so that he could play hide and seek with his own shadow among them, wheeling round misty ephemeral turrets that changed shape even as he charged at them; and diving like a frightened gull along a cliff face in front of the brilliant whiteness of the cloud walls, a minute black speck against the tremendous depths of the sky.

He remained at about twelve thousand where breathing was easy, enjoying the freedom of flight, watching the fabric ripple on the spars of his wings and enjoying the clarity of the upper air and the faint warm smell of his engine, then, leaping giant-like round a cliff of cloud, he almost flew into the tail of a Rumpler that was using the clouds to make its way over the British lines. The observer, who was wearing a yellow coat like his own, was pointing downwards and the pilot was staring over the side with him. They obviously hadn't seen him and obviously didn't expect to see him, and he pressed the trigger automatically, catching the whiff of cordite as the gun rattled.

The observer disappeared from sight into his cockpit, and the Rumpler's wings folded up with a bang he could hear even in the Pup, and the fuselage dropped like a stone, spinning a little as it did so because of the flapping wings, fragments of wood and canvas breaking off and floating away as it went down, and a shower of black objects that might have been plates for the camera falling out of the cockpit.

Ira watched until it vanished into the cloud, then the sky was empty again except for a few small fragments of wing that were still drifting downwards below him, and he sat in the cockpit of the Pup, staring round and above him, feeling certain there must be a trick somewhere and that at any moment a flight of Albatroses would drop out of the sun on to him.

But nothing happened and he began to marvel at the suddenness and the swiftness of it. A moment before there had been a machine, sitting just above him, the sun glowing through the wings so that he could see the ribs and spars and the Maltese crosses on the upper surfaces silhouetted through the fabric, a swift beautiful man-made bird, with yellow-varnished struts and a fuselage of brown, green and purple, containing two men like himself, perhaps as young as himself, probably not keeping their attention on their job because they were enjoying some private joke, or because one of them was worried about his wife and children in Germany. Then, almost before they had realised it, the whole structure of their machine had fallen in on them, and they were fighting for life, one of them probably still conscious on the whole of the long dreadful dive for earth and knowing all the time that there was no hope for him.

Already they were probably pulped carrion on the soured earth of the battlefield below, perhaps charring in a smoking wreck somewhere among the barbed wire and shell holes. Remembering how a few days before it might well have been himself made Ira feel very frail and vulnerable, and he shuddered. The elated feeling had vanished and he turned for Huyzes in a subdued mood.

He decided to leave his report until after lunch and, in the end, he forgot to put one in at all, and Sillito came into the mess in the evening asking if anyone had destroyed a Rumpler over Fluquières as Wing had reported one crashed and couldn't find whom it belonged to.

Ira admitted it was his and, afterwards in the hut, Forde gave him a curious look.

'You shifty little 'orror,' he accused. 'You knock down more 'Uns when you're not on the job than most people do when they are. Rumplers, too! And in a Pup! Anybody who knocks down *anything* in a Pup these days deserves a medal.'

Ira gestured. 'He wasn't expecting to meet anyone,' he said. 'I felt a bit as though I'd cheated.'

Forde gazed at him, bewildered. 'Some'ow, y'know,' he said, 'I don't think you've got the right spirit at all about this old war. Despite all those base wallahs trying like billy-o to put the offensive spirit into us.'

'Don't you get the wind up, Ira?' Colyer asked. 'The minute I see a German the one thing that goes through my mind is that he might kill me.'

Ira had been on the point of shaking his head, then he realised that the prickling of the hair on his hands and the hollow feeling in his stomach as he approached battle was nothing else.

'Of course I do,' he said.

Forde was still staring at him, still puzzled. 'You never give me the impression that you 'ave any feelings at all,' he said.

'It's men we're shooting at,' Ira protested. 'Not partridges.'

Forde frowned. 'You give me the impression, in fact,' he went on severely, 'that the 'Uns are just flopping about the sky waiting to be shot down. But you obviously don't think that way. You're a funny feller.'

'You're always saying that.'

'Well, you are. You do a 'ell of a lot of damage, but you don't seem to take much pride in it.'

'I'm not going to make a profession of it. Killing people's not what flying's all about.'

'It is at the moment,' Avallon pointed out.

Ira gestured, feeling out of his depth. 'When it's finished,' he argued, 'everybody'll just forget about all these aeroplanes we've destroyed, and we'll all just be people again, going about our business. Colyer'll go back to his father's business, you'll go back to being a lord or whatever it is that lords do, and Toby'll go back to selling corn or milking cows. I'll go back to . . .' He paused, wondering what he would go back to. The only thing he was certain about was what he wouldn't go back to.

He blinked. The future suddenly seemed to stretch away blank and bare as a wilderness. When he had first started his apprenticeship before the war he had often felt that the way to security was a hard one to tread, and he had rushed into uniform feeling that at least it would be a change from what had looked like being a very dull life. Now, thinking about it again, he realised that the war had only put off the bleakness for the time being and eventually he would have to face up to it again, and he felt depressed with the weight of his future. It contained nothing, not even the certainty of surviving, and he found his shoulders drooping with the responsibility of it all.

He looked up and saw Forde staring at him.

'Well, go on, lad,' Forde urged. 'What *will* you go back to?'

'I don't know,' Ira admitted slowly. For the first time since 1914 he found himself groping into the darkness that the war stretched across the future, wishing with all his heart that he had had the luck to establish himself before it had come so that he would know where to aim when it ended. Joy of life and the acceptance of its possible end had been the wealth of his days for too long, and it left a hollow aching void that was as real as pain.

'You'll 'ave to think about it eventually,' Forde persisted. 'The war won't go on for ever. The Brass-'Ats might make a mistake and leave a few of us alive. What'll you do if you're one?'

Ira grinned, trying to make the best of his doubt. 'I could always take a pub,' he said. Then his grin died and he went on, puzzled: 'Only no one would let me have one at my age. In any case, a log book full of crashed Huns won't help much, will it?'

Forde looked at him pityingly. 'You're such an innocent little feller, Sunny Jim,' he said. 'I've 'eard that people with the sort of fame that war brings sometimes make a lot o' capital out of it afterwards.'

'They do?'

'Suppose they gave you the V.C.?'

'Don't be barmy. They don't give those things away to chaps like us.'

'They gave one to Ball,' Colyer said.

'He had to get himself killed first.'

'All right,' Forde said. 'Suppose it was just the D.S.O. then, like George Stoke? Even a D.S.O. looks good on business notepaper. People like to 'ave decorations and titles among their lists of directors. With the M.M. and the Pomme de Terre with cabbage leaf you've already got, it should look pretty good. I reckon someone'd be *pleased* to 'ave you grace his board.'

'I don't know the first thing about business.'

'You're 'ardly old enough,' Forde agreed. 'But you'd soon get the itch.' He lit a cigarette and patted Ira's shoulder. 'From now on,' he continued gaily, 'I'm going to work for the betterment of Ira Penaluna. I'm going to see that you become a 'ero.'

Ira grinned. 'I'm not sure I want to be one,' he said.

'Couldn't we form a limited company?' Avallon suggested gravely.

'Good idea,' Forde said. 'See that 'e wins D.S.O.s, M.C.s and all the rest of the nonsense that's out of reach of us ordinary mortals. Drop 'ints to Sillito. Then, after the war, we push 'im into some 'ot-stuff firm, and sit back and live off 'im.'

He gazed sombrely at Ira. 'With our encouragement,' he ended, 'you could even put the wind up the 'Uns and bring the war to an end. And that ought to benefit us all. Even the 'Uns, because they don't enjoy getting killed just to please their politicians and generals, any more than we do.'

2

The lull after the battles in the north seemed to be ending, and the war appeared to be on the move south, with a marked increase in the number of men and guns round Huyzes, and the number of lorries that moved eastwards along the road towards Cambrai. Forde began to grow nervous.

'I expect some rotten staff wallah who wants a new medal to go with his best suit's beginning to think of earning it,' he said.

The Bristol squadron across the field disappeared so that they had the place to themselves again, and Colyer was full of theories about its departure.

'North,' he said. 'They've moved north for the new offensive.'

'I suppose you got that direct from the general?' Forde said sarcastically.

Colyer looked surprised. 'Everybody knows that's where they've gone. That's where the offensive's going to come.'

'And they sent for you special and told you all about it? Lad, I don't care what's 'appening up there, it seems to me that there's a bit of dirty work at the crossroads 'anging over our 'eads down *here*, too.'

As it happened, they were both right and Colyer came hurrying to the Bull and Bush that evening with instructions that a squadron-sized patrol was ordered for the following morning. Sillito, who rarely flew, had decided to lead it himself.

'What's the world coming to?' Forde said. 'If *I*'d been out as long as 'e 'as, you wouldn't catch me going up.' He seemed tremendously impressed by the idea of everybody going up at once. '"Deep into German territory."' He quoted orders in awed tones. '"Looking for trouble." In Pups, too, for God's sake!'

The sweep was not a success. Not a single German came near them, though there were a few DIIIs in the distance flying across their front, which vanished at once when they saw the number of machines ranged against them. Even the pilots of the British SEs they saw seemed startled, because Pups had long since become obsolescent and it was unusual to see so many of them at any one time.

'Perhaps they thought we were tryin' to write off a few,' Forde suggested. 'After all, they're about as dangerous as flying perambulators, these days.'

They had done no damage but they had also suffered none, and were just deciding that big formations were at least fairly safe when they were informed by Sillito that the offensive they'd been expecting for so long was likely to break at any time and that they were forbidden to go beyond the sound of the klaxon that summoned them for emergencies.

'Pity,' Forde observed. 'I've 'eard that pig's in pup again.'

Atwater's ballads came into their own at last, and Forde performed his upside-down act with the piano for the new arrivals who'd never seen it, while Avallon not only proved to be an expert on Chopin but also knew a method of heavy gambling at chess he'd picked up in the Guards, so that everyone started complaining there weren't enough sets. Rumours that they were to refit with Camels started, but nothing came of them and the weather deteriorated into the blue mistiness of autumn. Finally a week later, orders came that they were to move north to the Ypres front.

'Sillito said Estrée Blanche,' Colyer announced. 'Or a new field called Huclier.'

'Sounds like the name of a disease,' Forde commented. 'Like mange or thrush.'

Ira was in low spirits. He hated moves and didn't look forward to uprooting himself. They had dug themselves in well at Huyzes and the huts were filled now not only with comfort but with their memories. Even their private ghosts haunted the cemetery in the village and the idea of taking over a new field with huts of unknown comfort and unknown ghosts chilled him a little. He had grown used to the field, too, and could fly in with his eyes shut now, and he noticed that Colyer, too, had begun to worry about the new and unexpected obstacles he would have to master in the north.

For some time nothing happened and Ira began to hope that the order was nothing but a rumour, but then he noticed that Sillito and Stoke and the clerks were busy packing up files and burning documents and superstitiously he began to wish they'd stop. Huyzes was safe—not only for him but also for Forde and Colyer and Avallon—and he was suddenly terrified of something happening. The idea of flying from another field seemed fraught with peril. It was a feeling he couldn't explain, but it was as though he were aware of vast changes coming that endangered them all and he wished—as though it would make a difference—that he could stop this destruction of old papers. But the first of the lorries disappeared abruptly and suddenly there were no comfortable chairs in the mess to sit on because all the best ones had gone ahead to set up a new mess for when they arrived.

He spent a miserable day with all his kit packed and nothing to do. But mail had arrived and there was a letter for him from the daughter of one of his mother's friends, who had once momentarily touched his heart. She wrote chiefly out of kindness and it was a letter as devoid of affection as it was full of news, but it made him feel lonely and deprived and, when everyone else began to take advantage of the empty evening to write to girl friends and wives, he sentimentally began to read into it all sorts of things it didn't contain. Caught by the nostalgia of being away from home and the always present possibility of being killed, he managed a heavy epistle in reply, but when he read it through again he found himself blushing at what he'd written and tore it up quickly and sat frowning with bewilderment at the gap in his life.

The following morning, still waiting orders to move, the squadron did two patrols. The first one was uneventful, but Jacobs, an aggressive South African Jew in A Flight, had to crash-land on the way back when his engine cut. C Flight took the next patrol and Wales shot down an Albatros while Ira shared another with Forde. The evening patrol was flown by B and, although Colyer came back with his machine full of holes, they had lost no one. The next morning, still waiting to move, C Flight flew another patrol which came to nothing because of mist and low cloud, though it cleared later in the morning for A Flight. Since he had no machine, Jacobs flew Ira's.

They had just left when the commanding officer of a new squadron arrived with his clerk and his mess officer to take over their huts, and Sillito was still arguing with him, grimly determined to hang on to squadron property against the intruders, when a delayed telephone message brought the orders for the move.

Ira travelled to the new field on the Moto-Rêve with Colyer on the pillion, and they rode behind the squadron tender containing Stoke, one of the clerks and Sillito's dog. At Villeselpe they ran into French troops moving north, and when they stopped at Ercheu for lunch they found themselves surrounded by Americans in French uniform. Ira was not surprised to find Courtney among them, his rusty hair on end, his hawk nose aggressive in his smiling face.

He brought glasses and they toasted each other's countries and each other's fighting services until they all began to grow noisy.

'Now that your people are arriving in France,' Ira asked, 'won't you want to transfer to your own air force?'

'No, sirree,' Courtney said. 'They tell me our outfit's full of stiff-necked regulars who don't know the first thing about fighting. I met one in Montdidier recently and he gave me the old horse-feathers about smartness and duty.'

They all laughed and Courtney went on. 'All that goddam talk they put out back home about supplying thousands of war-planes. Hell, we're still flying French machines! We might as well stay where we're comfortable.'

As they moved northwards again, the countryside took on a delapidated air, as though it had grown old in war, and Arras had the look of a strong man dying of a wasting disease. The main street was narrow with tall houses, but there appeared to be no inhabitants anywhere except for soldiers, and everything was broken with unglazed windows, shattered rafters, torn wall paper and a debris of bricks and furniture. Further north it grew even worse with the terrible humility of suffering. They were in an area now that had been devastated so often it had become a waste land, and Ira was glad when they turned west away from the lines towards Huclier.

The village was red-brick and single-storeyed, and after the wooded slopes of Huyzes the Belgian countryside looked depressingly shabby. The field to which they were directed was a large uneven meadow with a few poplars at one end.

Colyer eyed them nervously. 'Why do they always pick 'em with trees in the way?' he demanded bitterly.

There was a farmhouse which they were to use as a mess, with pigs and cows to draw Forde like a magnet. French peasants were still collecting from the landing area rotting stooks of corn that looked as though they'd been left out all summer, and women in black and old men in blue smocks eyed them hostilely. There was another squadron refitting with Bristols at the other side of the field, still living in tents despite the cool nights, and when they went across to their mess to get to know the lie of the land they were informed that Werner Voss, second only in skill to Richthofen, had been killed.

'56 Squadron got him,' they were told. 'McCudden's lot.'

'Well, I'm sorry for him,' Colyer said, 'but it makes one less valley of death to ride into.'

The place seemed friendless without the dogs they'd left behind at Huyzes, but the ground crew had already erected the Bessoneaux and Stoke had managed to set up his office in one of the outbuildings. The squadron flew in during the evening, minus Jacobs, who, it seemed, had had a bullet in his engine and had crashed again.

Ira was furious because his machine had carried a lot of extra gadgets and he had always tuned it himself, but Forde told him it didn't matter as they were finally going over to Camels.

'Two guns and a hundred-and-thirty-horse Clerget,' Avallon said. 'Turn like bats and climb like larks.'

'And kill everybody who tries to fly 'em,' Colyer added gloomily. 'They've got a nasty trick of taking off sideways, I'm told, and when you try to straighten 'em out they do a sideways dive into the ground. No flowers by request.'

For once the rumour proved true and Sillito ordered Ira to go to Candas the following morning to pick up the first of the new machines.

'Find out everything there is to know about it,' he said. 'And stay until you can handle it.'

The instructor at Candas was quite frank. 'It's no good kidding you they're easy,' he said. 'They're not meant to be. Somebody back home has suddenly realised that if aeroplanes are easy to fly they're also easy to hit. So they've built us one that isn't. You've got to keep your wits about you all the time or she'll go out of control.'

The new machine was a snub-nosed, hump-backed, wicked-looking aeroplane, with none of the sweet lines of the Pup. It seemed to be all engine, and, with the dihedral only on the lower wings, had a curious uneven look about it.

'It's easy to kill yourself.' The instructor, a sardonic man sparing with words, confirmed Colyer's fears. 'So you've got to be firm with them or you'll go into a spin at the first opportunity. They're tail-heavy as hell and so light on the controls the slightest movement of the stick will throw 'em all over the sky.'

'That's quite a list of vices,' Ira observed.

The instructor looked at his ribbons and shrugged. 'It's the beginners who suffer,' he said. 'Because they're difficult to get off the ground and put down again, and there's bloody little chance if you do crash 'em.'

He leaned across the fuselage, his hand stroking the varnished fabric. 'You'll not find it much different from a Pup,' he said. 'Just a hell of a lot more powerful.'

There was much more space in the Camel's cockpit, and it had a hard business-like look about it. The instructor leaned over Ira's shoulder.

'Just remember,' he advised. 'Go easy. She's a bastard taking off. You'll find she'll swing like hell.'

'Which way?'

The instructor grinned. 'You'll soon find out. Just be ready to give her opposite rudder to correct it. But when she's up there'—he jerked a hand upwards—'she'll do all you ask: Go round vertical and snap out of it just as quick, if you want. Try turning to the left first and keep her well throttled back. You know what to do if she falls out into a spin.'

Ira waited as the propeller was swung and listened to the crackling hiss as the engine warmed up, then he taxied away and moved about the field, turning right and left to check the rudder. There was another Camel marked with a large white K about a hundred yards away, also moving cautiously about.

He sat for a moment, setting his thoughts in order, then as he opened the throttle, the engine howled into life and the Camel roared across the ground at full speed with the tail well up, the engine spraying castor oil back over him in a fine mist. Somewhere ahead there was another Camel climbing in a curious crab-like movement and he supposed it was the Camel marked K which had taken off just ahead of him.

His hand moved to the fine adjustment, then he pulled the stick back to hurtle into the air with an exciting rush such as he'd never experienced before in any other aeroplane, soaring over the hangars like a lift. He seemed to be up to three thousand feet in no time and he noticed that if he relaxed the pressure on the stick the tail dropped at once and the machine seemed to shoot upwards again almost vertically.

It was a bright day with a few puff balls of autumn cloud about, and he noticed with surprise as he looked down that the green of summer foliage had changed almost overnight to the brown of autumn.

Just ahead, he saw the Camel marked K levelling off and trying a few hesitant turns.

He tried a turn himself, carefully closing the throttle a little because the speed seemed tremendous, and immediately he found the controls becoming sloppy. He corrected quickly, lifted the nose to the horizon and tried again, and began to make turns with increasing confidence.

Straight flight was harder than he'd expected and he noticed that the wind was on his cheek as he crabbed through the sky. After half an hour he cut the engine and glided down, misjudging the speed a little so that he bumped badly as he touched. The instructor came across to him, grinning, as he burped the engine on the thumb-button to bring the machine into line, and a mechanic moved forward to wipe off the film of oil before the dust settled on it.

'How do you like it?' The instructor leaned over while he sat in the cockpit, memorising the fittings and listening to the sizzle and click of the cooling engine as it dripped spots of clear yellow oil to the grass. 'I think she's the best we've had so far.'

Another pilot was sitting in the K Camel now and, as Ira climbed from the cockpit, he opened the throttle and they saw him roaring past, crabwise across the ground, the engine spluttering. The instructor winced visibly as it scraped past the hangars, but it was climbing now, the engine picking up, still moving sideways but safely off the ground.

The instructor turned to Ira again. 'With Camels,' he said, 'you end up either dead or another Ball.'

He squinted upwards at the K Camel which was now a small cross in the sky over the aerodrome, talking to Ira over his shoulder all the time. 'Unfortunately,' he was saying, 'you can't catch anything, so you just have to use surprise. That's why all the long-range stuff's left to the SEs and the Bristols and why the artistic boys like this chap McCudden won't have a Camel. But if you're cunning you can do a hell of a lot with 'em. Even save your life, because the Hun never knows which way you're going.'

He broke off, lifting a hand to shield his eyes from the sun as he stared at K. 'That stupid ass's going to break something if he's not careful,' he commented.

K's nose had dropped and it has flicked into a spin, and the instructor began to walk hurriedly on to the field.

'That's a bloody silly thing to do at that height,' he snapped.

K was at two thousand feet now and still spinning, and for half a minute Ira watched it drop lower and lower, then it hit the ground with a thump not fifty yards away to vanish in a cloud of dust, flying pieces of aeroplane and clods of turf. A wheel bounced lazily towards him and what appeared to be the cowling whirred up into the air.

After the scream of the engine, the sudden silence seemed enormous. Ira's instructor had stopped dead.

'Full engine,' he said in a flat voice. 'Must have watched all the way down till the light went out. That's how *not* to fly a Camel.'

Back at Huclier, everyone crowded round the new machine, listening as Ira talked, and after a while the American, English, took it up. He landed looking white and startled. Atwater followed, returning to earth with a colossal bounce after wildly misjudging his speed. Forde came down looking even more unhappy than English but the Camel survived without anything being damaged.

A second Camel arrived the following day and for the next week, the squadron re-equipped until everyone had a shining new machine. Some of the pilots recently out from home were a little nervous of them at first and their early attempts to fly in formation were laughable, but no damage was done and English actually managed to surprise one of the new German Pfalzes while leading A Flight and shot it down. Then the inevitable happened and one of the newcomers crabbed into the trees at the end of the field when taking off and everyone began to eye the Camels more warily, Colyer making a point of landing well up the field and pancaking in his efforts to keep plenty of space between his undercarriage and the trees.

'Reminds me of a chap I saw at Colney,' Forde said, watching him thoughtfully. 'Landed a 'undred feet up in a BE. Shoved 'is wheels through 'is undercarriage and broke off all four blades of 'is propeller. Didn't know anything was wrong till he jumped out and then he almost broke 'is back. The ground was only two feet below.'

Much to Forde's delight, they had arrived in the north just as the great offensives in Flanders seemed to be dying down.

'Suits me fine,' he said. 'It's a belief o' mine that the wisest warriors are those who arrive too late to be involved in the bloodshed but not too late to miss the glory.'

A tremendous amount of noise still went on, however, and a great many lives were still being lost, and the area over which they flew was a featureless landscape pockmarked with shell holes that crowded together so closely they ran into each other. They were all filled with water and all the litter and debris of the recent battles lay about them—smashed guns and aeroplanes, broken wire entanglements and shattered vehicles. In Ypres, recognisable by its star-shaped citadel, there didn't seem to be a wall standing that was running north and south, and everywhere around was as flat as a sheet with no houses, no trees, nothing. Filthy water from the rains that came down in what was normally a wet countryside had spread over the lost land with the contents of all the ditches and dykes which had been broken down by a barrage that had created an obstacle for its own troops. Tanks, carts, guns, horses and men had sunk into the green slime and even flying over it was a depressing business so that they all began to wish they'd never been moved.

With the new Camels and the SEs and Bristols which were now appearing in numbers, however, the Germans seemed to have lost the superiority they'd won in the spring, and they managed to avoid casualties, but, as though to put the seal on the danger of Camel flying, Howard, the leader of A Flight, killed himself as he returned from patrol, doing a shoot-up of the field which laid everyone flat on their faces. As he pulled his machine up, his wings folded abruptly and the Camel dived into a barn at the far side of the aerodrome with a whack that could be heard all over the field.

'Bullets through the main spars and centre section struts,' Sillito announced in the mess as the new arrivals brushed up their buttons and boots and departed for the cemetery. 'Pity. We could have done with him. Orders have come through to fit bomb racks and practise low-flying.'

Forde stared bitterly after his long lonely figure as he departed.

'Ground-strafing,' he said uneasily. 'Dog-fightin' with infantry. The bastards oughta know that a 'Un on his feet can turn better than I can in an aeroplane.'

3

During the night rain rattled on the roof and Ira turned over in his blankets convinced there would be no flying the next day. But the following morning, while it was still dark, they were awakened by the roar of the klaxon and he sat up in bed, wide-eyed, as though coming out of a nightmare.

'First time I've ever heard it sounded in anger,' he said, startled.

The hut was already a chaos of scrambling men, all searching for equipment and clothes and getting in each other's way, with Forde hopping about on one leg to drag on a sock and cannoning off the other three, so that it was like trying to get dressed with a drunken hippopotamus in the room.

Colyer was on his knees, reaching under his bed for his boots. 'Must be something big,' he said excitedly, and Forde stopped his lumbering dance to turn on him, heavily sarcastic.

'Curb your bloody enthusiasm, lad, for 'eaven's sake,' he said. 'Normal people can only think what a nuisance it is 'aving to wage war at all, let alone at this time of the morning. You don't 'ave to get shining eyes and a beating 'eart about it.'

He put his head out of the door and withdrew it with a grin, his hair wet. 'Good for flowers and flyers,' he said. 'Ceiling at nought feet, by the look of it. Rain'll stop play, you see.'

Sillito was waiting in the mess for them and by this time the light had increased until they could make out heavy clouds hanging low in the sky. Ira was hopeful that there'd been a false alarm, because it looked far too gloomy for flying, but there appeared to be no sign of a cancellation. He ate breakfast in an apprehensive silence, because he knew that troops filled every village in the forward zone and there were horse-lines in every field, and that they'd been flying up and down the line every evening for some time past making as much noise as possible to drown the tanks' engines as they trudged their slug trail across the countryside to new positions in woods near the front.

Forde was in a sorrowful mood as they headed towards the hangars. 'What a waste of all that lovely rain,' he complained.

C Flight was the last to leave, and, as they took off, two machines from A Flight were already limping back with spluttering engines. They climbed through mist and cloud behind Kelly to fifteen thousand feet and turned over Hollebeke to head north. There seemed to be a lot of two-seaters out artillery-spotting but surprisingly few Germans.

One man turned back with a faulty engine, then, in the distance, they saw what appeared to be a swarm of bees over a jampot which they recognised as a dog-fight and Kelly led them down towards it. By the time they arrived, however, it had broken up and all the machines had dispersed, leaving a single column of smoke staining the sky to show where someone had gone down in flames.

Kelly climbed again until they were over Pilkem, where they saw a group of Pfalzes in the distance and passed a flight of SEs heading east looking for trouble. Over Hooge they found an LVG, but it managed to dodge into the murk and they flew round like terriers at a rat hole as they waited for it to reappear. It had long since vanished homewards, however, and they climbed again over Wieltje where Kelly led them down on to a flight of silver-painted Pfalzes and triplanes.

The German flight broke up at once and Ira saw Kelly on the tail of the German leader. He took up a position himself behind one of the triplanes and it banked steeply as he fired, gradually turned over on to its back and dropped into a spin.

Back at Huclier, A Flight was still making out reports. They had lost a man, but he'd telephoned from an artillery post to say he was safe, though he'd wrecked his machine running into a trench. B Flight had returned without loss.

Another squadron patrol followed in the afternoon then, at dinner that night, unexpected orders came through that they were to move back to Huyzes the following day because of some new battle that was said to be brewing up further south. There were wild cheers, partly because they were going back to familiar and unspoiled territory after the soured land of Flanders and partly because there was a chance that with a bit of luck they might miss *both* battles.

Forde was delighted. 'I reckon I must be the despair of the V.C. department of the *Daily Mail*,' he grinned. 'There they are, rushing round tryin' to fit me up with a battle, and 'ere I am always somewhere else.'

He was so overjoyed, he played the piano upside-down for the benefit of the men from the Bristol squadron across the field and as a sing-song started, Atwater was called with ironic cheers to sing one of his ballads. The breathy tenor that had once graced Methodist church halls had become a joke that only Atwater failed to appreciate, and his upturned eyes and clenched hands were now a standard act in any binge in the mess.

By the following evening they were back on the original field at Huyzes, the cheers dwindling to bitterness as they discovered that a Canadian squadron of SEs newly formed in England and just arrived in France had taken up residence in their old huts and that they themselves were taking over the dilapidated dirty huts at the far side of the field that had recently been evacuated by the French pioneers.

'I thought everything else was pin-pricks,' Forde said heavily. 'This is a pike-thrust through the 'eart.'

To Colyer's relief, the Canadians, with true colonial arrogance, had topped the trees at the far end of the field and asked permission afterwards, but only the rapturous welcome of the dogs made their return really worth while.

They had lost a large amount of their mess furniture in the move and the huts alongside the sunken road were still dirty despite delousing by squads of Chinese labourers who had moved into tents near the village and made a great deal of noise every night with their high-pitched singing.

'Like a lot of cats fighting,' Forde said.

His only pleasure was that he had arrived back in time to see the pig at the farm litter, and he took to vanishing for long periods to lean on the gate of its stye with a look of calm country joy in his eyes.

It soon became obvious to Ira that they hadn't dodged anything by the move. The offensive in the south was on its way, and both German and Allied bombers passed overhead during the night, seeking out each other's railheads and ammunition dumps and making sleep impossible as the hut shook to the drone of their engines or the thump of their bombs.

Then the SE squadron across the field unexpectedly received orders to move and as they hurried to reclaim their old quarters, Ira, Forde, Colyer and Avallon swept back into the Bull and Bush.

A book on accountancy had been left on Ira's bunk by the previous occupant and he picked it up and began to study it. It seemed to be filled with bewildering information about bankruptcy and solvency and, though he found it dull and uninteresting, he remembered Forde's insistence that he should decide what he was going to do after the war and began to turn the pages. It seemed to offer possibilities, however boring, but he pushed it under his pillow to read when no one was looking, faintly ashamed of it and not anxious for it to be seen.

As September drew into October, the weather grew worse, and there were long periods of rain and low cloud that stopped everybody flying but the bombers. From time to time, Wing turned up a job for them and one of the flights went out and groped about in the mist for ground targets, but air fighting grew less intense and most of the casualties came from accidents.

'We're losing more fellers from the weather than from the fighting,' Forde pointed out gloomily.

Certainly the faces in the mess had changed and there seemed surprisingly few of the original members left. Colyer was able by this time to rate himself an old hand and even people more recently arrived than Avallon were beginning to put on airs in front of newcomers.

Kelly reached the end of his tour and, like Stonehouse and the others, his attitude was one of relief that he had survived. His replacement was a man called Wagner, who looked saturnine and cynical enough for Forde to start a rumour that he was a German spy who had wangled his way into the R.F.C. to get details of the new machines. In fact he turned out to be a very mild ex-schoolteacher who had served in the trenches and grown tired of the mud, the discomfort and the shelling.

With Kelly gone, Wales was given C Flight and Forde became his deputy. He seemed to take his responsibility heavily and worried himself sick about landing them all in an ambush when Wales went on leave.

'You'll 'ave to bear with me, Sunny Jim,' he said. 'I'm not a 'ostile type, like Kelly was. Even the Low-Wing Monoplane's better than me. I just 'aven't got the knack of knocking 'Uns down.'

'You'll get it,' Ira said.

Forde smiled. 'Not me,' he insisted. 'I must be the unknackiest feller in the world, in fact, because I've only knocked down about three, if you include all the fifths, quarters, sixths, halves and twenty-fifths I've been credited with, and that isn't exactly hotstuff shooting for a scout pilot. What is it that makes you blokes who run up quick scores different from the rest of us?'

'I haven't run up a quick score,' Ira protested.

'It's a bloody sight quicker than mine!'

Ira considered. 'Perhaps we can all shoot a bit,' he said.

Forde smiled. 'Stalkin' two-seaters isn't just shootin',' he said. 'Is it guts?'

Ira shrugged. He had never thought of himself as brave and even, at times, when the hair on his hands pricked and his stomach felt empty—as it always seemed to before take-off—he had even considered himself a coward. 'Everybody who flies has to have guts,' he said firmly. 'Especially the chaps who fly FEs.'

Forde looked worried. 'Well, being aggressive then?'

Ira grinned. 'You'd soon go west if you were aggressive in an FE. It's just knowing how to play dirty. Like being a bully at school. Anybody bigger than you, you give a wide berth to. Anybody smaller, you wait round a corner for, with a bigger club than he's got and hit him hard when he's not looking. It's a rotten war, isn't it?'

Forde was not a good leader. He was uncertain like Wyatt and Ira had a suspicion that the rest of the flight discussed him as he had once discussed Wyatt.

When Wales returned from leave and Forde went off in his place, Ira took over as deputy, but the following day Wales went down with a stomach upset he blamed on too much hard-living on leave and Ira put up the leader's streamers.

'No stopping to waltz with the enemy,' he said as he gathered the flight round him before leaving, and he was surprised how easy it was to give orders to men older than himself.

As they climbed, two flights strong, through the cloud, he felt well able to deal with emergencies and realised how lucky he was to have done his first tour of duty before the business of air fighting became too deadly.

Over the lines there was a pyramid of cumulus, clear-cut and white as a shining iceberg and, deafened by the hissing crackle of his motor, he picked his way through the clefts and gorges, intoxicated by the sheer beauty of it. Near La Fère, Archie fired at them and the double cough of the exploding shells made him jump. He'd been so busy thinking what a fine fellow he was he'd almost forgotten Archie and, concentrating on the job, he caught an infinitesimal movement below him, a shift of shadow across the earth. The ground was misty and ashen-looking and it was hard to see things against it, but he was able to pick out a moving flight of aeroplanes below.

He pushed his goggles up to satisfy himself that the sky was empty above him, and was pleased to see the rest of the flight were all with him. The aeroplanes below had turned into DIIIs in a variety of gay colours, their spade-tails catching the sun as their position changed, and he dropped headlong through the sky behind them, his ears full of the scream of wires and the howl of engines.

The DIIIs grew in size with surprising rapidity, then their black crosses seemed to fill the gun sight. As Ira fired, the Camel shuddered and the leading Albatros turned outwards, trailing a thin plume of leaking petrol that made a curving trail behind, then it began to fly straight and level again and he saw a red glow like the end of a cigarette under the fuselage. The black smoke came at once, dragging like a dark streamer from the stricken machine, then a flare of flame, and he saw the pilot raise his hands, his mouth open as he cried out in fear or pain.

The Albatros, now just a mass of oil-stinking smoke from wing-tip to wing-tip, went down in a slow spiral, small burning fragments detaching themselves to follow it in smaller spirals, and it passed so close to Ira he heard the roar of the flames as it dropped out of sight and caught the sickening stench of the smoke as he flew through it. Then it seemed to disintegrate and out of the smoky red centre of the glaze he saw burning pieces of wing appear and the front half of the fuselage with the wheels attached going down end-over-end, and the tail section, broken into pieces, fluttering down behind.

Colyer had been close behind him as the Albatros had burst into flames and he was silent and thoughtful as they walked back to the Bull and Bush.

'I think I'd rather shoot myself with my revolver than die like that,' he said.

Forde returned from leave with all the latest magazines, a new set of gramophone records, a bright red face and dark rings under his eyes.

'Don't know whether I'm pleased to be back or not,' he said. 'I don't really look forward to being shot at in the coming brawl but I must say the air seems clearer out 'ere than at 'ome. London's full of staff wallahs, and all the civvies seem to think it's a sort of great sporting event out 'ere. 'Ow many Germans 'ave you killed, they ask. As if it's a football score.'

Ira listened to him impatiently. Now that his own leave was imminent, he was filled with a longing for England, for neat green fields after the sickening debris of the war, and conversation that wasn't of aeroplanes or the lustful talk of women.

'When do *I* go?' he demanded abruptly, interrupting Forde's jeremiad.

Forde stopped dead. 'You in a 'urry?' he said severely.

'Yes.'

Forde's expression melted. 'Tomorrow morning,' he said. 'Colyer when you come back. What shall you do? Chase a few frisky 'arlots?'

'Yes.'

'You're a rotten liar,' Forde said mildly. 'I expect you'll go to the theatre and fall for someone in the back row of the chorus.'

Forde had stayed in London rather than go home and had seen all the latest shows from *Chu Chin Chow* to *The Maid of the Mountains* and had found a young widow out at Hampstead who had satisfied his needs.

'Nice young woman,' he said. 'Name of Rachel Timms. She'd be pleased to 'ave you to tea, lad. I told 'er about you. 'Usband was a farmer like her dad. We went out to 'is place one day. They 'ad some lovely 'Erefords.'

He seemed a little puzzled by her devotion. 'She's probably got a screw loose somewhere,' he said, 'because a scout pilot's no insurance for the future. It just sort of 'appened, though. After we'd combed out and buttoned up it seemed the most natural thing in the world.'

'Why don't you marry her?' Avallon suggested. 'Quite a respectable institution. Thinking of it myself, actually.'

Forde smiled wanly. 'Matter of fact,' he admitted, 'I did get rather fond of 'er and she seemed to like to 'ave me around, and it was nice 'aving somewhere to go for a bit of peace. My family are still full of the pious 'ope that I'm killing Germans and wanted me to go to church to pray for victory. It seemed easier just to go to 'er place and sit in front of the fire.'

He was full of hints and useful tips for Ira. 'Just keep away from Piccadilly,' he advised. 'You know what those young women who 'ang around there are up to, don't you, and you're too young for that lark.'

'If you're stuck for something to do,' Avallon offered, 'you could always drop in at Greatyers. Family converted it into a hospital. Always room.'

'Handy in case you stop a Blighty,' Forde observed.

'Sister Nancy works there. Be pleased to see him.'

'I've got a cousin in Birmingham,' Colyer suggested. 'She used to frighten the life out of me. She wouldn't be boring.'

Forde held up his hand. 'No young women of doubtful reputation,' he announced.

'Why not?'

'Because, so far, 'e's managed to remain pure in 'eart and unsullied in mind.'

'No choice of mine,' Ira pointed out. 'Perhaps I'll go to Cornwall. Do a bit of shooting.'

'Don't you do enough 'ere, for God's sake?'

'Might sail, then. Might fish. Might just walk.'

'Walk?' Forde looked shocked. *'On your feet?'*

Avallon shook his head sorrowfully. 'Feet were made for pressing accelerators and rudder bars, not walking.'

'And what a waste of a 'ero,' Forde said. 'Tramping round all those empty acres looking for some jolly Cornish Jenny to invite you into the conservatory.'

There was a lot of noise in the mess that evening and Ira remained in the hut to pack. The idea of being back in England so overwhelmed him with nostalgia he lay on his bunk staring at the ceiling. As the noise in the mess grew louder, he considered investigating it, but, since he didn't drink much, he decided it wouldn't be worth leaving in the morning with a hangover and he huddled instead over the book on accountancy. He was already finding that it bored him, but he had struggled on with it, absorbed more by the effort he was putting into reading it than by the contents, and he didn't hear Forde return.

He became aware of him finally, standing alongside him, peering over his shoulder.

'What in the name of God's 'Oly Trousers are you up to *now*?' he demanded.

Ira felt foolish. 'Trying to learn something,' he said.

'Whatever for?' Forde seemed to think he'd gone off his head.

Ira gestured. 'Well, the war's not going to go on for ever, is it?' he said. 'You said so yourself. Some time I've got to earn my living. I can't just go back to school.'

Forde indicated the book. 'You can't do *that*, though,' he said firmly.

'Why not? They get a lot of money. My stepfather's one.'

Forde shook his head, took the book from him and tossed it across the hut. 'Not that, lad. Not that. I just can't see *you* adding up figures in your head for some rotten profiteer.'

Ira sat up indignantly. 'Well, what *can* I do?'

'As life's short and sweet at the moment, you could concentrate on enjoying your silly self. On the other 'and; if you really want something to think about for the future . . .' Forde went outside the hut and came back with a handful of earth. He took Ira's hand and slapped the earth into it.

'That's what matters,' he said. 'Soil. Muck. Think about that, lad. Soil and cows and pigs. *They*'ll never let you down like 'uman beings will. They'll always be grateful for what you do for 'em and never do the dirty on you—'cept by dying sometimes when you don't expect 'em to. Ever thought of being a farmer?'

Ira considered. It sounded like a good open-air life and the idea of accountancy had long since begun to pall.

'I don't know anything about it,' he said.

'*I* do,' Forde pointed out. 'It's bred in the bone, lad. I could take over a farm anywhen I liked and make it go.'

Ira's eyes shone. 'Could you really?'

'Sure I could. And not 'orse-and-cart stuff either. When this lot finishes I'm going to put what I've saved into a farm.'

'Would you have enough?'

Forde gazed steadily at him. 'I've saved hard,' he said. 'But *two* of us would be better. Then we could have something worth having.'

What he was suggesting dawned on Ira at last. 'You mean, *you and me*?'

'Why not? We get on all right.'

'You'd be carrying me on your back.'

'I don't think so. Farms are going to be mechanised after this lot.' Forde dragged a book from his shelf and began to point to pictures of strange machines that didn't mean a thing to Ira. 'This is what the Yanks are using these days. After the war we'll be ploughing with tractors not 'orses, and 'arvesting with mechanical reapers.'

Ira stared at the pictures dubiously. 'I'd be all right if I could fly 'em,' he said.

Forde swung at him with the book. 'You're a natural mechanic,' he said. 'You'd make 'em work. Save us pounds. Fancy the idea?'

Ira grinned. 'It sounds wonderful,' he said. 'It sounds wonderful just to know what's ahead.'

4

Frail stars were still glittering icily overhead through the wisps of mist as the tender arrived at the railhead. The village street was shadowed and silent, but there were half-seen figures moving about in the growing light, steel helmets and rifles sharp against the horizon. Voices came from the darkness and now and again a match glowed over a cigarette. There was an air of expectancy about the whole place that set Ira's pulses thumping.

The train to the coast was abysmally slow and the windows

wouldn't shut so that it was bitterly cold in the thin morning air. In Ira's compartment there were two gunners, three infantrymen and an elderly colonel who commanded a supply dump. They talked listlessly of the Allied chances near Ypres, but the colonel didn't think much of the war, or the troops either, and bored them all stiff telling them why.

It was late in the afternoon when they reached the coast after a journey that left Ira aching and desperate for food. He was already bursting with impatience, but the talk about farming with Forde the night before had given the view from the train a different meaning and he found himself staring with new eyes at cattle as they slipped past. They made him feel warm and he thought of Forde with deep affection because he'd unexpectedly given depth to his life, something he felt it had never had before.

The idea of farming grew on him and he began to think of old houses and slow-moving horses and hear thick country accents like Forde's. Then a squadron of SEs flew low overhead and his eyes swung instinctively towards them, assessing their clean lines, their speed, and wondering how they'd fare against the new Albatroses that were coming out.

He stared at them until they were out of sight, pleased to watch them, and by the time they'd vanished he realised he'd forgotten all about the cows in his pleasure at seeing aeroplanes. He suddenly wondered if he were right to enjoy flying so much, but it made him feel good and filled his world with colour—warmth, meat and drink to him.

Guiltily he looked round for more cows and studied them earnestly, surprised to find they were of a different colouring and size from the last lot, and with delight he realised they were a different breed and sat back, pleased with his perception.

The first sight of England was of a shining rain-wet quay with the arc lamps still burning in the grey morning light. There was a dull fretting wind that rattled a sheet of loose corrugated iron on a roof somewhere and all the dock workers seemed to be standing in doorways out of the drizzle with their hands in their pockets.

'Too wet to work,' one of the gunner officers said bitterly. 'No wonder we're always short of bloody shells.'

The train to London was jammed and the corridors were packed with men, and at Victoria the khaki stream headed off the platform into the arms of mothers, wives and girl friends. Ira took a taxi to Waterloo and caught the train to Malden. His mother had received his letter to say he was on his way and was waiting for him at the gate as he appeared round the corner at the end of the street.

His stepfather had a pleasant house in a row, large and comfortable but incredibly crowded with knick-knacks, and after the outdoor life of France it seemed suffocating. His mother was tearfully pleased to have him home, but he felt he hardly knew her. Her husband had taken a day off from the office to see Ira and, though they had never got on particularly well together, he made a great effort to be friendly and man-to-man.

He offered Ira a drink. 'I suppose you've got used to this sort of thing now,' he said.

Ira nodded. 'Oh, yes,' he lied. 'You should see what I put away at the front.'

There was a colossal meal waiting for him and he wondered how they had managed it from their meagre rations.

'What are you going to do with your leave?' his stepfather asked. 'Go to a few shows? Take a few girls out? There's a jolly pretty one lives next door.'

'Edward!' Ira's mother looked shocked. 'Ira won't want to know *her*. She's older than he is, anyway, and she's got a dreadful reputation.'

Ira's interest was roused at once. 'How long has she lived there?' he asked.

'Just moved in,' his stepfather said. 'Her father's something in the City. Travels about a lot.'

Ira's mother filled his plate again and stared at the furry moustache he'd been trying not very successfully to grow. 'I don't think I like your whiskers, dear,' she said. 'Especially now that your nose . . .' She came to a stop and her eyes filled with tears as she regarded its changed shape.

Ira had thought his moustache looked rather dashing. He had grown it chiefly to stop people asking his age, and though Forde claimed it looked like pubic hair, he defended it briskly.

'Everybody grows them in France,' he said. 'There've even been orders out regretting the tendency of all ranks to shave the upper lip. I think they feel a set of whiskers frightens the Germans more.'

His mother studied it again. 'I think if I were you I should cut it off, dear,' she said, and he mumbled something that was neither willingness nor unwillingness and got down to his food again, at the back of his mind the certain knowledge that he would have to get out of the house as soon as possible, if only to avoid disagreeing with his mother who seemed determined to think of him only as a schoolboy.

'Thought of going to Cornwall,' he announced abruptly, and his mother looked up, her expression one of hurt and disappointment.

'For a day or two, dear?' she asked.

'No. For my leave. To St Blazey.'

It seemed an opportunity to find out something about farming and, in addition, he had a female cousin in St Blazey about his own age whom he remembered nostalgically as pretty. He had been tongue-tied in her presence the last time he'd seen her but he had an optimistic feeling that he might now be more at home with her.

His mother was frowning. She had never really got on with the black Cornishmen from her first husband's family. They were deep-sea sailors and had a dubious history that amounted almost to piracy, and what was more they had looked as though they had.

'Those people,' she said stiffly.

'I like Cornwall.' Ira made a feeble attempt at defiance. 'After all, it's where I came from.'

'So did I, dear,' his mother said. 'But not from St Blazey way.'

Ira was squashed by the reproof. 'Might like to do a bit of fishing,' he said lamely. 'Bit of sailing.'

Fishing and sailing were pastimes Ira's mother's relations had never followed. She had hardly ever seen a fish except on a fishmonger's slab, in fact, and she classed boats with aeroplanes as dangerous things that without warning had a habit of removing male members of the family abruptly beyond reach.

'I should stay in London, dear,' she said with a surprising firmness. 'Enjoy yourself in the places you know.'

During the afternoon Ira pottered about his room, his mother joining him from time to time to be nostalgic about things that no longer interested him. She brought out articles he'd forgotten he possessed and tried to get him absorbed in them, but the only emotion he could feel for them was one of surprise that they'd ever been able to amuse him. She even tried to persuade him to leave his uniform off and wear a school blazer, but he was terrified that someone would think he'd dodged military service and offer him a white feather, and found every excuse he could think of to avoid it.

Without wishing to alarm her, he asked a few tentative questions about girls he knew, thinking wistfully that he might find the courage to look one of them up, but they all appeared to be married or in some other part of the country.

'You remember that teacher you had when we first came here from Cornwall?' his mother asked.

Ira recalled a young woman he remembered being desperately in love with, despite the fact that at the time she had seemed to be of an extremely advanced age.

'Married, dear, and widowed already.' His mother shook her head. 'Marriage's what that thing next door needs. There always seems to be a new young man outside waiting for her. Always officers, and you know what *they*'re after.'

Ira wondered how his mother knew what officers were after, and if the girl next door would be interested in a new breed with wings on his chest. He viewed the possibility with a mixture of excitement and trepidation.

During the evening his mother knitted khaki socks for him while his stepfather read to her from Dickens. The house seemed as silent as the grave behind the loud ticking of the clock, and Ira began to feel he'd burst if something didn't happen.

Eventually he found a battered book on the shelves entitled *The Evolution of the British Farm* and took it down enthusiastically. But it was utterly beyond him, and in the end he put it limply aside, defeated, and decided to go for a beer to the local pub. He found it harder than he thought. His mother still clearly regarded him as a schoolboy and every time he thought he was making headway towards an announcement she brought him back with a jerk to a point in his life when he was wearing a school cap and carrying a satchel.

They retired early and Ira went to his room despondently. His mother sat on his bed to talk to him.

'We're going to do everything we can to make this a good leave,' she said. 'We've booked for *Chu Chin Chow* tomorrow night. You'll like that.'

While she searched his drawers for clean pyjamas, Ira sat with his ill-fitting jacket off, staring at the floor. It looked like being a very dull leave. Like the last one in the spring. In *that* waste of boredom there had been only one highlight when he'd been taken home to supper by a dark-eyed girl he'd met at a social at the Church Hall. Her family had been on holiday and it had only been later that he'd realised what she'd been offering him on the sitting-room sofa and had kicked himself all the way back to France.

'That dark girl . . .?' he found himself saying.

'Which dark girl, dear?' His mother had been spreading the clean pyjamas on the bed and the query stopped her dead.

'That dark girl I met at a church social or something . . .?' He was intentionally vague.

'She's married, dear. Did you like her?'

Ira retreated back into himself, unwilling to strip his emotions naked.

'Oh, no! Just wondered, that's all.'

'There's Claire Turner . . .'

Ira looked up quickly. 'Who's Claire Turner?'

'She's the daughter of a friend of mine, dear.'

'Oh!' Ira's interest waned at once. His mother's friends' daughters were usually offered for his inspection as models of propriety and were invariably unexciting.

'I don't think so, Mother,' he said. 'In any case, I've got to go to Brooklands to see some chaps from the squadron who were posted home.'

'I wish you wouldn't, dear.'

He was startled at the sharpness in her voice. 'It's my job, Mother,' he pointed out.

She frowned. 'I wish it weren't. Your father was an aviator, too.'

The following morning he was awakened early with a cup of tea.

'It's only seven o'clock, Mother,' he bleated, blinking disgustedly at his watch. 'We always sleep in when we're not on duty.'

His mother was not intimidated. 'Early to bed, dear, early to rise,' she said gaily.

After breakfast he swept leaves in the garden for something to do, and then, in the hope of escaping, announced that he had to do some shopping. But his mother insisted on going with him and he spent a miserable morning being dragged round the shops and being introduced to her acquaintances. They had very indifferent coffee in a crowded little teahouse and he listened to all the talk of babies, marriages and widowings with a sullen indifference.

There was a girl across the room who looked passably pretty and as bored as he did, and he made eyes unashamedly at her for half an hour, surprised to find he didn't blush any more. Then he remembered he was wearing his voluminous best tunic and began to wonder dully if she were as repelled by it as he was. As they left he announced he was going to buy a new one.

'But, dear,' his mother said, 'you've already got a perfectly good one!'

'It doesn't fit,' he said, stubbonrly rebellious. 'It never did.'

'You're still growing, dear.'

'No, Mother, I think I've stopped. Besides, I don't like it.'

She sighed. 'Very well, dear, I'll come with you.'

'No, Mother.' Having once defied her, he found it was growing easier. 'I'll go on my own.'

Her face fell and he felt cruel at once, but she seemed to realise they had at last reached a point in his life when she could no longer insist. The tailor was more than willing to rush the tunic through and though his was not a West End establishment, and Ira knew the result would never look the same as Avallon's, at least it would fit him better than the one he hated so much.

After lunch he went to his room to avoid being taken out again and fell asleep on his bed until tea-time. It seemed to please his mother, because she was providing care and comfort, and, when he protested at her fussing, she retaliated by reminding him that he was really all she had.

'I lost your father,' she said. 'I have no one else.'

Her words made him feel mean, but before tea was over he was desperate again. As they washed up together, his mother reminded him that they were going to the theatre and removed his tunic to press and clean it, paying special attention, he noticed, to his wings and ribbons.

'I shall be so proud of you, dear,' she said in a quick switch of loyalties that puzzled him. He knew she hated flying, but she now seemed to be reaching for the added glamour it offered her when she was seen with him. He decided that civilians were as mixed up about the war as soldiers.

He enjoyed the first half of the show, but during the interval his eyes were roving round the auditorium and, seeing all the girls, he felt deprived and began to wonder in such desperation what he could do about it he hardly noticed the rest of the performance.

On the way home they sat opposite a family in the train which included a girl of his own age who eyed him with interest the whole way. He began to feel frantic. London seemed to be packed tight with pretty girls and it seemed impossible to get to know any of them. As they drank their bedtime whisky—very weak and watery—he resolved that he must do something. Two whole days of a precious leave had already fled by without event.

He was young, desperate to get to know a girl and being ridden full tilt by a new and unexpected lust. From time to time he tried to examine it, but it was new to him and sprang entirely, had he only known it, from a consciousness that his life might well be short and the need to feel that, if it ended abruptly, what had passed hadn't all been an arid desert of empty emotion.

The following day, without accepting any argument, he announced that he was going to Brooklands to look up some friends.

He found a few of the older men who remembered his father and recalled him as a boy sewing fabric for fragile aircraft, hanging about in the shadow of Sopwith and De Havilland and having his first flight with Cody. Then he saw a few men he knew acting as instructors. They were depressed by the failure of the Battle of Passchendaele and didn't seem much happier with their lot than when they'd been in France, and called their pupils 'Huns' because they managed to kill instructors with such monotonous regularity. He was welcomed to the mess, however, and saw Stonehouse there, a wonderfully brand-new Stonehouse, no longer living on his nerves, plumper already and actually enjoying life.

'Pat Kelly's dead,' he said. 'Did you know?'

It came as a shock to realise that the knob-faced Irishman was dead already.

'His M.C. came though just after he got back and he was showing off a bit,' Stonehouse said. 'He flew through a house and killed two kids.'

Ira felt much more at home in a Flying Corps mess and stayed to lunch. In the afternoon they allowed him to fly an SE5, a handy little aeroplane with a Hispano engine. It was strong, stable as a horse and cart and could zoom fifteen hundred feet without trouble.

Stonehouse invited him to a party in the West End he was going to in the evening, but Ira refused, feeling his mother would worry where he was.

Stonehouse shrugged. 'Well, if it ever suits you, I've got a flat in Kingston. Come round any time you like. There are usually a few willing girls there.'

Ira caught a train home in the early evening and they sat round the fire for the same routine as the previous day. Later, the clouds that had been hanging over the city cleared and the rain stopped. About nine o'clock the air-raid warning sounded and Ira's stepfather went round the house to make sure no light was escaping.

'They're coming earlier these days,' his mother said nervously. 'They killed a whole family in Battersea last month.'

Feeling he owed it to Forde, Ira had been pushing stubbornly through *The Evolution of the English Farm*, but he now put it thankfully aside and moved the curtain to peer out at the searchlights probing the sky.

'Ira!' He jumped at his mother's voice, just as he had as a boy when he'd been caught out in some mischief. 'Put that curtain back at once! You'll have us all killed!'

Ira put the curtain back meekly. 'I think I'll go for a walk,' he announced in desperation.

'Suppose you're caught in the raid?'

'We're getting them every night in France at the moment, Mother. I'll know what to do.'

His mother still seemed unwilling to let him go. 'We'll leave the door on the latch,' she said. 'Just knock on our wall when you come in so we'll know you're home.'

Outside, the dark autumn streets were empty and Ira walked under the bare trees, his feet shuffling ankle-deep through the blackened leaves. In the town centre he found a small red sign which read 'Swan Inn' and, deciding that at least everyone wasn't dead, pushed his way through a heavy curtain into a dimly lit bar. The place was full of men in uniform.

The landlord seemed anxious to talk. 'What's happening at Ypres?' he asked indignantly. 'You don't seem to be making much impression on the Germans there.'

'No,' Ira said. 'They're a rotten lot. They don't play fair.'

The fire in the grate was enormous and Ira took off his coat and hung it behind the door. The landlord's eyes widened as he saw his wings and medal ribbons.

'The next one's on me,' he announced. 'How did you get *them*?'

'Flying,' Ira said shortly.

A youngster of his own age was wearing the uniform of the Guards with three stripes on his sleeve, and they started swopping yarns. Another sergeant from the Middlesex Regiment joined them, then an officer from the Yeomanry, and they all agreed that it was much harder work being on leave than it was being in France.

'All they ever seem to talk about over here is making money,' the Middlesex sergeant said.

'Chap I know who was a shipping clerk'—the Yeomanry officer took up the story—'he made enough to buy himself a house. Formed a company with another clerk. Army contracts. Buttons, I think.'

'No wonder they always fly off your trousers when you bend down,' the Guardsman said. 'Every time we duck, all our buttons burst, and there we are, in No Man's Land, with our trousers round our ankles. No wonder Jerry's winning.'

'How's the Push in your part of the line?' the Middlesex man asked.

'Gets pushier every day.'

They fell to exchanging names and were surprised at how many of their contemporaries were no longer alive.

They called for more beer and the group began to grow noisier. Another sergeant joined them, and they found themselves sitting at a table with a Service Corps officer and a dark attractive girl. The officer was rather drunk and not very lucid, and the Guardsman finally dragged it out of him that he'd spent the whole of the war in charge of a transport dump in South London.

There was a sudden silence round the table and, as they all stared at him, Ira began to feel sorry for him. The Guardsman began to be rude and, conscious of the dark girl's eyes on him, Ira told him to shut up and, for a while, as the officer mumbled something about more drink and disappeared to buy it, they argued among themselves about whether he was just lucky or a deliberate dodger.

'After all, there are plenty of decent chaps who haven't been in the fighting,' the Yeomanry officer said generously.

'And a bloody sight more who don't want to be,' the Middlesex sergeant snorted.

The dark girl had been listening to the argument silently, making no comment, and when it stopped they discovered that the officer who'd been with her had vanished.

They all apologised at once and the dark girl laughed. 'It's all right,' she reassured them. 'He was very dull and a bit drunk. There's only one problem. Who sees me home? I can't walk in the dark alone.'

Since she lived nearby, the task fell naturally to Ira, and he managed to get her coat on without wrenching her arm. The searchlights were still probing the sky as they left, but the air raid seemed to have come to nothing, and the girl slipped an arm through his as though it were the most natural thing in the world.

'I'll show you the way,' she said.

They could hear the drone of an aeroplane engine somewhere above them and the girl gestured at the sky. 'One of ours?' she asked.

'Could be,' Ira said. 'They've fixed up one or two for night flying.'

'I think we'd better hurry,' the girl said. 'My father gets upset about me being out, but I can't very well sit at home every night and listen to him going on about the war. Do *you* have trouble with parents?'

'My mother still thinks I'm a schoolboy.'

'How old are you?'

'Twenty-two,' Ira lied, adding a little more for luck.

'I'm twenty-three. My name's Peggy Phillips, by the way.'

'I'm Ira Penaluna.'

'Well, it's unusual at least.' She seemed to think what she had said sounded rude and hastened to qualify it. 'All the girls in London seemed to be called Peggy or Polly and all the men Tom or Jack. How long are you on leave?'

'I've got five days left.'

'What are you going to do with it?'

'I *was* thinking of going to Cornwall.'

She squeezed his arm. 'That *would* be a waste.'

'That's what I was thinking,' Ira said.

She indicated a road to their left. 'Down here.'

'I go this way, too,' Ira announced.

'That's useful. It's the first time I've talked to a flier. All the others have been something ordinary like infantry or gunners or navy. My father's always going on about me. But it gets so lonely. Do you get lonely?'

'Chiefly on leave when I'm home.'

'What's it like in the Flying Corps?'

'Exaggerated. I mean, in the newspapers.'

'Really? How?'

Ira tried to explain. 'All that "intrepid birdman" stuff,' he said. 'All those "heroic death dives". Most of it's written by chaps who don't know anything about it. We spend most of our time frightened to death or bored to tears with each other.'

'You don't look as though you're the type who'd be frightened easily.'

'I am.'

'What by?'

'Girls mostly.'

She laughed and, with a warm excited feeling, Ira decided he was doing rather well.

'Down the next road,' she pointed out.

'That's funny,' Ira said. 'I live down here, too.'

She gave a little chuckle. 'I live at Number Twenty-Four.'

Ira stopped dead. 'You'll be . . .'

'I'll be what?'

'I've heard of you.'

'I'm sure you have. Everybody has. But it doesn't worry me much. You're dead a long time and you're only young once.'

They set off walking again, her hand in his, and Ira's heart suddenly began a slow thump. They stopped outside a large dark house hidden among trees and Ira glanced next door, noticing that his mother's light was still on. She was obviously waiting for him.

They crept silently down the drive of Peggy's home and into the kitchen. There was a small fire in the grate, which she stirred up. As she reached for the kettle, a male voice came from upstairs.

'It's all right, Father,' she called from the kitchen door. 'I'm just making myself a drink.' There was a pause and Ira heard faint mutterings from somewhere above them. 'It isn't late,' she went on. 'I'll be up soon.'

She shut the door and beamed at Ira. 'He's always going on. It's because my mother's in Bournemouth recuperating. She's always ill. She enjoys being ill. I think she's frightened of a bomb dropping on her. I tell them I have to work, late.'

They smiled at each other like conspirators.

'Where do you work?' Ira asked.

'Ministry of Munitions. It always sounds good when I tell them I have to stay to get another shipment off to France. They don't argue. And you can't sit indoors twiddling your thumbs all the time just because there's a war on, can you?'

She handed Ira a cup of cocoa and indicated the single-ended sofa at the back of the kitchen. Ira sat down and she moved close enough to him for her knee to press against his.

'Rather useful living next door, isn't it?' she said.

'Yes.'

'Sorry I haven't anything stronger.'

'Cocoa's fine.'

Her face was close to his. 'How old are you, Ira? Really?'

'Twenty-two,' he insisted.

'You've got a funny nose.'

'I broke it. Flying.'

'Do you want to kiss me?'

He tried to make a professional job of it, but he was still a little uncertain and it wasn't terribly successful. To his surprise, she didn't seem to mind and lifted her arms to put them round his neck.

'I've never been kissed by a pilot before,' she announced. 'It's quite a new experience.'

5

When Ira's mother brought him a cup of tea the following morning she gave him a reproachful look.

'You were very late in, Ira dear,' she said. 'And you didn't knock on the wall.'

She was just going out again when Ira called her back.

'Mother, why did you christen me "Ira"?' It was something he'd often wondered about but never really worried over until the previous night when Peggy Phillips had commented on it.

His mother eyed him, surprised. 'Wrath, dear,' she said. 'It means "wrath". It was a family name. It suited the Penalunas, I'm afraid.'

He frowned. 'Then why "Abel"?' He had seemed as a child to have more than his fair share of the sort of names that would arouse ribald mirth in a schoolyard.

His mother paused, considering. 'There were so many "Cains" in the Penaluna family,' she said. 'I felt an "Abel" might restore the balance a little. I don't think it did. You're very much like the rest at heart, dear.'

As the door closed, Ira sat with the tea in his hand, thinking for a moment about what she'd said. He supposed he *was* a Penaluna, all right, and somehow he did feel more of a Cain than an Abel.

The thought reminded him of Peggy Phillips and his eyes became distant. It had been quite a heavy session on the kitchen sofa and he had a feeling that he'd acquitted himself well.

He came out of his reverie with a jerk as he realised he'd spilt tea on the sheet and, as he'd always done, he dived for a handkerchief and guiltily sponged it clean. Then he saw he was still behaving like a schoolboy and decided he'd better stop before the habit took hold.

At breakfast, when his mother announced they would be going visiting, he put his foot down and said he couldn't.

'But, dear,' she protested, 'these are people I've told so much about you.'

'I'm sorry, Mother,' he said firmly. He found, however, he hadn't the courage to tell her he'd arranged to meet Peggy Phillips for lunch, and offered instead the excuse that he had to go to the tailor's for a fitting.

She was clearly disappointed, but he was determined not to be pushed into any more dull days. London seemed to be bursting at the seams with eligible girls and he was determined to get to know one or two of them.

He delightedly stuffed *The Evolution of the English Farm* back into the shelves where it had come from, deciding to have another go at it when he had time but knowing perfectly well that he never would, and set off for the town. He was pleased to see that his tunic was coming along nicely—so well, in fact, he wondered uneasily if it weren't a little *too* well fitting and rather Frenchified—then he took a train into the city where he found the streets full of Australians, New Zealanders, Indians, Canadians, Belgians in tall forage caps, and a number of lost Russians wondering what to do with themselves now that revolution had taken their country out of the war. There were also a few Montenegrins and Portuguese, and even Americans in tall old-fashioned choker-collared uniforms and hats like Boy Scouts. For the most part they were cheerful, friendly and faintly ashamed that their country had taken so long to get into the war.

Shysters sold iron crosses and spiked helmets at every alley-end and all the smart women seemed to be on the arm of a wounded officer. The place was full of gloom in a way France never was, despite the proximity there to destruction and death, and the only thing anyone seemed able to talk about was the failure in Flanders. There was also a great deal more concern with military punctilio and more prostitutes than he'd ever seen in his life before, but the weather had become unexpectedly warm and Peggy Phillips appeared full of smiles at their rendezvous, and at once the bricks and mortar around him seemed to lose their greyness and began to breathe with him, sharing his delight in the thought of having a girl of his own.

He had to rely on her to name the restaurant, because he'd never eaten in the West End in his life before, but she knew of one near her office and when they'd finished they sat over the coffee and she allowed him to hold her hand under the table as though he'd known her for years.

Feeling a thousand years old, wise beyond his time and tremendously experienced in war, wine and women, he suggested wildly that they meet in the evening for another meal, his mind already roving ahead to being alone with her on the kitchen sofa again.

'Not a meal,' she said. 'But if you like to be at the end of the road about nine-thirty, I can find an excuse to slip out.'

He saw her back to her office, lingering with her hand in his until she had to drag it away, then he mooned about the city all afternoon, wondering why leaves were so dreary compared with active service, and went home full of excuses for not being able to stay in.

'Met a chap I learned to fly with,' he said. 'Asked me round to meet the family.'

'Why not bring him here?' his mother chided. 'You know you can.'

'It's his last night,' he explained quickly. 'He's going back tomorrow.'

Followed by her reproachful glance, he found his coat. His stepfather followed him into the hall. 'How are you for cash, son?' he asked.

'I've enough for the train fare.'

'Would a pound be any use?'

Ira stared at him and smiled. 'Always,' he admitted.

He felt the note being pushed into his hand. 'And, Ira'—his stepfather gave him an understanding look—'this friend of yours you learned to fly with: don't keep her out too late.'

Ira grinned and his stepfather patted his shoulder. 'Don't worry about your mother,' he said. 'Just be kind to her and I think everything will be all right.'

Ira nodded, feeling guilty and faintly ashamed. There were a lot of things he didn't know much about, he decided, and people were probably nicer than he'd ever thought, and he realised how young he still was, despite his war service and the two medal ribbons on his chest. Most of the time, his youth didn't worry him much—not even when Forde was doing his Father Time act in the Bull and Bush—and most people in France accepted him as one of themselves and didn't ask questions. It was only when he was thrown up against some unexpected kindness like his stepfather's generosity that he realised that the fault lay with himself rather than with the older generation, and that the gap between them was enormous and difficult to bridge.

He was still pondering the problem when he caught a whiff of perfume, and felt an arm slip through his, and immediately he became a mixture of mature manhood and uncertain boyishness. He was conscious of being in the presence of experience and felt vaguely that he could only be accepted if he proved himself. But this thought of proving himself terrified him also, and his mind became a maelstrom of emotions in which sex played a larger part than the nobility he'd always expected of love.

They spent half an hour in the Swan, then decided to head for the fields. They turned away from the town, Ira unable to control the shivering that kept shaking him from head to foot. But, even as they pushed open a farm gate and headed into the shadows, a freezing rain began to fall and they were driven into another pub where they sat in a corner holding hands, their knees together under the table, Ira ridden full pelt by his desires.

'We'll go home,' Peggy whispered outside as she pushed him away. 'Father'll be in bed.'

They walked with their arms round each other, and she stopped in the shadows under the trees to give him experienced kisses that made his blood run hot. But her father was in the kitchen when they arrived and Ira felt his heart sink to his shoes.

Phillips was a dark saturnine man in his fifties who seemed to regard Ira with deep suspicion. Despite all Peggy's hints that he might be tired, he remained a fixture in the kitchen.

He produced a grudging drink for Ira, but he was still there as it approached midnight, and Ira was becoming desperate.

'I bet you flying chaps need lots of sleep,' Phillips said. 'All that height.'

It seemed a clear hint that it was time to depart and Ira rose reluctantly, seething with frustration. Peggy followed him to the door.

'I'm sorry,' she whispered as they stopped in the porch. 'He seems to have taken a dislike to you.'

'That's all right,' Ira said between his teeth. 'What about a show tomorrow?'

'That'll be wonderful.'

She kissed him hurriedly and immediately his pulse quickened and his arms tightened as he pressed against her.

'Naughty boy,' she giggled, pushing him away.

'It's such a waste of good leave,' he said bitterly, but she had already closed the door behind her and he was talking to a blank wall.

For a long time he stood in the darkness, remembering the promise in her eyes and aware of a great battering ram of desire.

'For God's sake,' he muttered hoarsely as he turned away.

His mother was still awake when he returned, and called softly to him as he crept upstairs. Bitterly, he went to his room without answering and sat on the bed, brooding over the wasted evening and feeling unnecessarily virginal and desperate to put matters right.

He woke the following morning to realise that his mother had brought him a cup of tea which stood by the bed cold. He couldn't remember her appearing and, deciding that perhaps his stepfather had been having a quiet little chat with her and anxious to please, he forced it down.

He left the house after breakfast and this time he noticed that his mother made an effort to give him an understanding smile.

He bought tickets for *Chu Chin Chow* despite the fact that he'd already seen it once, ate a lunch of sandwiches in a pub in Piccadilly and, out of sheer boredom, passed the afternoon in the British Museum. It seemed a stupid way to spend a leave, but he was terrified of an air raid keeping him out of reach of his rendezvous.

He reached the appointed spot almost an hour too soon and walked up and down outside Peggy's office, brooding on the other men who passed with girls on their arms. They all seemed so self-assured and confident he wondered what one did to acquire such poise.

Peggy appeared at last and they took a taxi to the Café Royal where they had one too many aperitifs and ended the meal unable to stop laughing. The fit continued even into the show, where they laughed at all the wrong places, and, although he knew it would cost him a fortune, he took a taxi home. On the way Peggy was as eager as he was and their mouths searched for each other in the blackness, and as they stopped the taxi at the end of the street to emerge more than a little dishevelled, the driver gave Ira a knowing look and grinned.

As they entered the drive, Ira immediately saw the light in the kitchen.

'*He*'s there,' he said furiously.

'Oh, Ira!' She turned to him, soft and clinging. 'I really am sorry. Let's sit in the summer house. It'll not be very warm but at least we'll be alone.'

'Won't he wonder where you are?'

'He thinks I'm out with a friend.'

'Pity you didn't say you were staying the night.'

She was silent for a second. 'What would you have done if I had?' she asked slowly.

'We could have gone somewhere.'

'Where, for instance?'

'An hotel.'

She giggled. 'Ira, what ideas you do get!'

The summer house was dark and smelled of damp, but there was a cane chair in there, and she pushed him into it and sat on his knee. For a while they were silent, then as they shifted position, Ira's elbow caught a bundle of rakes and hoes and the lot fell on them with a clatter. He found his ardour dying at once.

'Oh God,' he said.

She giggled in the darkness. 'He's going away tomorrow night,' she said. 'He has to go to Bournemouth to see Mother. He goes on the late train. He thinks I'm staying with a friend.'

'Doesn't he ever suspect?'

'Probably, but I have to do something. Next time you come home I shall probably be in a flat of my own.'

'I might not last that long,' Ira said gloomily, convinced he was going to spend the whole of a short life as a virgin.

She shivered and jerked at her collar. 'It's cold in here,' she observed.

'It's not very comfortable either.'

As he set off home, Ira was beetle-browed and surly, convinced there was a conspiracy against him. He only had one more night and he began to wonder if he wouldn't have been wiser to have found some girl among his mother's circle of friends, after all, and seen what could have been done with her. But his first meeting with Peggy had seemed so promising he had pursued it day by day, each time hoping for better luck.

He'd been surprised, in fact, by his own boldness and the way his shyness had not proved an obstacle, and he put it down to the fact that Peggy was clever and as keen on him as he was on her. It seemed obvious at once that this was an essential part of the whole business and he nodded to himself, feeling he had uncovered a great truth.

Pleased with himself, he searched his mind for some of the clever things she'd said, but he found he couldn't find any and began to wonder gloomily if he hadn't just been blinded by his own enthusiasm. Then he remembered Stonehouse and his nearby flat, and his invitation to meet the willing girls he claimed were always there, and he was suddenly so frustrated he set off to walk to Kingston, his shoulders hunched against the cold. He was young and hard as nails and it didn't seem far.

There was no sign of life as he rang the bell and he decided in despair that Stonehouse must be out, but a light eventually went on under the door and Stonehouse appeared in pyjamas.

'Come in, old son,' he said. 'I'd turned in early. We had a hell of a party here last night.'

'What sort of a hell of a party?'

Stonehouse grinned. 'Picked up some girls from the chorus at Drury Lane,' he said. 'When I woke up this morning, the place was full of silk stockings and balloons and things. There was a girl asleep in the kitchen and another on the settee.' He stared at Ira. 'What's up, old son?'

'Nothing.' Ira was wondering what malignant fate had led him to Stonehouse's flat on the wrong night.

Stonehouse was holding his head now and remembering with wistful faraway eyes. 'We had some Yanks here, too,' he said. 'And you know what they're like. They started playing strip poker and when everyone gets down to underwear, you know how *that* ends.' He jerked a head at his bedroom. 'I was in there with a blonde piece.' He frowned as though his head hurt. 'The chap I share with's away. You can sleep in his bed.'

Bitterly, Ira made his way to the other bedroom. There was a balloon hanging from the gaslight, and a silk stocking tied round the lampshade. They seemed to suggest debauchery and he went to bed feeling desperate.

The following morning he went to Brooklands with Stonehouse and ended up in the early evening with him in a pub near Piccadilly. Stonehouse was going to a party at Hounslow and suggested that Ira should join him, but Ira's mind was full of Peggy Phillips and the big old house next door to his mother's, empty of everyone but the two of them. Despite Stonehouse's promises of girls, he decided that the chances of two tremendous parties in three nights were pretty slender and that a bird in the hand was worth two in the bush. He settled for Peggy Phillips.

Stonehouse was all for priming him with drink before he went and, though he didn't drink much, it was considerably more than he'd intended. He stopped on the corner of Regent Street to light the pipe he'd begun to affect, staring resentfully at all the men escorting girls. It seemed so easy for everyone else, he reflected, feeling as virile as a bull yet without the confidence to do something about it.

A prostitute dressed in white with a fur hat stopped in front of him with a penny-in-the-slot smile.

'Hello, soldier,' she said. 'Can I do anything for you?'

Lost in his own thoughts, Ira started as she spoke, then he shook his head and moved away, red with embarrassment.

A hundred yards further on, he stopped and turned, staring back, his eyes sultry and shivering inside his clothes at a surge of adult masculinity. He was wondering if it wouldn't be worth while going back to the girl in the fur hat and making arrangements to get it over and done with. At least, he wouldn't go back to France feeling he was going to die inexperienced.

Some unexpected streak of puritanism held his feet, however, and deciding he wouldn't know how to open the conversation, anyway, he gloomily set off for the station.

He arrived in Malden two hours too soon and found a hotel where he could buy a meal. He ate it with his eyes all the time on the waitress, and eventually found himself at the Swan a good half-hour before he intended. To his surprise he found Peggy there already, sitting with a girl friend and an officer of the London Scottish with three wound stripes on his arm.

'It's all right,' Peggy said quietly as they vanished. 'Father left an hour ago for Victoria.'

Ira couldn't wait to get her away from the lights of the pub, but there was an air raid going on in the city and they could hear the drone of engines and the thud of anti-aircraft guns. She seemed eager to watch.

'Don't you think we ought to be under cover?' Ira suggested.

'Under covers, I think you're meaning,' she said with an arch little giggle.

They walked home hurriedly, and she let them in at the back door. The kitchen fire was still burning and the room was warm. He reached out for her at once and pulled her to the sofa.

'That was sudden,' she said as he released her.

'It's what we came for,' Ira said. His voice was hoarse and he cleared his throat. 'We've been waiting all week for a chance to be alone.'

She slipped into his arms again and they kissed, then without warning she pushed him away.

'What's the matter?' Ira asked, wondering what he'd done wrong.

'Nothing,' she said. 'Just too hot. A jumper and skirt aren't the best things for romping on a sofa. I think I'll go and change.'

Ira's heart thumped suddenly. He'd heard of this point in the proceedings before, and he recognised it as a critical moment.

'I'll come and help you,' he said, surprised at his own brashness.

She eyed him sideways, then she smiled. 'You're learning fast,' she said.

He grinned. 'Hope your father enjoys his holiday.'

She chuckled. 'When you've been married twenty-five years I expect it's not just the holiday he's after.'

He followed her upstairs in the darkness, his heart thudding, aware of a choking feeling in his throat and noticing the cold beams of the moon on the landing and the old-fashioned decorations.

She opened a door and, crossing to the curtains, pulled them quickly, the rings rattling on the bamboo pole. There was a gas fire in the hearth and she stooped to light it, then rose and turned to him, smiling enigmatically. He was still wearing his coat.

'Take your coat off, Ira,' she encouraged. 'You won't need it here.'

He removed the coat and laid it carefully over a chair, aware of a curious precision in his movements. Now that he'd arrived at the critical point in the affair, he found his courage was barely up to it. He'd been working for this moment all week, but now, even with his blood hammering in his veins, he felt inexperienced and uncertain.

'Shan't be a moment,' she said.

She seemed quite unperturbed by his nervous stare as she reached up and pulled the jumper over her head, and stood before him, her bare shoulders gleaming under the strap of the slip she wore.

'You'd manage better without your jacket,' she suggested, kicking off her shoes.

Ira was stricken dumb, his mouth dry, his throat constricted, his fingers clumsy, and she took pity on him and unfastened the buckles of his Sam Browne for him.

'You need me to look after you,' she said softly.

He reached for her awkwardly, but she pushed him away. 'Don't rush,' she chided. 'There's plenty of time.'

Ira nodded. 'It's warm in here,' he said, surprised how slight and small she seemed without the jumper, and how cool her flesh was under his fingers.

'I think it'll be much more comfortable on the bed,' she suggested.

As he clutched her again, she subsided on to the pillow.

'You're doing very well for a beginner,' she murmured.

Choked with emotion, he began to fumble with straps. Staring up at him with that maddeningly knowing smile on her face, she reached out to pull him towards her and it was a moment or two before they became conscious of the taxi clattering away in the road outside. A man's voice was talking at the entrance to the drive, and they both sat bolt upright, passion fading rapidly in fear of discovery.

'Father!' Peggy was already hitching straps back into position. 'The old idiot's come back. It must be the air raid.'

She gave Ira a push and, as he fell off the bed with a bump, she ran to the window, so slim and desirable he felt sick with frustration.

'Something must have gone wrong!' She gave a little panicky cry as she reached for her jumper and shoes. 'Hurry!'

Ira was grabbing for his Sam Browne as she darted backwards and forwards across the room, from the mirror to the window, jabbing at her hair with a comb. His brows were down in a grim line and he was numb with fury and nauseated by the disaster as she pushed his cap at him and tossed his coat in his face.

'Back stairs,' she said. 'He'll come in the front door!'

He allowed her to push him in front of her, choking with rage. They could hear a key in the front door now.

'Tomorrow,' she was saying.

'I go back tomorrow,' Ira bleated.

As he fumbled his way in the darkness to the back door, he heard her voice from the front of the house, as gay and indifferent as if he'd never been there.

'Father! You didn't go!'

Besotted and wretched, he made his way silently to the road, keeping to the shadows of the shrubbery. He was cold with fury, with his lack of experience sitting like a stone in his chest. His mother had not even gone to bed when he arrived.

'Is that you, dear?' she called.

'Yes.'

'Where've you been?'

'Out,' he snapped, and headed for the stairs.

Inside his room, aware that he'd been rude and that his mother's query had been an invitation to a chat, he flung his cap and coat down on the bed and stared round the room, feeling as though he'd like to punch a hole in the wall.

There was a faint knock, and his mother's voice. 'May I come in, dear?'

He grunted a reply and she poked her head round the door.

'I had a message for you but I didn't know where to get hold of you. It was that girl I told you about, dear. Claire Turner. You met her once. I always thought you were rather keen on her.'

Ira searched his memory and couldn't even recall any girl he'd been keen on.

'What did she want?' he asked, almost choking over the words.

'She was visiting her mother this afternoon and wondered if you'd like to go and have dinner at her flat with her. Her friend's away and she was alone. She's rather fast and it sounded rather daring really, but you've grown up now and it's wartime, so I suppose it would have been all right.'

Ira groaned. His mother stared at him. 'Are you all right, dear?' she asked.

'Yes, I'm all right.'

As she disappeared, Ira caught sight of himself in the mirror, glaring, then he picked up his coat from the bed and hurled it at the wall in fury. It brought down the picture of *Hope* huddled on top of the world, that had been in his bedroom as long as he could remember, and it bounced on the dresser, clearing it of his mother's knick-knacks which descended with it in a noisy shower to the floor.

His mother called up the stairs. 'Are you all right, Ira?'

'Yes. Just knocked something off the dresser.'

'You've not been drinking, have you?'

'No. Just a bit fed up.'

'About going back tomorrow, dear?'

'Yes.'

'Never mind, dear.' His mother's voice floated through the door, vague and gentle. 'You've had a wonderful leave, haven't you?'

6

The last day of Ira's leave proved as futile as the rest of it had been. In a desperate attempt to put things right, he telephoned Peggy Phillips at work, but she seemed to regard the whole thing as a huge joke and couldn't stop giggling, and in a fury he slammed the receiver down in the middle of the conversation. He felt ill-used and shadowed by a set of malignant fates.

At Boulogne he followed the notices directing returning men to their units and new drafts to their bases. He was still unsettled. Peggy had seen him off at Victoria, full of apologies for her laughter, but she'd talked too much, mostly in clichés, and he'd realised she was always a little arch and devious. They'd held hands on the platform until the train had left, Ira all the time with a feeling of dishonesty at his *volte-face* and conscious of the uncomprehending look in her eyes.

It made him glad to be back. England had been full of artificiality—artificial prosperity, artificial gaiety, artificial patriotism, even artificial emotion, it seemed—and it left him with a feeling of disillusion, sadness and a tremendous wish to be swallowed up again by the squadron.

All round him men were heading for trains—infantry, artillery, cavalry, engineers, signalmen, Service Corps, Medical Corps, Navy, Marines, Flying Corps. The new drafts stood out like sore thumbs among them, their buttons shining, their boots polished, their puttees neat, their packs squared off as though they'd been lined with cardboard. There were a few contemptuous glances at them from the old hands in their goatskin and sheepskin jackets and the greasy-edged overcoats hacked off short with jack-knives to keep them out of the mud of the trenches, and where the new drafts arrived in military silence, the air round the old hands was full of catcalls.

'I thought they'd killed you off!'

'How's the shooting on your part of the front?'

'Have they killed that little bastard in your mob who wanted to win the war on his own?'

They set off on a slow clanking train up to the front, passing roads full of jammed waggons, gun limbers and marching men. Then they began to see captive balloons hanging in the air, and at Roye Ira was glad to see the familiar face of the Crossley driver.

'Hello, sir,' he said. 'Nice to 'ave you back.'

He fussed round Ira, establishing him in the front seat of the tender and putting a sack over his legs to keep out the draught.

'Gittin' a bit chilly these days, sir,' he said. 'But all that rain seems to have stopped and there's been a lot of flying. What was it like at 'ome?'

The question brought back all the missed opportunities of Ira's leave and he didn't answer. His brows went down in a puzzled frown and the driver pulled a face to himself as he climbed into his seat. He'd long since grown used to men arriving from leave with hangovers or in the throes of agonising new love-affairs, and had learned to hold his tongue.

Ira was still brooding on missed chances, and his lack of experience of physical love lay cheerless and humiliating under his heart. The driver didn't attempt to converse and they sat in silence as the Crossley jolted over the pavé between the gun limbers and lorries and marching men.

At Huyzes, Ira went to the Bull and Bush to dump his bag before reporting his return to Sillito, but as he opened the door he stopped dead. There were two youngsters in there with unfamiliar faces, and there seemed to be nothing about him that he knew. He was just about to back out again when he recognised the calendar hanging over the wash-basin with a picture of a Kirchner girl on the front and he entered slowly, aware of ominous changes.

'Who're you?' he asked cautiously.

The two youngsters had leapt to their feet, ramrod-straight before him. 'I'm Milton,' one of them said. 'That's Lucas.'

Ira was looking round him and he noticed that Colyer's watch had gone from the nail where it always hung, and the photograph of his girl friend from beside the bed. His eyes moved slowly and he saw Avallon's kit standing in a dark corner of the hut. He looked quickly at Forde's corner, but everything there seemed normal enough.

He was just working out the imponderables of the situation, a sense of heavy foreboding taking away the pleasure of being back, when he heard aeroplanes overhead. He went outside, followed by Milton and Lucas.

Atwater greeted him from the door of the next hut. He was leaning on a stick with his foot in a carpet slipper. He said he was now leading B Flight but had sprained his ankle in a crash-landing when his engine cut on take-off. His eyes on the sky, Ira hardly heard him.

Lucas and Milton appeared alongside him.

'That the patrol coming back?' Milton asked.

Ira nodded. The sky looked burned white and empty and the machines were too far away to be recognised, but he counted five, which seemed fairly normal. He returned to the hut and wrenched off his coat and cap and went outside again.

'I say'—Lucas, a fresh-faced boy with pink cheeks, stared enthusiastically at his ribbons—'you're quite an old hand!'

The machines were turning over the trees at the end of the field now, and Ira watched them with narrowed eyes, his heart thumping suddenly. Lucas seemed not to notice the expression on his face and was peering at his ribbons.

'That's the M.M., isn't it?' he was saying. 'And the Croix de Guerre! How did you get . . .?'

Milton nudged him quickly, and they edged away. The aeroplanes were coming in to land now, their engines burping as the pilots blipped the cut-out buttons on the joysticks. Squinting to catch the letters on the fuselage, Ira watched them until they turned, Monkey Brand and the other dogs streaming behind, then he saw Forde's J and his bulky shape in the cockpit and was aware of an immense weight being lifted off his shoulders.

As he started to unpack his bag, he saw the two youngsters watching him. 'Sorry about the rudeness,' he said gruffly.

They exchanged glances and he studied them, feeling generations older than they were, then tried to make conversation because he knew Forde would have done so, to help them find their feet.

'Flown Camels before?' he asked.

'In England.' They moved closer, like puppies eager for friendship.

'How long?'

They told him. It didn't seem much, but they seemed less interested in themselves than in him.

'Got any Huns?' Milton asked.

'One or two,' Ira said.

'Is it very difficult?'

Ira smiled. 'Not really,' he said. 'You just point your guns at them and pull the trigger and down they go.'

'I bet it's not as easy as all that.'

They were still talking when the door burst open and Forde appeared, bulky against the light, smoky grime on his chin. He was frowning, and was about to toss his equipment down when he saw Ira.

'Sunny Jim!' He clasped him warmly, so that he disappeared entirely into his vast embrace, then Forde seemed to feel he was being unnecessarily emotional and pretended instead to kiss him like a French general, first on one cheek then on the other.

'Back to the fold, lad,' he said.

Ira indicated the two newcomers. 'What happened to the others?'

Forde grimaced. ''Uns have been a bit 'Unnish lately,' he said in a flat voice, bending over the equipment on his bed as though he didn't wish Ira to see his face. 'Things have changed. The 'Un's getting the new DV now and we don't fly in twos and threes any more. The Richthofen mob are around again, too, and they work in a bunch, so we have to do the same. It's nothing to see fifty or sixty machines milling round at once. We've lost three fellers since you left. Two from A Flight. They were 'it by a blight. And Archie put a piece of shrapnel in the other cheek of Basil's be'ind in a balloon raid. 'E'll lean like the Tower of Pisa.'

'He did before. Won't it straighten him out?'

'Bigger piece. All unbalanced again.'

'Rotten luck.'

Forde shrugged. 'I'd willingly compromise with God for a nick in the backside to be safe 'ome,' he said.

He stripped to his underwear and started to wash his face. Ira stood near him while the two youngsters listened quietly like strangers from their corners.

'Things are quietening down again now,' Forde went on between snortings and blowings into the water. 'I dessay the 'Un's decided to settle for a quiet winter. By God, I 'ope so. I've only a couple of months now before I can expect to be posted 'ome and if he does, I might just make it.'

They were silent for a moment, then Ira raised his head. 'What happened to Colyer?' he asked quietly.

Forde paused, then he straightened up and drew a deep breath. 'Crashed coming back,' he said. ''E wasn't so 'ot on

Camels, y'know, and he never mastered those bloody trees. The bloody thing caught fire and there wasn't enough left to tell whether he'd been wounded first.' A spasm of anger and fear crossed his good-natured face. 'I 'ate it when they burn,' he said.

After tea they decided to go into Roye for a meal and Ira started up the Moto-Rêve, watched wistfully by Lucas and Milton. As they ate, he brought up the subject of the motor cycle.

'Are we going to include the two new boys in the combine?' he asked.

Forde shook his head. 'I reckon we'll keep it to ourselves,' he said slowly. 'It won't be the same without Colyer and Basil, and I find I 'ave greater need of it these days.'

He seemed faintly ashamed of the admission. 'Me!' he went on. 'I thought I was the sort that didn't *ever* get the 'ump. I knew I was no bloody militarist but I never thought I was the sort to start to crack.'

'You're not starting to crack,' Ira said, a little worried by his words.

Forde shrugged. 'I 'ad two nasty crashes,' he said. 'Two in a week. I ended up in No Man's Land after a scuffle with some particularly spiteful 'Uns and 'ad to wait there in a shell 'ole with a couple of stiffies till dark. I wanted to be sick. Then some rotten sod punctured one of me tyres in a fight and I turned a somersault when I landed. It shook me up a bit. I must be tireder than I thought.'

He gave a wan smile and Ira noticed there were dark circles under his eyes and that, despite his bulk, his face looked thinner and older than he remembered.

'I'm glad you're back, lad,' he said sincerely. 'It'll be comforting to have you around again. I've got a new feller called McKenna just behind me, and he's a bit of a win-the-war merchant and seems more eager to get 'Uns than look after my rear end.'

'Has he got any?'

'One. It was probably a mistake but it's made 'im all lustful for blood.' Forde sighed, despite his uniform, looking more like a farmer than a military man. 'I always think I'd 'ave done better in those medieval wars, when only the proletariat got killed and the officers never did anything 'alf so unpleasant as crossing swords.'

'The wars went on longer in those days, though,' Ira pointed out. 'Perhaps that's why. One lasted a hundred years.'

'Oh, well!' Forde smiled. 'I expect they pensioned you off when you'd done your forty years, and allowed you to go 'ome and dally with the maidens.' He paused. 'Did you see my Rachel, by the way?'

Ira felt guilty. 'Didn't have time,' he said. 'I read a book about farming, though.'

Forde didn't seem to hear him. ' 'Ow about young women?' he asked.

Ira hesitated, then he smiled. 'There was a corker lived next door.'

Forde eyed him stolidly. 'And did you?'

'Did I what?'

'I'm not going to write it in letters of gold for you, old sport,' Forde said. 'You know damn' well what "Did you?" means. We've discussed it often enough.'

Ira hesitated again. 'Yes, I did,' he said.

Forde eyed him sadly. 'Sunny Jim,' he said, 'you're the rottenest liar in Christendom. You didn't, did you?'

Ira frowned. 'How did you know?'

'Your face. It was like a shutter 'ad come down across it. Disappointment. Frustration. Anger. Bewilderment. Whatever you like. I can read you like a book.'

Ira described the whole week in detail, with all the frustrations brought about by Peggy Phillips' father, his own mother, and Stonehouse's missing girls. Forde almost fell off his chair laughing and his merriment seemed not only to bring him back to life but also put the week into its proper perspective. Ira began to laugh, too.

'Just wait till we get posted to 'Ome Establishment,' Forde said. 'We'll set the town alight. Dark-eyed 'ouris . . .'

'Dark-eyed what?'

'Houris. Much the same reelly as you were thinking about. Nautch girls . . .'

'What the hell are nautch girls?'

'They're interesting too.'

'Can you get 'em in England?'

Forde gestured. 'Mark II type. Paler in shade and per'aps a little obsessed with Mummy and Daddy and going to church and what the neighbours might think, but I believe there isn't much difference when they're stripped to the buff.' He lifted his glass. 'Here's to 'Ome Establishment! We'll have a flat somewhere, just you and me, where parents can't interfere, and start looking around for that farm. 'Ere's to it.'

'Here's to surviving,' Ira grinned.

Forde was suddenly sober. 'Amen to that, Sunny Jim,' he said.

7

It was growing cold in the evenings now and mist crept from the river bottoms between the knuckly hills to fill the huts with a smoky autumn smell and lie in the folds of the field, so that parked aeroplanes appeared to float without wheels on a sea of grey vapour. The mess fire wouldn't have warmed a rat and, as the huts grew damp, there was a perpetual hunt for fuel for the stoves.

There were several days of uneventful patrols, with rumours from the dying Battle of Passchendaele filtering down to them to make nonsense of the vast claims made in the newspapers that arrived from home.

'The 'ole bloody business seems ridiculous to me,' Forde said, staring bewilderedly at the map on the wall of the mess. 'All we've done is capture a village which isn't there any longer and push our way into a more dangerous salient than we 'ad before.'

It was clear to Ira that they'd not dodged much by moving south again because troops were already moving up to the front once more with guns and ammunition, and the rumbling of tanks was heard again in the evening. The hope he'd secretly entertained that perhaps the generals would lay low and reserve their diminished strength after the dragging failure in Flanders waned even further when orders came that ground-strafing practice was to start again.

'I wonder who's killed most of us,' Forde asked sourly. 'The 'Un or the General Staff?'

A week later at dinner Ira noticed ominously that Sillito had a brigadier with a toothbrush moustache as his guest and began discussing in whispers with Forde what it meant. It obviously meant something unpleasant and they both lost enthusiasm for the meal as they guessed that the brigadier was there to give them a pep-talk.

They were not surprised when orders contained the information that the attack was to start the next day. As soon as Sillito had finished, the brigadier got to his feet. He was a short fat man with purple cheeks and eyes like boiled blue marbles.

'It's up to you chaps,' he announced. 'This is the battle that's going to finish the Hun . . .'

'What again?' Forde murmured. 'They told us that last time. They've been telling us since 1914.'

They were awake until midnight, their thoughts occupied with the following morning as they studied special target maps marked in red, or worked at the hangars with the fitters and riggers to make sure their machines were ready.

They were supposed to be in the air by dawn, and as the klaxon woke them, they could hear a multitude of engines churning somewhere in the mist.

'Tanks,' Ira said, sitting with his head cocked. 'It's started.'

For once there was no barrage. This time the tanks were to go straight in without it and punch a hole a mile wide in the German line. They were briefed to bomb aerodromes, batteries and troops on the move, and despite mist and rain and a cloud base at not much more than a hundred feet, they took off in formation and flew east, never much more than fifty feet off the ground.

Following Wales blindly, trying to keep him in sight, they passed over masses of horsemen and infantry standing by white arrows laid out on the ground, then, as they swept over the trenches and the deep dug-out system of the Hindenburg Line, Ira saw that the barbed wire had been flattened where the tanks had forced their way through.

Almost at once he ran into a thick fog where the smoke screen mingled with the mist, and flashing overhead at ninety miles an hour, he caught brief pictures of grey dragging juggernauts followed by infantry that huddled in the blue-grey exhaust smoke. The clouds seemed to have sunk even lower by this time and they were having to skim low over the ground into a curling puther from smoke-shells that made his eyes sting.

Passing over trenches full of men in grey uniforms, they broke formation and climbed to drop their bombs. The whole earth below seemed to be enveloped already in smoke and leaping flashes of flame, then they were whirling about in the mist, within yards of each other as they tried to place their bombs and turn out of the blast to zoom away. In a split-second glimpse Ira saw two aircraft collide head-on with a smash that was almost like an explosion, then, locked together, they dropped like a stone into the smoke and he saw a flare of flame before he passed out of sight.

There was little hope of finding his target in the confusion and he released his bombs where he could. An aeroplane shot past him in the greyness, missing him by no more than a few yards, and while his heart was still thudding in his chest with fright, he almost hit a tree. Swerving violently, he took the top twigs off with his wheels and zoomed until he was clear of the smoke to catch his breath.

Glimpsing a column of men marching towards the battle, he headed further east and, joining another Camel, swooped down on them from behind, his guns rattling. The Germans returned his fire from the ditches and he saw splinters fly from his centre section and whip back over his head, and he began to be buffeted by the disturbed air from the explosions below into a wild rocking flight that was accompanied by flying lumps of wet mud. Bullets crackled about his ears as machine guns opened up and he saw the Camel on his right fall away in a steep turn that became a dive until it crashed among men who were still digging with their finger-nails and staring over their shoulders at it in fright, striking one wing first so that it whirled on to its nose and went rolling over and over like a catherine wheel in a scattering of wreckage.

He felt shocked and exhausted from the effort of holding the Camel at a reasonable level above the ground. Despite the cold, he was sweating profusely and, with his compass useless after all the twisting and turning, it was impossible to fix his position by the sun because of the murk. Lost, he climbed above the cloud again and began to head west, and almost immediately ran into a group of green-painted Pfalzes. They seemed as startled as he was but his reactions were quicker than theirs and, as one of them went down streaming smoke, he slipped beneath them through the cloud, his guns empty, to pick up the Bapaume–Amiens–Albert road and head home.

At Huyzes, dazed by the din and shaken by the confusion, everyone was counting noses. The machine-gun fire had worried them all and they were excited with barely hidden fear, putting on a noisy façade of gaiety to hide their uneasiness.

'You can't tell when they're shooting at you or from where,' English said loudly. 'And I swear to Christ they're getting better.'

'They're gettin' a lot of practice,' Forde pointed out dryly. 'I can't make out 'ow they didn't 'it me.'

Atwater's smile was just too wide and looked like a death's head grin. 'They must be rotten shots to miss anything as big as you,' he said. 'Try shaking yourself. See if anything drops out.'

The undamaged machines took off again as soon as they'd been patched, rearmed and refuelled, to do the whole thing all over again, not once but again and again until dark. The following day and the day after that were the same until Ira was nauseated by his own fear.

The sky remained hidden by low cloud and the ground obscured by mist. The fire was appalling and he watched with disbelieving eyes as Forde spiralled down into the smoke. He was convinced he was dead and couldn't think how to approach the future without him, suddenly realising he had always regarded Forde as he'd regarded his schoolboy heroes—mature wise boys whose ability, skill or courage he hadn't ever queried because they didn't get ink on their fingers or scuffle round the playing fields at lunch-time.

He was in a panic of worry about him, but by night-time Forde had returned, covered with mud, white of face and uncharacteristically edgy. Ira's greeting brought life into his sad, slow, shaken smile.

Their targets remained batteries, trenches and aerodromes, and they roared through the mist and rain whenever the weather let up sufficiently to allow them off the ground. Machines returned with leaves or the remains of telephone wires entangled with their undercarriages and Forde's edginess began to become nervous bad temper.

'They'll kill us all at this bloody rate,' he complained.

But the news that the tanks had broken through led Wing to insist that they flew, whatever the conditions, and the terrible excitement of success kept them going so that they continued to take off into the murk, hoping always that further east the weather would clear.

Most of their flying was done at no more than fifty feet, out of sight of the sun, and once more Forde vanished. One moment he was there and the next he was gone and, though he didn't believe it possible, wild thoughts that he had been picked off by some unseen German raced through Ira's head. Then Wales's engine started giving trouble and he had to turn back and Ira had to forget Forde to lead the remaining machines into the mist to drop bombs among the chaos of lorries, limbers and carts that was building up beyond Cambrai. But in the murk they became split up and he found himself alone and climbed out of the mist to find his bearings on his map.

As he circled, through a break in the cloud he spotted tanks below him and noticed they were not moving east any longer and that a lot of them appeared to be disabled. Nearby an RE8 slogged through the filth, the observer leaning over the side, marking the front line on his map, and for a while Ira watched a couple of Pfalzes which were making threatening moves towards it and went down finally in a curving dive to drive one of them into the ground. The observer of the RE8 waved thanks to him, silhouetted against the ragged sky and the low-driven clouds, then, even as Ira waved back, a shell hit the two-seater. There was a flash and a puff of smoke and a couple of dark objects tumbling downwards, then nothing else but a piece of wood and canvas twisting slowly to the ground.

Feeling sick, swearing loudly to himself in sheer terror, Ira went down again into the smoke. The air was bumpy with shell fire and the hitherto undamaged countryside seemed to be crumbling beneath the barrage as houses fell apart like collapsed piles of children's bricks. An explosion lifted his tail and he regained control with difficulty, aware that the whole left side of the fuselage had been somehow stripped bare of fabric, then holes appeared in his wing and a flying wire broke with a twang like a double bass.

The machine was rattling and clattering now like a can full of stones and before he could swerve to avoid it he saw he was diving straight into a machine-gun nest. In a panic he kicked at the rudder bar so that he wasn't going the way his nose was pointing, in the hope of putting the gunners off their aim, but more splinters flew and more fragments of fabric began to flap, then oil sprayed into his face and a frightful grinding started somewhere in the engine as the machine began to vibrate as though about to fall to pieces.

His ears filled with the wail of flying wires, he saw a gap in the smoke between two trees and headed for it and, deciding to take a chance on not being strapped in, he unclipped the buckles of his harness. Just as he did so, there was a crash and the sound of splintering wood and twanging wires as his wings were ripped off, then the fuselage, with Ira still inside it, was bouncing along the ground, the undercarriage wiped clean away, until it came to rest in a hedge bottom.

He scrambled out and dived headfirst into a ditch. There were several British soldiers there, cowering from the showers of dirt and stones the shells were throwing up.

'You crashed, sonny?' someone shouted in his ear and, half-crying with rage, fright and self-pity, he turned on the speaker in a fury.

'No, you bloody idiot, I always land like that! And don't call me "Sonny"!'

For some time, covered with guilt at his rudeness and shame at his fright, he cowered from the awful concussion of the shells, each iron clang seeming to lift his feet from the ground, then the sergeant in charge decided they'd have to bolt for better cover.

'The wall there,' he said, pointing, and they all leapt from the ditch and began to run, Ira struggling along in a daze of fear in his heavy flying boots. A shell fell just behind them and a corporal running alongside him went head over heels like a shot rabbit. Terrified, Ira stopped because the sergeant stopped, and they half carried, half dragged the corporal after the others. Flopping down in the shelter of the wall, blown and gasping, Ira looked at the sergeant, his face grimy, wanting to bury himself in the earth for safety.

'Thanks, sir,' the sergeant said. 'Unfortunately, I don't think he's going to make it.'

The man they'd rescued had been hit between the shoulders and was already turning grey, and after a while he died. The sergeant seemed satisfied with his new position, however, but Ira had recovered his wits by this time and had decided it was safer flying and that he ought to try to get back to Huyzes.

The shelling slackened off a little eventually and thankfully he began to head for the rear. As he began to realise he was out of danger, he remembered again that Forde had vanished and began to feel sick with worry. Though he made him feel like an awkward colt most of the time, Forde's solid farmer's air of knowledge, good sense and imperturbability was also helping him to grow out of a clumsy adolescence without pain.

Falling in with a wounded officer, he saw him delivered to a dressing station that almost turned his stomach over. But someone gave him a mugful of whisky which made him feel better and he forced himself to search among the wounded for Forde. He was told there was a pilot among them somewhere and he pushed his way through the misery until he found a boy of his own age who had broken both his legs in a crash and was writhing in agony.

He turned away, his worry heavy in his mind, and set off towards Huyzes. Then, as he reached the main road, he saw a bulky shape just in front, limping a little and also heading west.

'Toby!'

The man in front turned and, running heavily in his flying boots, Ira caught him up and they fell joyfully into each other's arms.

Back at Huyzes, since they had no machines, they were told to report to Candas to collect two new Camels, but during the evening news came in that the Germans were hitting back and that every available pilot was to be used to stop them. Immediately, Sillito decided to send two new arrivals to Candas instead and Ira and Forde were given their machines to fly.

Forde sighed, 'I'll be 'appy when the bloody battle's over,' he said wearily.

The torment went on for another week that left Ira edgy and morose. Ground-strafing was too much a matter of luck. It was impossible to tell from hour to hour where the front-line troops were and it was only possible to identify the uniforms of the men firing round the angles of broken walls from low down where they were just as likely to be the wrong ones.

'You can't dodge,' Wales said bitterly. 'Some of those bloody staff types who're so keen on ground-strafing ought to come and try it occasionally.'

He was white-faced and strained-looking these days and he had grown so tense he refused any longer to live in the same hut as Atwater. 'I just can't stand his bloody singing any more,' he announced.

They were all touchy with sheer weariness by this time. Dislikes became more marked and men whirled on each other in unexpected bursts of temper. Others who had been friends ever since flying school stopped talking to each other and just as unexpectedly made up their quarrel again. Emotionally and physically they were spent. It was an easy fact for Ira to face because they all felt the same.

They looked like ghosts and moved like drugged bees and the growing suspicion that the offensive was going the same way as all the others, after all, made them bitter with the grinding fatigue.

'Bloody staff,' Forde said. 'Made a mess of it as usual.'

He was sitting on his bunk, staring at the floor, the grey cordite marks still on his chin, his eyes empty of anything but weariness and hopelessness, a cigarette hanging from his limp fingers. He looked drained of energy, a vast shapeless bulk in his flying clothes.

Ira stared at him from his own bunk, conscious of the nag of anxiety for him. Until the last few days he had felt that nothing could happen to Forde, but now he wasn't so sure and couldn't see how he could protect him. The fear was aggravated by exhaustion and by a cynicism and a callousness towards death that he'd never felt on his last tour of duty. It worried him a great deal and he realised that what at first had been less fear than sheer unwillingness to risk his neck had gradually become a dumb weariness at the repetitious chancing of his life and finally the accepted misery of wind-up.

'If *you* feel like that,' Forde said, 'what must the rest of us feel like?'

'What makes *me* so different?' Ira demanded.

Forde sighed. 'I dunno,' he said. 'But something does. You 'it what you shoot at for a start.'

'I'm still scared,' Ira said.

Forde managed a slow twisted smile back at him. 'Well, if a lad like you, who's smart with his guns and flies like a sparrer with a moggy after it—if *you* can get the wind-up, what about me? With me, it's a regular gale.'

Ira frowned. 'It's not knowing where the bullets are coming from,' he said.

'*And* the low flying and not knowing whether the next tree you see's going to be the one you 'it. *And* the mist that stops you seein' it in time.'

Warburton, the batman, put his head round the door. 'Something's happening, sir,' he announced. 'The major's got a visitor. Staff, looks like.'

'Bloody staff,' Forde said again. 'Oughta 'ave all been drowned when they were still pups.'

A few moments later the klaxon sounded and they rose wearily, reaching for their gloves and helmets.

'This one'll be all right,' Forde said doggedly, trying to smile. 'This one'll be easy.'

It turned out to be a disaster. Two men were lost, one flying into the ground and the other simply disappearing into the mist. Forde's reaction was heavy humour as he pretended to fill in what he called his standard letter for C.O.s writing to bereaved parents.

'Dear Sir, Madame or Miss, as the case may be. I regret to inform you that your son is dead, missing, believed to be a prisoner of war. Cross out what is not necessary. He was very popular, fairly popular, most unpopular. Take your pick and apply pen. His end was regretted, cheered, quite unnoticed. He has not paid his mess bill and a cheque would be most welcome.'

'Suppose he has?' Ira asked.

Forde shrugged. 'It could go into the mess fund to keep the rest of us in drink.'

The act seemed to revive their spirits a little, but the laughter was short-lived, because Sillito arrived with the news that the offensive they'd been supporting had failed.

'So much for the final battle,' Forde said sadly.

After all the disastrous offensives of the past, reserves had not been ready for the tanks' speedy advance and the Germans had been able to stop the cavalry in its tracks when it had finally arrived.

'So now we're going to have to do it all again in reverse.' Sillito's high frosty voice was bitter. 'Because the Germans are mounting a counter-attack against the bulge we've made.'

8

Like all attacks, the German counter-move also came to nothing and finally both sides were back where they'd started, exhausted by casualties and the destruction they'd caused.

'All for nothing!' Forde said heavily. 'All those fine fellers killed! All that damage done! What a bloody fine effort!'

As they drew breath, thankful to find themselves alive, flurries of snow began to fall, turning the ground white. Eventually, it changed to sleet and the earth was covered with a grey slush that was icy cold in the biting wind. Towards the west, as the fighting eased off, they could still hear rifle and machine-gun fire and occasionally groups of tanks lumbered past the field from the parks in the rear on their way to the front.

The weather remained bitterly cold, with more snow flurries from time to time, and the countryside became drab with winter. In the middle of the gloom the M.C. for which Sillito had recommended Ira came through, together with one for English and one for Atwater, and the awards were made the occasion for a celebration.

Forde scrounged the ribbon from Stoke's best tunic and took Ira's jacket to one of the riggers for it to be sewn on. Milton and Lucas were too awed to comment on it.

'It's like a rash,' Forde explained to them gravely as they gaped. 'Once you get the disease, it spreads all over your body, and you start sproutin' 'em at every corner. Until you get the infection you remain dull in plumage, but once it starts, you get so your friends 'ave to shade their eyes.'

He gave Ira his French general's kiss. 'For the honour of

the Bull and Bush,' he said. 'It's nice to see 'em around—even if they're only on your friends. At least, it means one less that the staff 'ave bagged for themselves.'

There was a wildly determined air about the drinking because they were celebrating not only the awards but the respite from the killing and their own survival. Atwater headed determinedly for the piano and, leaning heavily on Forde's shoulder, worried his way through *The Toreador's Song* as though he felt the stirring words referred to him personally. Forde turned to Ira as he stopped.

'I wish 'e'd sprain his tonsils,' he muttered.

The noisy ballads started, but as they yelled them at the tops of their voices they were only scoffing at their own routine of daily hazard and reducing the possibility of a messy end to the level of a schoolboy jingle. The tunes Forde played were more nostalgic than in the past, though, and less noisy than they'd once been and Ira noticed that when English and a few others bore down on him for his upside-down act he brushed them away with the excuse that he had a headache. English didn't seem to mind. He was very drunk and was telling a story about an American he knew who'd been given the M.C., but who, as he'd joined his own air force since, wasn't sure whether he ought to wear it with his new uniform or not.

'Any guy who's gone through what I went through to get this,' he announced firmly, 'has the right to wear it in his goddam bath if he feels like it.'

Forde's attempt to get Ira drunk failed miserably because Ira kept pouring the drink back into Forde's glass and in the end it was Forde who ended up worse for wear. Pushing the determined Atwater away from the piano, he took the front off with slow deliberate movements and began to pick out a tune. By this time, however, his fingers were clumsy and, in the end, shaking with frustration, he raised his huge fists to his shoulders and brought them down with all his strength. There was a pained twang from the piano and one of the felt hammers leapt out through the strings on to his lap.

Everyone was hooting with laughter as Ira pulled him away.

The hammer dropped to the floor and he tossed it back into the piano and struggled with Forde to the Bull and Bush.

'Why can you do everything better than I can?' Forde asked hollowly as Ira lifted his legs on to his bed. 'You can even drink better than I can and you're only a lad.'

'That's just the point,' Ira said. 'I can't. I pour it in the flower vases. Haven't you noticed how the flowers in front of me always wilt?'

Forde was owlish now. '*Your* new gong's better than those other fellers',' he said. 'They only got theirs for long service. You got yours for 'eroic action against the enemy.'

'You're drunk,' Ira pointed out.

Forde grinned. 'Me temples are clanging together like cymbals,' he agreed. 'I find I like to get drunk these days, though. I sleep better. I think those two kids think I'm a howling coward. I'm not, am I?'

'Just terror-stricken, like the rest of us.'

Forde smiled tiredly. 'From you, that's all right. I'll be glad when they post me 'ome, all the same, lad. I'm fine when I'm flying, but I'm a nervous wreck when I'm not.'

It was raining the following morning and, sitting up in bed, grey-faced and heavy-eyed, Forde was overjoyed.

'One day nearer 'Ome Establishment,' he said. 'One day nearer being able to live without risking my precious 'ide against the 'Un.'

To his disgust, the cloud began to lift by breakfast-time and during the morning it broke up completely and patches of blue sky appeared.

'Flying's on,' Wales announced sourly. 'A Flight's got the morning job. We're up after lunch.'

'Thank God the days are short,' Forde said. 'Eighteen hours a day flying weather like we 'ad in the summer got me down.'

A Flight took off almost immediately and C Flight were to leave as they returned.

'That's the worst of this job,' Forde commented heavily.

'We go over the top twice a day and three times on Sundays. Your nerves expand and contract like watch springs.'

They left the field as A Flight appeared on the eastern horizon and Wales led them towards Moy. The cold purity of the air lifted Ira's heart. Beneath the blue arc of the sky the majesty of the cumulus reflected the sun in a dazzling light, full of fire and shadow, with tremendous towering heights, pile on pile of them, all of them unbelievably splendid. Everybody on both sides of the line seemed to have been caught unawares by the unexpected break in the weather and the sky was empty. Wales led them in and out of cloud formations, looking for lurking two-seaters that might be trying to sneak over the lines under its cover.

As they turned back towards Huyzes, Ira spotted a faint movement below them near Cerizy, and moving alongside Wales, rocked his wings and pointed. It was a group of Pfalzes which seemed to make no attempt to save themselves and before they knew what had happened Wales and Forde sent two down in flop-winged dives, while Ira's target disintegrated in a puff of smoke and flames. Nauseated, he saw the pilot drop clear, turning over and over to float on the air as though he were swimming, his size dwindling to nothing as he vanished beneath them.

They had all seen the incident and they were subdued as they landed. Forde was frowning heavily and Ira was silent. Wales was noisily talkative.

'Air superiority,' he said. 'That's what does the trick. Not skill. Just air superiority.'

'Fat lot of satisfaction that'll give that bloke that jumped,' Forde growled. 'And in any case by tomorrow *we*'ll probably be jumping because the 'Uns 'ave brought out some new and 'orrible engine of war that's given *them* air superiority.'

Wales frowned and turned away quickly and Forde eyed him sadly as he headed for his hut. 'It's time the Low-Wing Monoplane flew 'ome,' he said. 'It's not the fear of death that's worrying 'im, it's the constant flinching from it. I know. I feel like that, too.'

The following morning the weather was clear again and bitterly cold and remained so for the whole of the week. English, the American, was posted to Home Establishment and, though he was thinking of joining his own air force, he, like Courtney, had heard strange stories of majors transferring from the infantry and being set over men who'd been flying for months.

Ira shot down another Pfalz in a skirmish over St Quentin and, late in the evening, accompanied by Forde, crashed a two-seater near Belle Eglise. When he offered to share the score, Forde shook his head.

'Keep it, lad,' he said. 'If we're going to win this war, *somebody's* got to do it and you're much more efficient at it than I am.'

The fighting seemed to have entered a phase of consolidation after Cambrai, but the winter days failed to halt flying, and A and B Flights lost men in a series of running fights. Always it was the new unknown men who seemed to go, but their departure still unsettled Ira. Even after three and a half years of war he hadn't yet got used to the indignity of death and all too often was close enough to see his friends mutilated, burned or crushed.

Forde tried hard to stand on the sidelines, uninvolved, making his comments in his heavy good-humoured way, but Ira noticed that suddenly his remarks were more cynical and sharper-toned. He was under treatment for stomach pains now, but he still drank heavily and was too lethargic to do anything else but read magazines. Although he received regular letters from his widow in London, he wrote few in return.

'The spirit don't even move me to try,' he admitted. 'I think some of the stuffing's leaked outa me somewhere.'

He had lost the heavy colour from his cheeks and there were shadows of washed blue under his brows, and sometimes, when he didn't realise he was being watched, Ira saw a white edge come into his eyes.

When the Wing medical officer arrived on one of his visits, Ira tackled him. 'Why can't he go home?' he demanded.

'He can. But he won't.' The doctor was an Irishman and

sentimental about courage. 'Like so many of you, he's afraid of letting the side down.'

The following day was Ira's day off and Wales took the flight off without him. He got up late and answered a letter from Peggy Phillips, careful not to commit himself to too much enthusiasm, and the letter was lame and an effort to write. When he'd finished, he dragged the Moto-Rêve from its stand and rode into Montdidier. He returned just as C Flight appeared over the trees at the end of the field. Sillito and Stoke and a few others were counting the machines as they dropped from the broken cloud.

'One—two—three . . .' Sillito stopped and glanced at Stoke. No more machines appeared and he turned and began to walk quickly towards the hangar, a long ungainly figure lost in loneliness.

The Camels had obviously been in a fight. They were trailing wires and torn fabric and as they arrived the ambulance roared up and mechanics and orderlies began to lift Wagner from his cockpit. Sillito was looking round for Wales.

' 'E won't be coming back.' Forde's heavy face was sick-looking and drawn. 'They jumped us. Mixed Albatroses and Tripes. I think it must have been Richthofen's mob.'

'They went north after the counter-attack.'

'Well, they must 'ave left a few be'ind to 'old the fort because they all seemed to be red. There was smoke going down over Cambrai, so that must have been Wales, because McKenna went into the river. Full engine. I thought something must 'ave 'appened to Wagner the way he was flying. Will he be all right?'

Sillito shrugged. 'Better come to the office and make your report. Wing'll be interested to know the Circus has moved into this area. They might even offer us some help.'

When Forde had finished making out the report, Sillito gave him a cigarette. 'Pity about Wales,' he said. 'You'll have to take over his job.'

Forde frowned and said nothing. After a while he sat up. 'I've 'eard there's better, sir,' he said slowly.

Sillito stared at him over his thin red nose and Forde went on. 'I haven't got what you'd call an impressive score,' he pointed out.

'Can't be helped.' Sillito frowned. 'We'll have to replace Wales from the squadron. They're so busy forming new outfits in England for the spring offensives, there'll be no experienced men from there.'

'How about young Penaluna?' Forde asked. 'He makes me look like an amateur.'

Sillito began to pull at Monkey Brand's ears. 'I considered him,' he admitted. 'He can do it, and he'll be taking over when you go home.' He paused and his hand moved slowly over the dog's neck. 'Even so, he's only a boy.'

'Boys are running squadrons these days,' Forde said doggedly. 'Give it to him. I don't want it. Responsibility'll make him grow up.'

'You realise you're giving up a third pip and more pay? I thought you deserved them before you went home.'

Forde smiled. 'Me life's of more concern to me at the moment than promotion,' he said. 'And I'd be responsible for a lot of fellers I don't feel fitted to protect. I'd love to think I'm a born leader, but I'm not. I'm a born led.'

'You did that,' Ira accused Forde when he returned from Sillito's office.

'Dessay I did,' Forde agreed. 'But 'oo else is there? Only me, still ploughin' round the 'eavens like a fart in a bottle, trying to do some damage. Forget it, lad, you were born to be a 'ero, so let's hear those stentorian commands ring out. It don't make you a general, so your pals'll still speak to you.'

He seemed a little concerned that Ira might wish to move out of the hut.

'Not me,' Ira said, and Forde grinned.

'Well, I didn't think you'd want to share with Atwater,' he agreed. 'Not with his bloody caterwauling.'

The thought of being responsible for all the other men in the flight—not just occasionally but all the time—brought Ira to earth with a jolt and it struck him as strange that despite his youth and troublesome virginity, he had the yea or nay of older men's lives.

There was a lot of cloud about the following day that could hide an enemy and the sky between the white piles of cumulus was clear and steely-blue. It was the sort of morning when trouble could arrive fast and Ira called everyone into the hangar to explain what he intended to do. He went through all the signals for the newcomers and, remembering the mistakes he'd made himself in the past, took the trouble to explain to the men who'd taken the places of Wales, McKenna and Wagner what to do if they had a gun stoppage or engine trouble, and how to tackle a two-seater as a flight. Afterwards he drew Forde to one side.

'Think it made sense?' he asked.

'More than I've 'eard for a long time,' Forde said with a smile. 'I 'ope you shoot down thousands of 'Uns and bring the war to an abrupt end. I daresay we've all got a better chance if we forget the usual sporting approach and decide what the 'Un had for breakfast before we start.'

Ira watched carefully as they prepared for take-off, anxious that no one should get into anyone else's slipstream, and at ten thousand feet he turned south, still climbing along the lines. There were a few groups of fighters about, but he carefully avoided action with them until, over La Fère, he saw a swarm of triplanes heading for a couple of RE8s and dived on them, firing while still out of range to frighten them away.

There were Lafayette Spads over Moy worrying a two-seater and, squinting into the sun, Ira saw a glittering of wings that turned into another group of triplanes waiting their opportunity. He affected not to see them and continued on his course until he saw them make their move. Then, as the triplanes pounced, he rocked his wings and went down after them.

The Spads were still busy driving the two-seater to the ground and the triplanes, as intent on their prey as the Spads, didn't see the Camels diving almost vertically on to them. Before they could do any damage, C Flight were among them and the triplane in front of Ira went down in a spin that ended abruptly as the wings folded up and it fluttered down like a scrap of crumpled paper, trailing blue smoke, fragments of wood and fabric breaking off to spiral down after it. A second machine never pulled out of its dive and Ira saw it disappear into the Oise with a tremendous splash.

It turned out to be a good day for the squadron generally and, going out late in the last light of the afternoon, Ira knocked down a lonely Pfalz.

'I think they're getting worse,' Forde said. 'It must be because they push all their best men into the hot-stuff outfits.'

The following week brought several vicious skirmishes with the Richthofen Circus and two more men disappeared. Then, towards the end of the week, Courtney turned up again. He seemed to pop in and out of Ira's life like the Demon King in a pantomime.

'I've come to bring thanks from our outfit for your help the other day,' he said. 'And to ask you down for a celebration. It's nearly Christmas and Nungesser's with us.'

The Americans had hired a Frenchwoman to do the cooking and she produced *coq au vin* in the best style, with more wine than any of them could drink. Cheerful jeers and insults were flung across the table in both French and English, and a dispute arose as to whether or not the Camel was better than the French Spad, and they swopped machines to try them out, and Ira found himself being challenged by a French major to a mock duel with Nungesser.

Nungesser, a sturdy blond man with scars on his face, gold-fenced teeth and decorations that seemed to hang to his knees, was unconcerned, but Courtney was eager to show off his prowess, and Ira was pushed forward unwillingly. Because of his injuries, they had to lift the Frenchman into his machine, but he took off in a climbing turn that seemed to indicate there was nothing wrong with his flying.

It was noticeably colder as they flew back to Huyzes and Ira cowered out of the draught in the deep cockpit. That night he was glad to leave the hut to sit in the mess where there was a huge fire. He began to look forward to Christmas, and Lucas and Milton, the two new pilots in the Bull and Bush, began to make paper trimmings and hang them from the corners of the hut. Two days later, however, Lucas was forced down behind the German lines after a brush with the Richthofen Circus, and the following day Milton vanished, too.

Forde, who had begun to count the days to his posting home, crossed his fingers quickly and wrenched down the trimmings as though they were some evil fetish.

'Poor little bastards,' he said thickly. 'A fat lot of good *their* Christmas spirit did 'em.'

It was suddenly hard to stir him out of his gloom. Take-offs and landings had become for him part of a tired old legend which aged him daily. He was often sick, too, and was drinking doses of chlorodyne before every flight to counteract the effects of the castor-oil fumes from the engine.

Now that he was so close to his posting home, everyone was trying to help him, and Ira gave up his days off so he could watch him in the air.

Cheered, Forde went through his log book, totting up everything he had done since arriving in France. 'Three 'undred and twenty-eight hours,' he announced solemnly. 'Including fifty-odd on One-and-a-half-strutters. I've laid my 'ead on the block ninety-seven times over the lines and been in forty-odd fights, and shot down seven 'Uns including all the little bits. I dessay I've earned my keep.'

Winter arrived with a vengeance and blizzards clawed at the huts. Snow blocked the roads and made life miserable because it became impossible to obtain coal for the stoves, and all traffic stopped because the lanes were full of drifts. Ira wore his flying boots and scarves in the hut and waited for the disaster that the wretched weather seemed to presage. Patrols had become an agony because the cold affected the guns so that they refused to fire, and he sat in the sky so frozen he didn't care what happened to him.

Everybody was set to work shovelling to keep the hangars

and a strip of runway clear, but when they took off rime blew off the surface of the wings into the faces of the mechanics leaning on the tails, and there was a series of accidents due to frozen engines.

Icy moss hung on the stone walls and the sky was leaden, with flocks of black crows hovering over the countryside in the flurries of snow. Huyzes-le-Grand seemed deserted, its roofs stark against the sky, the slushy snow hidden by the mist. Water pipes split and threw petrified fountains down the walls and, with the coal running out and the marshy ground in the valleys covered with starred puddles of ice and the wind cutting like a razor in thirteen degrees of frost, the Bull and Bush became the coldest place on God's earth.

Christmas Eve came in a whirl of snowflakes and they took off for the afternoon patrol from a field bleakly marked by wheels and skids. They were twelve strong, twelve drab blunt machines rising and falling as they hurtled through the grey afternoon light, moving up and down like horses on a roundabout as they fought in a gusty wind to hold formation.

The afternoon was heavy with low-bellied clouds like wet sails, majestic and threatening and filled with purple valleys and icy pinnacles. Ivory castles were set above dark chasms full of secret pathways and, below, Ira caught fragmentary glimpses of the squared hedgerows against the snow, and black ruins sticking up out of the whiteness like broken teeth among the scars of the trenches. It was possible to pick out everything—lorry parks, dumps, even latrines—simply by the tracks around them, and the trenches were sharp zigzag lines cut through the whiteness.

They climbed higher and higher, picking their way like mountaineers among the towering clouds, with only odd glimpses of a corner of a wood, a winding river, or a broken township emerging beyond the misty edges of the cloud beneath them.

Ira's eyes roved restlessly about the reaches of the sky. He was heavily conscious of the nearness of Forde's home posting and was eager not to him have come to harm, and his eyes were alert for the black slow-shifting specks against the cloud or the sky, or the brief shadows against the land which probably meant death.

Eventually, Atwater saw a group of twelve Albatroses below and fired a Very light to draw attention to them. Immediately, Ira's breath came faster and the hairs on his hands began to prickle with the old sensation of hollowness in his stomach which he knew was fear. He shifted direction slightly, hands and feet moving against throttle and rudder as he glanced backwards to make surc the aeroplanes behind him were closed up. He could see the black crosses on the machines below now but he held on to his patience, listening as everyone behind him tested his guns, then Atwater rocked sideways as a signal that everyone should pick his target and dropped out of the sky like a stone.

The earth raced towards them as they fell, and as Ira fired the Albatroses wheeled and scattered, his target dropping out of the fight at once, streaming smoke. Tracers criss-crossed the area where they had been and he pulled his shuddering machine from the dive, twisting his head right and left, trying to watch his own men and keep an eye on the enemy at the same time.

Then he saw that a bunch of Albatros DVs had joined the fight and his heart thudded in his chest as he recognised them immediately from the red paint they wore as the Richthofen Circus.

Inevitably the size of the battle drew in other protagonists and a squadron of SEs smashed through the middle of the mêlée, then another flight of Albatroses and yet another until the sky was full of aeroplanes. Ruddering wildly, he saw an Albatros chased by an SE, which in its turn was followed by another Albatros painted all red. The first Albatros burst into flames and plunged towards the earth, but, even as it pulled out of its dive, the SE staggered under the blast from the guns of the all-red machine. Skidding about the sky in a maniac fashion, he found himself face to face with an Albatros and he could see the winking flashes from its guns and fragments leaping from his centre section. If he turned away he knew he would present an excellent target, but at the last moment it was the Albatros which wavered, and he saw his own tracer striking it, and it dropped below him in a fluttering spin then turned over on its back and fell towards the cloud through the twilit sky.

The fight was scattered over an area two miles wide now. An SE, followed by two Germans, wheeled below him, then, finding a scrap of rising mist, plunged into it and, dropping on top of the searching Albatroses, Ira saw one of them fall near the river through a gap in the haze.

The clouds were drawing closer together now, as though the night were pulling the curtains across a stage at the end of a performance, and the flashes of the guns below flickered through the dusk. Above them, the last of the light was catching the summits of the mountains of mist, and the sky, with all the debris of battle cleared, was calm, unmoved and untainted by the war, unheeding, superb and beautiful.

As they turned for home, hedge-hopping at tree-top height, Ira saw three or four fires burning on the ground which he knew were aircraft, and they landed at Huyzes, throwing up clouds of snow from their slipstreams as they taxied across the field towards the hangars. As they crowded together, they were all grateful to be alive, and noisy with triumph.

'Where did they all come from?' Forde asked. 'I reckon God musta been watching over me to bring me through a fight like that.'

As they talked, Sillito arrived to say that five German machines had been reported downed, and the three that Ira had destroyed had all been identified. Only one man from Atwater's flight was missing and he had already telephoned to say he was safe. Forde began rubbing his hands at the prospect of the celebration.

Ira was still trembling from the excitement when they reached the mess. B Flight was round the fire making toast and drinking anything but tea and when the missing man turned up soon afterwards, they were so grateful to be able to celebrate Christmas without a ghost at the feast, a tremendous party started. Forde was drunk early in the proceedings and Ira and a visiting doctor from Wing put him to bed, his broad features set in the death-mask of a whole dying generation. He woke just after midnight, muttering with a nightmare, and as Ira lit his lamp, he saw him lying on his pillow looking strained and ill.

'I think I'm losing me revs a bit, lad,' he said.

On Christmas morning, with the wind rattling the stovepipe, Ira was awakened by Forde shouting that it was snowing again and that they'd be able to celebrate properly without having to worry about flying. He seemed almost himself again and they sat up together, yelling greetings, to find the windows plastered with white and the field covered with mist.

There was a church parade during the morning that Ira tried to dodge, but Sillito had a regular soldier's attitude to such things and his thin red nose poked into all the corners to dig out the shirkers, his narrow face disapproving as Ira tried to offer an excuse. Ira was a little bitter that he should be such a stickler for regulations at such a time, but as they returned to the mess, Stoke brought the news that Sillito had been posted and was to leave at once for a job at Wing. Immediately, Ira changed his opinion of him and Stoke even began to tell a story of how in 1915, as an instructor, he'd fallen heavily for a female charity worker and had hired out an R.F.C. trainer for joy-rides on behalf of a local hospital. It didn't sound much like the sober, frosty-faced Sillito, but Ira gave him the benefit of the doubt now that he was leaving and there were last drinks at the bar and hurried handshakes, then he was gone, and the absence of his disapproving stare made them all behave like schoolboys for the rest of the morning.

Christmas dinner was late because the mess sergeant was also taking advantage of Sillito's departure and was drunk, and watched the serving of the meal leaning in the doorway at what appeared to be a forty-five-degree angle. The turkey was tepid and the bread sauce cold and they drank flat champagne and port that tasted of shellac, and only the sergeant's incredible list enabled him to get away with his crime because Forde began to lay bets on how many more drinks it would take to bring him down. They forgot the indifferent meal in the enthusiasm of the wager and the sergeant finally went down with a crash as Forde offered him a fourth whisky.

While they were polishing off the port, Forde, who was in a wild mood, had the idea of getting the ducks off the neighbouring pond drunk and before long he had them crash-landing at full revs into the bushes alongside the mess. They played noisy Snap at a franc a call until someone announced that the mechanics were giving an impromptu concert in one of the hangars and they streamed across the field to watch it. There were songs on the banjo, harmonies and jokes that grew weaker and smuttier as the concert progressed, then despite the cold, the squadron blacksmith stripped to the waist to show a muscular white torso, did a few strongman acts and offered to let all comers punch him in the stomach. The mechanics sent up the smallest of their number, who lashed out viciously before the blacksmith had his muscles deployed and they had to carry him to the sick bay to bring him round.

The bar was open when they assembled in the mess again. Forde was still drinking heavily, his great face wreathed in smiles and a dangerous look in his eye that worried Ira.

'Next week'll be 1918,' he said. '1918, lad, and if my relief comes before the spring offensives I might still be alive at the end of it.'

Towards tea-time the weather cleared a little and a few pilots went up, dragging a veil of snow behind them as they took off to stunt over Huyzes-le-Grand for the benefit of the villagers. Then, as they were all beginning to gather in the mess again for more drinks, Forde was called to the telephone. A few minutes later, as they were grouping themselves round the stove, they heard an engine start by the hangars. Ira assumed it was one of the flight-sergeants working at a recalcitrant engine in an excess of zeal and took no notice, but a few moments later he heard an aeroplane take off.

The doctor from Wing strolled to the door to look. Two seconds later he reappeared.

'Come and look at this!' he said.

They streamed outside into the biting cold. One of the sergeants was standing nearby staring at a Camel that was just pulling out of a dive into a loop. As it reached the summit of its climb, it half-rolled and came streaking down towards the mess.

'Who is it, for God's sake?' Atwater asked, a bottle of whisky still in his fist.

The doctor frowned. 'The sergeant says it's Forde. The stupid clown'll kill himself!'

After all the past days of watching him like a hawk, after the tremendous fight the night before, Ira's heart went cold as he watched. The Camel was hurtling towards them now at full speed and it zoomed up over them with a roar that set the windows shaking. At the top of its climb, it turned and dived again and they all flung themselves flat on their faces as it roared over them, its wheels just above their heads, its slip-stream blowing a cloud of snow into their eyes. As they lifted their heads, it banked round the trees at the end of the field and came howling back.

Ira stared at it narrow-eyed, then, as the Camel came hurtling back at him, he flung himself flat again, to jump up as though he were on springs, surrounded by whirling snow, as it passed overhead.

One of the squadron lorries was coming from the village and, as the Camel flashed towards it, they saw the driver jump out and run, and the Camel leapt over the lorry and turned at the end of the field for another run. As it howled towards them, the noise set up a hare in the middle of the field, and the Camel turned to chase it. As it banked, just above the ground, a wing-tip touched in a puff of snow.

'Oh God!' Atwater jerked out.

The Camel began to wobble in a horrifying manner and as they started to run, it levelled off, banged down, and began to slide sideways across the field, shedding undercarriage, wings and tail in flying fragments. Gouging a great wound in the turf, it finally slithered to a stop, the fuselage practically denuded.

As they came to a panting stop alongside the remains, they saw Forde's huge frame huddled in the cockpit, dressed only in his uniform despite the cold. They pulled him out, working frantically, and laid him in the snow. There was a great gash in his cheek that had laid his teeth bare and Atwater shoved through them with his bottle of whisky, pushed his head back and poured the spirit into his mouth. It promptly ran out through his cheek, and Forde came to life with a jerk, spluttering and gasping.

'You bloody idiot!' Ira said, almost in tears as the ambulance screamed up. 'You might have killed yourself.'

'Not me!' Forde was shaking with laughter that scattered huge drops of blood on his uniform. 'I'm unkillable, lad! I've survived! That was Sillito on the telephone. He rang up like a real gent to put me outa my misery. My relief's here! I've finished flying.'

Ira felt like hitting him with Atwater's bottle. 'And in bloody fine style,' he snorted.

Forde lay back against Atwater's knee, his torn face livid as the doctor worked over him, a vast smile on his lips.

''Ome,' he said. ''Ome! Bein' alive! Bein' alive when the war ends! Ever thought of that, lad? It's like 'aving your future given back to you when you thought it 'ad been taken away. It's like finding you're alive when you'd decided you were dead. Still'—he raised his head and grinned as they lifted the stretcher into the ambulance—'I oughta known better than try to dogfight with a bloody rabbit. They're more manœuvrable than a Camel at that 'eight.'

Part Three The Friendless Sky

I

If anything, London seemed more different than ever. Piccadilly seemed to contain only foreigners and prostitutes, but there was remarkably little gaiety and it was even hard to get drunk because there didn't seem to be any drink anywhere. The newspapers, when they weren't conducting their win-the-war campaigns, were issuing firm resolves on behalf of the nation, grim warnings and dour expressions of determination. 'Carry on' seemed to be the catchword now.

By this time, almost every family in the country had had experience of death, either at first hand or through friends or relatives, and there seemed only women, old men and children left. Apart from businessmen—and there seemed an enormous number of them in London—everybody else seemed to be in the Army, and their places had been taken by Americans, but nobody seemed to care very much and it didn't make much difference.

After the fiasco of Cambrai nobody believed in anything any more. Russia was out of the war and the French Army was said to be still in a state of mutiny, which more than balanced the arrival of the Americans, and the only thing people seemed to hope for now was that the war would die of sheer inanition.

Ira wasn't sorry to be home. Stoke had followed Sillito to Wing and Atwater had vanished to England shortly afterwards, leaving him the oldest member of the mess, and it had been a sobering business when he'd tried to remember the men who'd been at Huyzes when he'd arrived. He'd found that he could recall nothing but shadowy forms and hollow voices and only a few had stood out in his mind.

With promotion had come an extended tour, an unexpected D.S.O., and another medal from a vague Belgian dignitary; and a burst of good flying weather had pushed up his score swiftly. But in his solitariness he had taken to flying alone a lot and had become graver and more withdrawn. No one joked any longer about his age.

His departure had followed a riotous binge in which the new Commanding Officer had said they'd have to drop a note to the Germans to say they could start flying again now that he was going and when he'd left the following morning half the squadron had appeared outside the Bull and Bush to see him off, with empty bully-beef cans and a tin chamber pot clanking behind the tender.

'Just like a wedding, sir,' the driver had said gaily.

His mother, pathetically proud of his ribbons, had laid on the usual meal for his arrival and he suddenly found himself surprisingly close to her. She was still afraid for him, however, and still couldn't see any future for a man who wanted to fly aeroplanes. It was an attitude Ira found hard to accept. Aeroplanes were a new and developing form of transport and he'd already decided that after the war someone was going to try to use them to carry passengers from one part of the world to another. Men were already flying regularly to France in the course of their duties and it seemed sense that eventually someone with money to spare would convert the big bomber designs into passenger-carriers to the Continent and beyond. Even in 1913 the *Daily Mail* had been offering prizes for the first man to fly the Atlantic, and the fact that no one had felt sufficiently well equipped to attempt it had not obscured the heady glimpse of the possible.

He decided he'd aged as a flight leader, and certainly too many things had happened for him still to be a boy. Guynemer was long dead with the German, Voss, and Richtofen was said to have been sent on leave in case he, too, was killed. Bishop was safe in Canada and only McCudden and Collishaw seemed to be still flying, and the story was that McCudden was due for home, too, before long. Even Courtney, the American, had been wounded and when Ira had visited him in hospital he'd found him surprisingly quiet. He'd been hit in the calf and chest, but, though neither injury was serious, wounds and pain had a habit of sobering a man and he, too, had realised that he wasn't immortal.

Forde was not at the address he'd forwarded to France and when Ira went to look him up, he was told he'd never turned up.

'He's with a widow he knows, somewhere near Brooklands,' the other occupant of the flat said. 'He's instructing there.'

When Ira eventually found him, Forde grinned sheepishly.

'I suppose I've got some explaining to do,' he said. 'I got rather involved, y'see.'

'The chap in the flat told me about it. You thinking of getting married?'

Forde gave him one of his old grins. 'She keeps dropping 'ints. Unfortunately, I 'ardly think this is the time for marriage, do you? Especially after she's already 'ad one try that ended a bit abruptly.'

Ira shrugged. 'With half Europe trying to knock each other's blocks off,' he said bluntly, 'I think we need more of it, not less.'

Forde eyed him curiously. 'My word,' he said, 'you've even taken to philosophisin'. That's a new turn for you.'

Ira laughed. 'It's the way Avallon's thinking, too,' he said. 'He's at Tern Hill and he says she doesn't mind a bit that he has to sit on a cushion all the time.'

Forde stared at him, puzzled.

'You've grown up, lad,' he said. 'It's not the medals. It's not because you've finally bought yourself a uniform that fits you either. It's something else. There's an air about you. An air of knowing what you're about. I always thought I was right to suggest you took over the flight. It's done you good.'

Forde himself looked well fed and plumper than ever, and the surgeons had done a good job on his face. Apart from a deep pink scar on his cheek, most of the marks of his crash seemed to have disappeared in a sleeker self-assured appearance.

'It's comfort,' he said. 'And release from fear. I shall never come out of this business trailin' clouds of glory. I dessay they'll give me a victory medal when it's over and I'll be 'appy to receive it, but I'm not eager for more. Life's become very precious to me and you're even makin' out a case for makin' an honest woman of 'er.'

There was an enormous mixture of men at Brooklands—Americans, Canadians, South Africans and New Zealanders, to say nothing of Frenchmen and Italians and even two Russians still learning to fly Camels. There were also a few faces that Ira remembered from his own training days, and people like English and Atwater, who still made a bee-line for the piano at every opportunity that offered itself. Jacobs was there, too, already planning for after the war was over. He'd been in the diamond-buying business in South Africa with his father but had no intention of going back to it.

'I couldn't go back to that, man,' he said, 'any more than I could loop round the moon. I'll buy an aeroplane or two. They'll be giving them away with the groceries by then and I'll take 'em back and start a passenger business. I've got a cousin who'll help me and a nephew up on the Rhodesian border. Kid called Shapiro. I bet he'd come in with me. He's already hot stuff with machinery. I suppose that's what *you'll* go in for.'

Ira shook his head. 'I'm going into farming,' he said, 'with Toby Forde.'

Jacobs stared. 'Farming? *You?*'

Ira said nothing, but Jacobs' comment set him wondering uneasily if farming needed some quality he didn't possess, and he began to feel disloyal that he should even consider anything else and pushed the thought from his mind. Buying a second-hand Douglas for the journey from Malden, he started work as soon as his leave was finished and, though he was good at instructing, he soon realised that the conditions were chaotic. Every instructor had different methods and every pupil learned to fly a different way. Since there appeared to be no proper measure of skill, it was impossible for one man to take over another's pupils and the need for setting up standards seemed to be so obvious he wrote a report on the subject and submitted it to the colonel. The colonel, however, was a man who rarely flew and seemed to dislike everyone with decorations.

'Perhaps you'd be better employed testing at the other side of the field,' he said shortly.

Forde was sympathetic as Ira unpacked his locker. 'That didn't last long,' he said.

Ira started his new job the following day and found that Gilliard, the Commanding Officer of the test squadron, was of a very different type. He had an Oxford degree in mathematics and considerable skill as an artist, and he had held a pilot's licence since the first days of flying.

'I understand you're Jack Penaluna's son,' he said as Ira appeared in his office. 'And that you know quite a bit about every aspect of flying.'

Ira agreed that he probably did.

'Well, I'm new to this job, too,' Gilliard said, 'so perhaps you're just what we need. I hear you were chucked out at the other side of the field for airing your views.'

Ira grinned and Gilliard went on cheerfully: 'How about doing the same for us here? No one seems to rate the job of test pilot very highly and most of the testing up to now's been done by men without any particular qualifications. And after some of the machines we've had to fly, I think it's a job that calls for a proper attitude to research. Could you do it?'

Forde gave him a strange look when Ira told him about the interview, then he beamed. 'I think he's right,' he said. 'You've got exactly what's necessary and you look beyond the surface to the things that really matter. I 'ope you survive this rotten war because you're probably the sort aviation needs. You just don't fly. You think about it, too.'

As he spoke, Ira felt another surge of disloyalty, remembering the farm they'd planned, but Jacobs' words had started a whole new train of ideas in his mind, and he knew that, where once he had regarded aeroplanes merely as sporting equipment as exciting as racing cars, he had now taken to regarding them as part of the future.

After a week of studying existing methods, Ira put in a report as requested, saying exactly what he felt about testing, and when he was called to Gilliard's office the following day, fully expecting to be hauled over the coals for his cheek, to his surprise, Gilliard offered him a cigarette and told him to sit down.

'That's a surprisingly bright bit of writing you've done,' he said. 'You've obviously given it some thought over a long time. Do you fancy being a test pilot?'

'I'm more of a practical flier than that,' Ira pointed out. 'But it seems to be a profession nobody's thought of much up to now.'

'Are you anxious to get back to France?'

Ira smiled. 'I don't know really, sir. But I think perhaps testing ought to be done by men who can't shoot as well as I can.'

'If it's medals you're after, you can get them for this, too.'

'No,' Ira said. 'It's not medals. It's just that I enjoy flying too much to be cold-blooded about it.'

'Perhaps you've got a point,' Gilliard agreed. 'However, until we find the right man, how about setting up some standards for us? I have a feeling we've stopped building aeroplanes by making drawings on the backs of envelopes and need someone articulate who can tell us what's wrong.'

The job turned out to be a strange one for Ira. It was slow and painstaking where flying in France had always been opportunist and demanded the intuition of a cavalry leader. For the first time he found himself deliberately doing things wrong with aeroplanes to find out how much bad handling they would stand, then setting the results on paper in words that could be understood by others who weren't always pilots. His approach had to be dispassionate and he had to crystallise his thoughts into intelligible sentences and outline them in clearly understood terms. It was actually too unexciting for his temperament and youth, but it was so different he found himself taking a pride in doing the job properly.

There were a vast number of weird and wonderful machines being offered by private contractors and designers and it was his duty to find which of them were worth pursuing and which ought to be thrown out, and he tried to see flying as an art with aerodynamics as a logic and sought means to rationalise the different skills and temperaments of the pilots who were going to fly the aeroplanes he tested.

He flew new and improved versions of the Camel, manœuvring them upside down deliberately to find out why young pilots killed themselves so often in inverted spins; belated triplanes which would never come to anything now because of the efficiency the new engines gave to biplanes; armour-plated Salamanders for ground support work; a strange machine called a Kennedy Kestrel with a back-stagger and queer X-shaped struts, which he detested from the moment he saw it; and once even a quadraplane like a Venetian blind that he just managed to get to the ground before it fell apart.

The weather was beginning to show signs of improvement when the German offensive on the Somme broke over the 5th Army and men returning from the front brought stories that the High Command and the Government had been warned a dozen and one times of its approach. The generals, it seemed, had failed to realise where the blow was going to fall, and the Government had failed to provide reserves.

London was downcast at the news and, despite the nonsense that was written in the newspapers about strategic withdrawals, it was obvious that a great many lives had been lost and a great deal of territory given up. By the end of the month, however, to everyone's surprise, the German attack began to peter out and people began to be cheerful again and even look forward to the end of the war. On April 1st, a rough, rainy day, the Royal Flying Corps officially became the Royal Air Force.

'Funny it should be April Fools' Day,' Forde commented. 'Hope it isn't an omen.'

There was a flurry of new medals to celebrate and they set about wetting the baby's head. But the following day Ira was taken off testing and sent to Birmingham to encourage munitions workers to an all-out effort to win the war. Other bemedalled men were doing the same, it seemed, but he loathed the job, not only because of the staring girls who listened to his embarrassed efforts at exhortation, but also because of the socially-minded women who invited him to their homes and regaled him with rationed foods he knew they'd bought on the black market.

He was glad to be back in London, but almost immediately he was told by Gilliard that he was to fly to France a highly secret prototype improvement on the Camel called a Snipe. It had only been brought out in January and no one had seen it yet and that was how it was to remain. He left at once from Brooklands for Lympne, landing at Clairmarais in the afternoon.

It was exciting to be back in the heady atmosphere of the war. Every road was filled with marching men, some of them tall, straight Americans in strange breeches and gaiters, strong young men who were fresh to the fight and actually looking forward to it. All round them guns and lorries were moving east, and there were troops in every field. At Clairmarais he was met by Sillito, still accompanied by Monkey Brand, who greeted him deliriously, and was sent on to Izel where he saw more faces he knew, among them Stonehouse, back once more at the stage of blue-ringed eyes staring out of a ghostly face.

He demonstrated the Snipe, showing off its good points and outlining its faults, and he was still making out his report in the squadron office when Sillito appeared by car.

'They've got Richthofen,' he said, and sat down abruptly, as though he didn't know whether to be elated or shocked.

They stared at each other, then Sillito gave a twisted smile. They'd known of Richthofen for so long, had so feared him and felt him immortal that the knowledge that he could be killed in combat like an ordinary human being was startling.

'Makes you think,' Sillito said. 'If they can get *him*, there's not much hope for the rest of us.'

'How did it happen?'

'Some Australian machine-gunners claimed him, but the medical chaps say it couldn't have happened from the ground. Then somebody from a Camel squadron—a Canadian called Brown—put in a report that he'd brought down a red triplane.'

'Smashed up?'

Sillito's narrow face looked puzzled. 'No,' he said. 'He crash-landed near the Bray–Corbie road and they found him still strapped in the cockpit, still sitting upright and holding the stick. He must have managed to put it down before the light went out. They carried him away on a sheet of corrugated iron and they've got him lying in state in a hangar at Bertangles. I'm going over to see him.' He looked up, faintly embarrassed. 'Pay respects and all that. Coming?'

They found the Fokker triplane at Corbie en route, but little remained of it but the framework. Superstitious pilots had taken every scrap of fabric from it to carry as good-luck charms, and mechanics were dismantling the Spandau guns that had sent so many airmen to their deaths.

'There can't be any mistake, can there?' Ira asked the sergeant in charge.

'None at all, sir.' The sergeant shook his head. 'We found his identity disc and a gold watch marked with his initials. There were papers, too—one of them a pilot's certificate.'

At Bertangles they were still arguing about who had done the killing. The Australian machine-gunners were still insistent about their claim and now, it seemed, an RE8 crew had said they had also shot at the red triplane.

A canvas hangar had been cleared and the body laid on a dais, and pilots and observers and ground crews from all the squadrons on the aerodrome were filing silently past, one or two carrying wreaths to add to the growing pile round the bier.

Richthofen was only a small man, not much older than Ira, fair-haired and half-smiling in death. His nose and jaw had been injured in his landing and he seemed frail-looking as he lay on the dais, so that Ira felt an intense wave of depression as he stared at him.

Late in the afternoon, when the light was beginning to wane, six pilots of the new Royal Air Force carried the black-stained wooden box containing the remains on their shoulders to an open army tender and, headed by a guard of honour of Australian infantrymen with their rifles reversed, the cortège passed slowly down the road beside the aerodrome. The war was still going on and the air was full of the sound of engines as machines landed and took off for the front. A grave had been dug in Bertangles cemetery near a poplar tree, and, beyond the hedge, they could see the wide spaces of the Somme uplands and the mass of Amiens Cathedral in the yellow sun of the late afternoon. Aeroplanes continued to roar overhead and from the east they could clearly hear the rumble of guns.

The cemetery was full of Allied soldiers, with a few mechanics from Bertangles, a few French women and children and old men past military age. As the coffin was lowered into the earth, a sharp word of command rang out and the volley of the salute drove the birds from the trees in a clattering lift of wings.

'I expect there'll be an outcry from the protest department of the *Daily Mail*,' Sillito said gruffly as they turned away. 'As for me, I just hope that if anything happens to me, the other side'll treat me as kindly.'

Ira's work kept him in France another few days, then he flew back to England for leave.

Forde seemed nervous when he looked him up. He had had a letter from Avallon, who was now flying SEs in France. He had married and he said that G.H.Q. appeared to have decided that ground-strafing was the thing that would win the war. In their efforts to use it to its limit they were pushing the casualty figures up enormously.

'They're forming squadrons specially for the job,' Forde said. 'I couldn't stand *that*.'

They celebrated Ira's return at a nearby pub and Forde announced that he'd found a farm.

'Rachel's father's,' he said. 'He'd like to retire. It's just what I've always wanted.' He glanced uncertainly at Ira. 'I hope it's going to suit you. 'E's got some lovely 'Erefords, and we've got to start thinking, because everybody says the war'll end next year and we've got to get in first.'

They bought an extra drink for luck, but a flood of men coming into the bar interrupted them. A munitions factory had opened nearby and the men had arrived from the Midlands to run it. They all seemed to know more about the war than they did themselves.

'There's another push coming,' one of them announced. 'And this time it'll take us to Berlin. It's going to be the biggest battle of the lot. We're only waiting for the kick-off.'

Forde stared sourly at him. He was a small man with a red face and a well-fed look about him. 'It's not a bloody game of football,' he protested. 'You can 'ave *my* place any time.'

'You wouldn't catch *me* flying,' the red-faced man said. 'I don't know how you do it.'

'I know,' Ira agreed gravely. 'Feathers are the very devil.'

Despite his firm rejection of the Kennedy Kestrel, Ira was still involved with experiments to see just how much it would stand. It was an unhandy machine, but there appeared to be some influence in high places because Gilliard kept asking him if he couldn't change his views.

'No, sir, I can't,' he insisted. 'That back-stagger hides the view behind and that's as good as a death sentence in France. What do they want me to do? Kill myself to prove I'm right? There must be somebody pretty interested in this machine.'

'Probably a relation of the Minister,' Gilliard agreed.

'I'll see if I can't write the damn' thing off.'

'That'd be one way of sorting out the problem.'

It was a warm day and, certain his work wouldn't last long, Ira didn't bother to put on a flying suit. He crossed Surrey into Sussex until he could see the sun golden on the sea, turned over Petworth, watching the light catch the plume of smoke from a moving train, and climbed as high as he could before kicking the Kestrel over, determined this time to prove he was right. The thought that he might kill himself entered his mind for a second, but he thrust it out again, feeling sure as he always had that it couldn't happen to him. Below him was a lot of what appeared to be parkland, hazy blue under the sun. At least, he thought, if the bloody machine comes apart here, it can't fall on anyone.

He dived until the wires shrieked and the Kestrel shuddered

with its speed, and watched dispassionately as the earth rose to meet him, then he manœuvred for a long time, diving, zooming, looping and rolling, doing everything that might be expected of the machine in a dog-fight. But it climbed as though it were sick—sluggish, ugly and ponderous—and he made a note of the fact on the pad strapped to his knee.

At the top of the climb he cut off power and pulled back the joystick until he was at stalling point, then he kicked at the rudder so that the Kestrel fell over in a spin, and the earth swung round him. Coldly, he counted the turns. One. Two. Three.

Then out of the corner of his eye he sensed that something had shifted position and he immediately corrected the spin to look, and went into a wide circle to examine the wings, tail, and the strange X-struts. Tightening the turn to put more strain on the machine, he could find nothing wrong, but he noted on the pad what he felt he'd seen. Then he climbed again and cut off power once more until he stalled into another spin. This time he kept his eyes not on the ground but on the machine and he saw the fault almost at once.

The fabric of the upper wing was wrinkling and the bracing wires were sagging and tightening as he turned, and he saw the strut move in its socket. It was almost imperceptible, but it was enough for an experienced eye to catch it at once.

He had just crossed his controls to pull out when he heard a noise like a pistol shot, clear above the engine, and the sky was blotted out as the wing collapsed. As he automatically cut the engine and switched off the petrol, he sensed rather than saw that the machine was going down in a fluttering movement like a leaf spinning from a tree. All round him there was a vicious clattering twanging noise as wires snapped and the torn fabric flapped in the wind, but somehow he'd managed to slow the rate of descent, though he knew he had virtually no control over the machine and, struggling against the collapsed wing which seemed to have folded over the cockpit, he thanked God for that tremendous back-stagger that left him space to push himself clear.

The trees below changed abruptly from a whirling green blur

to leaves, then he was brought up sharply with the rending noise of smashing foliage and he found himself hurtling through branches that snatched at his face, striking violent blows. One of them caught him across the right eye with a whack that knocked him silly, then he fell clear and landed flat on his back.

Dazed, stupefied and half-conscious, he tried to lift himself. But there seemed to be no strength in his limbs and he flopped back limply, aware of lights going out in his mind one after the other.

2

When Ira woke, he was too dizzy to move. Bramble thorns were sticking into his face and hands, but it was a wonderful feeling to be alive and he felt more like sleep than anything. At least, he thought with dazed satisfaction, he'd proved himself right. The Kestrel *was* no bloody good.

A light was on his face that he assumed was the sun and he closed his eyes, curiously pleased with himself.

'Are you awake?'

The voice jabbed at his consciousness and he realised that he was lying flat on his back on a hard bed under a light and there was a girl in nurse's uniform standing over him with a pair of tweezers in her hand. She was young and remarkably pretty.

He lifted his head heavily and gazed at her through the blur of blood that filled his right eye. Her cheeks were sweetly curving and her nose was straight and small and somehow she looked vaguely familiar so that he felt sure he'd seen her before somewhere, though he couldn't imagine where.

'How do you feel?'

He didn't answer and he realised then that she was working over his face, and it dawned on him at last she was plucking thorns from it and dabbing at the cuts and scratches with a pad of cotton wool and iodine.

'The doctor'll be coming soon.'

'Am I hurt?' Ira asked. He didn't feel hurt.

'Nothing broken,' she said. 'But you've done something awful to your eye.'

She dabbed again at his face and through the smell of the iodine he caught a whiff of the perfume she was wearing. She seemed a long way from the antiseptic-smelling nurses he'd known in the past.

'You're beautiful,' he observed. There didn't seem to be anything else to say.

She blushed and he thought what a change it was to be able to make other people blush instead of blushing himself.

'You're in an awful mess,' she said, and continued to pluck the thorns from his face. 'I wish the doctor would hurry. He has to come from the village.'

Sense was returning now and he felt like a scarecrow, with the blood on his face and his features a mass of criss-crossed scratches. Then he suddenly remembered the Kestrel and looked round for it. He couldn't see it anywhere.

'What happened to the Kestrel?' he asked.

'What's the Kestrel?'

'It's an aeroplane. The one I was flying. It fell apart.'

'Oh, that! I understand it's on top of a tree, with its engine missing. It's rather a mess.'

'I've been trying to smash that thing for days,' he said with lunatic cheerfulness.

The girl looked puzzled, and he went on with increasing awareness.

'Did I fall out of it?' he asked.

'They tell me you hit every branch on the way down and landed in a bed of brambles. They probably saved you from breaking your neck. You couldn't have picked a better place to fall.'

Ira frowned. 'Come to think of it, where *did* I fall?'

The girl jerked her hand and, turning his head, he saw iron trolleys and enamel dishes on a white-painted hospital table.

'This is Lady Avallon's place at Greatyers. You landed in the park.'

His eyebrows rose. 'Basil came here when he was shot in the behind. It's his family place.'

She stared at him, puzzled. 'Do *you* know Basil?'

'Yes, I do. Do you?'

'Yes. Actually.'

Then he knew at once why he'd felt he'd seen her before. He began to laugh and she stared at him anxiously.

'What's so funny?'

'You! You're Basil's sister.'

Her head jerked up and her eyes widened. 'Yes. As a matter of fact,' she said, 'I am.'

Ira grinned, delighted with himself. 'You even talk like him,' he said. 'I'm Ira Penaluna.'

Her face broke into a radiant smile. 'I'm Nancy!'

'He kept telling me I ought to drop in,' Ira said. 'It seems I did.'

Half an hour later, aching from stiffening bruises but virtually undamaged, Ira was sitting upright in a private room with a whisky in his hand while Nancy Avallon leaned over him, still picking the thorns out of his face with her eyebrow tweezers. It was his second whisky and, since it was on an empty stomach, he already felt drunk.

'There are millions!' Nancy said. 'They're all over your face.'

'There are a lot in my backside, too, but we'd better leave those to the doctor.'

She gave a hoot of laughter that was startlingly like Avallon's and studied his face again, the tweezers poised.

'We've telephoned the police,' she said. 'They'll get in touch with Brooklands. Sybil Mauncey'll be green with envy.'

'Who's Sybil Mauncey?'

'Friend of mine. Lives over there.' She gestured vaguely. 'She's had a cousin staying with her. He only had *one* medal.'

Ira grinned. Everything seemed to be functioning splendidly. Nancy Avallon had a flawless skin and the clearest eyes he'd ever seen. He was already smitten and to his surprise found he wasn't the slightest bit shy.

'Basil told us what a marvellous pilot you were,' she was saying. 'But surely it wasn't very clever to crash, was it?'

'I can fly 'em when they've got wings,' Ira said. 'It's a bit more difficult when they lose 'em. It was rather a do-or-die job.'

'What happened?'

'It fell apart.'

She looked concerned. 'Will you get into trouble for breaking it?'

'Not really. It wasn't difficult and I've been trying for a long time.' He looked up. 'Can I come and see you again?'

The blush came again, pleasing him. 'We've been expecting you for ages,' she said. 'Basil wanted you to be his best man, as a matter of fact, but you'd sneaked off to France.' Her face twisted in a grimace of concentration. 'Shut your eyes. There are about six in your eyebrow, and it's got an awful cut on it. It's in two pieces almost.'

He closed his eyes and felt the tweezers touching his face.

'Does it hurt?'

'Like mad.'

'Would you like another whisky?'

She poured him another drink from a large decanter, and chuckled. 'The way you're going at Father's whisky,' she said, 'you'll not wake up for a week.'

He came to in a bed of battleship proportions that seemed remarkably hard and uncomfortable, and found himself staring at a carved wooden ceiling in a room which, despite the warm weather, seemed surprisingly chilly.

He tried to remember what had happened, and vaguely recalled a doctor appearing and finishing the repairs that Nancy Avallon had started. Then there'd been a middle-aged woman with a smiling face and later a tall elderly man with a drooping moustache who looked like a portrait on the wall behind him.

He vaguely remembered having a meal, but then he came to a stop and hoped he hadn't done anything drunken and stupid, and while he was still trying to recall what had happened, there was a knock on the door and an old man in a faded tail-coat appeared. He was so old he was bent almost double.

'Good morning, sir,' he said. 'My name's Tickner. Miss Nancy wonders if you'll be getting up for breakfast.'

It was like being in a good if old-fashioned hotel and when he appeared later down a vast staircase, hobbling from stiffening bruises, he found Nancy Avallon sitting with a cup of coffee in the window waiting for him. The sun was shining on her hair and as she saw him, she rose, her face radiant.

'How do you feel?'

'Not bad,' he said, 'under the circumstances.'

'Feel like eating?'

'Not half.'

'We've got eggs and bacon. We get them from the farm. Father looks after them.'

Ira frowned. 'Did I meet Father last night?'

'Yes. He seemed suitably impressed. So did Mother. In spite of the fact that by that time you were pretty tight.'

'Where are Father and Mother now?'

'Father's at the farm. Mother's at the hospital, in the West Wing. I should be there, too. Nursing. But they gave me the day off.'

The ancient manservant, Tickner, appeared with a tray of bacon and eggs and they sat down and began to set about them.

'Somebody called Gilliard rang up last night,' Nancy said. 'To see if you were all right. He said not to hurry back. They're sending someone to collect the aeroplane.'

The mechanics appeared with a lorry as they were finishing breakfast and they went with them to the crashed Kestrel, riding in the cab with the driver.

The sergeant in charge stared up at the machine in its perch on the tree. It looked like a dead bird with its engine missing and its wings drooping, their fabric pierced by branches.

'Did you fall from there, sir?' he asked.

'Yes.'

'It's a long way.'

'It was the best thing I ever did,' Ira said.

The sergeant sent one of the men up the tree with a saw and

they began to bring the Kestrel down in small pieces. The engine lay in the brambles not ten yards from where Ira had landed.

'Good job it didn't fall on you,' Nancy said. 'It might have done.'

They walked back to the house together and Ira found that a remarkably comfortable relationship had sprung up between them already. Nancy was brisk and forthright and employed no feminine guile, and addressed him easily as if he were an old friend. She was vital, noisy and bursting with energy, yet she said nothing unnecessary and was intelligent enough for what she had to say to be worth hearing. It was as though he'd known her for years, instead of a matter of hours, and he began to wonder what he'd ever seen in Peggy Phillips.

Her parents had returned when they reached the house and there was a ceremonial taking of drinks in the library before lunch. Lord Avallon was an amiable old man who had lost three fingers at Mons in 1914, when he was already too old to go to France, and, despite Nancy's grimace, insisted on telling Ira all about it.

'Things are different these days, of course,' he said. 'All lorries and motor cars and aeroplanes. Francis doesn't seem to think much of 'em. Me eldest. Thinks they spoil the war.'

In the afternoon Nancy found a horse for Ira and they rode back to where the sergeant had now dismantled most of the Kestrel except for a piece of wing that was hooked to the topmost branches.

'Don't fancy risking anyone's neck to get that down, sir,' he said.

'I should leave it where it is, 'Ira said. 'As a memorial to its designer's lost hopes.'

On the way back to the house, they stopped the horses in a clump of trees. The weather was brilliant and there was a magnificent view. A small wheeling speck moved in the sky to the south.

'There's an aeroplane,' Nancy said.

'It's a Camel.'

She stared, squint-eyed, at it. 'Can you tell? I can hardly see it.'

Ira nodded. 'I can tell,' he said. 'The way it hangs in the sky. The sound. Everything.'

She indicated his ribbons. 'You've got an awful lot of those,' she pointed out.

'They give 'em away with the rations,' he said. 'French generals appear with their pockets full of them and they hand 'em out to anyone who wants one.'

'I bet they don't.' She studied the ribbons again, then she looked up into his face. 'I bet they're good for getting girls.'

'Not half. Fall over themselves.'

She seemed upset by the knowledge. 'Do they really?'

'Not really. Only teasing.'

'Well, don't start making eyes at Sybil Mauncey, will you? I should be livid.'

'Not me.'

She seemed surprisingly uncertain beneath the briskness.

'I bet you have lots of girls, all the same,' she said.

'No, not really.'

'Have you any girls at the moment? That is—I mean, *a* girl?'

'Only you.'

'What cheek!' She gave him a sideways glance. 'Actually, it's all right, really. I don't mind a bit.' She paused and went on quickly. 'There's a dance tonight. Would you like to go? You can. Technically you're a patient.'

'If you'll dance with me.'

She poked at the dry leaves of the previous autumn with her riding boot. 'I'm not much of a dancer,' she said.

'Neither am I,' Ira pointed out. 'So we ought to manage fine. Where is it?'

'Here,' she said. 'At the hospital. Mother organises it. Sybil Mauncey'll be there and the Vicar's daughters. Mind you don't get caught with *them*. They're so stupid it's ludicrous. Everybody comes. Mother says it's good for the convalescents and I suppose it is.' She looked up at him and went on in a breathless tone of eagerness. 'It'd be wonderful if you would go. Do you think you could possibly bear it?'

The dance started immediately after dinner. Nancy had put on make-up and the rustle of her dress was like the crash of artillery in Ira's ears. The great hall had been cleared and a huddle of aged musicians from Worthing had arrived by train to play fox-trots. A few girls from the village and neighbouring houses were standing about, a few of the more confident ones trying hard to persuade palefaced men to dance with them. For all Ira noticed of them, they might have been tailor's dummies. He turned to Nancy. They were both a little nervous of being alone in the centre of the vast floor and, at their first turn, managed to get their feet entangled.

'Told you I was a rotten dancer,' Ira said.

'No worse than me.'

In fact, Nancy was good enough to feel weightless in his arms and made him seem more skilful than he was, and he only lost step when they talked.

'Concentrate,' she urged in a fierce whisper.

For fear of tiring the patients, the dance finished early, and the girls disappeared back to the village in gigs and pony-traps.

'Let's go back through the gardens,' Nancy said, reaching for Ira's hand. 'It's so warm and I could do with some fresh air.'

As they stopped by the front door, they heard a distant thudding—so faint it was almost like the beating of a heart.

'It's the guns in France,' Nancy said. 'We sometimes hear them when the wind's in the right direction. Won't it be wonderful when they stop?' She looked at him. 'You *will* come and see us again, won't you?'

He had decided long since that he would.

'I suppose we ought to go in now,' she went on. 'Father bangs on the floor with his stick if he thinks we ought to be in bed. Nobody ever hears him, of course, because this place's so vast we're never underneath.'

She turned to him, in a way that was quite natural and unaffected, and reminded him of birthday parties before the war when there'd been girls in frilly pink frocks, and as she lifted up her face for him to kiss her, she seemed young enough to make him feel almost middle-aged. He kissed her gently on the lips, realising that it was the first time he'd ever properly kissed a girl his own age. The others had been older, taking control of the operation and telling him what to do, and it seemed more right this way and satisfying to feel experienced for a change.

Nancy seemed pleased. 'I wondered when you'd get round to it,' she said. 'I've been dropping hints all evening. Were you a bit scared?'

'Not of you,' he said. 'Of girls. I've never known when to start grabbing.'

She laughed. 'Always,' she advised. 'They all like it. I'm no different.'

He kissed her again for safety and for a moment they clung to each other in the darkness. Then she lifted her head, and, in the faint light, he saw her eyes were faraway. Her mouth widened slowly in a grin.

'Oh, Ira,' she said enthusiastically, 'wait till I tell Sybil Mauncey.'

3

Nothing in the world could have stopped Ira falling in love with Nancy Avallon. For once it didn't spring from excitement or the need for sympathy, and before a fortnight was out he was dangerously involved.

She was warm, happy and satisfying, and eager without archness, as though it were the most natural thing in the world that he should want to spend his time with her. He was delighted with himself and with her. She was all he'd ever asked and being with her was like looking through a magnifying glass that made everything sharp and clear and colourful. He was utterly bewitched.

Emotionally, he was alive for the first time in his life, and whenever he had a free day he roared on the Douglas down the country roads towards Greatyers. It was now almost midsummer and, apart from a few groups of marching men or a few army lorries, there was no traffic at all. Twice he flew down and landed on a prearranged strip of flat land near the house, Nancy appearing as soon as he roared over the garden. He stayed overnight, pleading engine trouble when he returned, and several times took advantage of invitations for week-ends, walking over the Downs with her side by side, laughing with her, both of them just happily aware of each other's presence.

On her birthday, her older brother, Francis, appeared with his wife from their house in Bath, on his way back to France after leave. He seemed almost to be playing the rôle of heir to a title, but then Ira realised he wasn't acting at all. His family history was fixed so firmly in his mind with all his thoughts, he clearly believed that everything that was worth doing could only be done by his own small sect, and because of this, war made special calls on him and demanded sacrifices which, because he was a member of a privileged caste, he had to make without hesitation or fear. He was like an older version of his brother Basil, but without his interest in mechanical things, a member of a wholly admirable but fast-disappearing group.

It had a heady effect to be so close to the wealthy and the influential, and Ira's relationship with Nancy developed quickly into a period of mounting, sustained elation. She always behaved as though she might not live to see the next day, happy in a breathless but controlled pleasure at everything, her head tilted with delight at her own cleverness as she did something that amused him. They wasted no time on irrelevancies and even their walking, even their holding hands, somehow became a perceptible caress they both felt but which was invisible to everyone else. Into the short time they'd known each other they seemed to have packed years of happiness.

He was so busy he saw little of Forde and felt faintly guilty as he realised he was ignoring him. From time to time, Forde tried to show him photographs he'd taken of the property he'd put their names to, but he was conscious that only half his mind, occupied as it was with the picture of Nancy's face, was paying attention, and he noticed a faint trace of bewilderment and resentment creeping into Forde's glance.

Nevertheless, he talked of his future to Nancy and was delighted to find she approved of his ideas of being a farmer, though her imaginings were strangely different from his own and included farm managers, hunt balls and shoots. It didn't seem to sound like what Forde had in mind and Jacobs' comments came back to him again as he realised uneasily that he didn't really see himself either muck-spreading or following a plough.

They were sufficiently in love, however, for the future not to matter, but, with most of the house given up to Lady Avallon's hospital and the family packed into one small wing, they were never able to be alone and they crept into the garden when it grew dark, light-headed at the warm weather, lack of sleep and their feelings for each other, clinging to each other in the summer house down the garden and exchanging racking kisses until their lips were numb, the emotion of their letters emerging in a burst of passion.

Although they talked of physical love, they never indulged.

'No,' Nancy kept saying as she pulled back, alarmed, from his insistence. 'Some time, but not now.'

His bank account dwindled alarmingly, but it made a pleasant change to be the dominant partner, and, though occasionally when she talked of foreign holidays he felt envious and jealous of the young men she mentioned who had so much money, it didn't last long because it was impossible to be offended or hurt by her.

Even in France the war seemed to be going well. The German attack in the spring had only lengthened their line instead of shortening it and the Americans were taking a large share of the fighting now. When the Germans had lashed out on the Chemin-des-Dames they had stopped them dead in their tracks and driven them back.

Gilliard told Ira he'd recommended him for the Air Force Cross for the risks he'd deliberately taken, and when it came through, Forde stared at it with a faint tinge of envy.

'Fame sticks to you, lad,' he said ponderously. 'Like the legendary excreta to a shovel. I reckon we ought to celebrate this one in style because it wasn't anything to do with 'ot-blooded battle but early-morning bravery.'

Nancy spotted the new ribbon the moment Ira arrived at Avallon's flat to pick her up. 'Oh, Ira,' she crowed. 'You positively glow with colour. What's this one for?'

'I'm not sure,' he said. 'I think it's for breaking the Kestrel.'

They met Forde and Rachel Timms at Murrays'. Rachel wasn't as pretty as Ira had imagined from Forde's descriptions, but Forde seemed very happy with her, and obviously approved of Nancy. Nancy herself was radiant with pride, her freshness almost setting her apart from Ira, because his own youth seemed to have slipped away from him somewhere in France.

As they saw Forde and Rachel off home in a taxi, she turned to him and asked in a hushed whisper, 'Are they married, Ira?'

'No.'

'I thought they weren't. Are they living together?'

'Yes.'

She said nothing and in the taxi to Avallon's flat he noticed a new ardour in the way she returned his kisses. As they descended and she passed him the key of the door, she was clinging to his arm as though she were suddenly afraid he might disappear.

They played a few records but they were all the usual ones—*If you were the Only Girl in the World*, *Lonesome For You*, and the songs from the London shows—and he found that the only thing he could remember as he heard them was Huyzes. Then it suddenly dawned on him there'd been no sign of Avallon's wife.

'There's nobody here,' Nancy admitted, blushing. 'She's gone to Greatyers for the week-end. I borrowed it for the night.'

'Oh!'

For a moment there was silence and they started talking again, quickly.

'Will you have to go back to France soon, Ira?' she asked in a small voice.

'We all have to do and die for a bit longer.'

'Do you want to?'

'Yes, because that's where I ought to be, and no, because of you.'

'Truly? Because of me?'

He put his fingers to her cheek and her unlined face looked young in its unselfconscious pleasure. He was touched with a new feeling of tenderness towards her. Her expression was lost and faintly afraid and he wanted to bring the happiness back to her eyes.

'Don't worry,' he said. 'It'll soon be over now and they might find me another Kestrel before then to smash up.'

Her eyes moved away. 'Don't,' she said.

He turned her face to his and she smiled wanly at him and put her hand over his where it rested on her cheek.

'One day, Nancy,' he asked. 'Will you marry me?'

Her eyes shone.

'Oh, Ira, what a silly question! But you don't *have* to ask me that, you know.'

'I haven't any money,' he interrupted.

She stared at him for a second, then she went on in a quiet voice. 'Lots of people will be living on their wives after the war,' she said. 'They're already talking about people going back to university to take up where they left off.'

'I shan't be going back to university,' he reminded her. 'I didn't ever go to university. I wasn't old enough.'

He had a feeling she didn't wish to be too serious but that her emotions had got a little out of control.

He glanced at his watch and they were both aware, as the movement made them realise the end of the evening had arrived, that they'd both changed in a brief fragment of time.

'I love you, Nancy,' Ira said.

She managed a small uncertain smile. 'I suppose you must,' she said, 'or you wouldn't ask me to marry you.'

'Surely you believe me?'

'Yes, I do. It's just this beastly war. It makes you cautious. There are times when I feel like a bitch on heat just because you all look so damn' brave.'

He leaned towards her, but she pushed him away and stood up quickly and moved away, uncertain of her own feelings. At the door, she stopped and looked back at him, still frowning, as though she were crushed by the wilderness of feeling they were blundering through.

'I knew everybody was away tonight,' she said, not meeting his eyes. 'I arranged it that way. And now I'm afraid. People don't meet as they should these days and when they do they get too sentimental about each other.'

He said nothing, allowing her to sort out her emotions because she seemed confused and younger than he'd thought her.

'It's all so silly,' she said in a low voice, angry with herself. 'Falling in love these days is like being on a bicycle back-pedalling. You put in a lot of hard work and get nowhere. Love includes having a future, too, doesn't it?'

He took her hand, but she pulled it away as though she were afraid of herself. 'I planned to have you stay,' she said, 'but now I'm going to make you go. Do you hate me?'

'No, Nancy.' In this new feeling he had for her, this baffling logic of love, he would have granted her anything.

She was still staring at him. 'Promise?'

He nodded. 'Cross my throat.'

She stared at him a moment longer, then she flung her arms round his neck and clung to him.

'Oh, Ira,' she said, 'now I know you must love me.'

4

He called for her next morning and they had lunch together before she went back to Greatyers, both of them quiet and occupied with their own thoughts.

He saw her off from Victoria before going to catch his own train at Waterloo. He was still a little dazed, and aware suddenly that never before in all his life had he said 'I love you' to any girl. When he arrived at Brooklands, Forde looked at him strangely.

'Are you in love with 'er, lad?' he asked.

'Yes.'

'Thinkin' o' marrying her?'

'I've asked her already.'

'Bless me soul!' Forde grimaced. 'The 'ero and the lady. It's the sort of thing parlourmaids read in penny magazines between knocks on the front door. She don't seem much like a farmer's wife, though.'

There it was again, that subtle hint that their futures were drifting apart. Knowing Forde, knowing how much he owed him for his wry humour and self-deprecating common sense, Ira hurried to deny it.

'Don't you believe it,' he said firmly.

'She hasn't put you off?'

'No,' Ira said with honesty. 'Not Nancy. I think she'd do whatever her husband did. I think the Avallons are like that.'

Forde smiled. 'That's all right then. I'm glad to see you 'appy. I used to think you needed motherin' in spite of all that blazing colour on your chest, but now I'm not so sure. You're beginning to take your first 'esitant steps as an adult and I think you're going to be all right.'

Nancy's letters came in a flood, ecstatic yet surprisingly calm, and when he rode on the Douglas down to Greatyers her family seemed to approve of him and the future looked good.

But the war persisted in intruding and the American boy English was instructing collided with another machine in mid-air, and in the afternoon they heard that Stonehouse had been killed in France, flying into the officers' mess.

Forde was visibly upset. 'I bet that spilled a few drinks,' he said.

While they were still recovering, Gilliard sent for Ira and told him he'd been posted back to France. Sillito, who, it seemed, had said too much on the staff about the policy of not providing parachutes, had been posted back to a front-line command, and he had asked specially for him. Ira recognised the squadron number as Avallon's.

'They've got SEs,' Gilliard went on. 'And they're giving you a flight. I told them they were bloody fools and that they ought to give you a squadron, but they insisted you were still too young.'

Ira was surprisingly shaken by the news. Forde was frankly and openly worried. 'When do you go?' he asked.

'End of the week. I'm to pick up some Americans at Hounslow and take 'em with me. To Tertry. It's Avallon's crowd. Sillito's running it.'

Forde's face wore a lost, nostalgic look. 'It'd be just like old times, wouldn't it?' he said. 'Sillito, Basil, you—and me.'

Conscious that time was short, Ira telephoned Lady Avallon's Hospital but was informed that the family had gone to London. He immediately went round to Avallon's flat, but it was empty and he decided that, whatever happened, the following day he would go to Greatyers. He'd already sold the Douglas to one of Forde's pupils, but he borrowed it back for the day and roared down the summer lanes through Guildford into Sussex. Tickner, the ancient butler, was in the hall when he arrived.

'Miss Nancy?' Ira asked, and the old man waved a hand silently towards the library.

The gesture seemed so unlike him, it puzzled Ira, and, thoroughly alarmed, he hurried down the long hall. Nancy was sitting in the window staring at a newspaper as though she didn't see a thing in it. She stood up as Ira appeared, but the eagerness had gone out of her manner.

'Hello, Ira,' she said.

'I've been trying to contact you, Nancy. What's wrong?'

'Francis has been wounded. He's in the Royal Free Hospital. Mother went down to arrange for him to be brought here where he knows the place. He's going to die.'

There was nothing to say in reply. It had happened so often before in the last four years.

'I don't think my father felt it could ever happen to an Avallon,' Nancy went on. 'The eldest son's always followed the father for generations. I believe he thought it would always be that way.'

She looked so small and pale, he put his arms round her silently and pulled her gently towards him. Up to that moment, she'd shown no sign of tears, but as he held her, she suddenly started crying.

'Everybody seems to be dying,' she said. 'Sybil Mauncey's cousin was killed in Italy two days ago. We heard while we were in London. Only *you* seem a permanent fixture.'

He hesitated for a moment, then he decided she was old enough and brave enough to know his news.

'Not any more, Nancy. I'm going back to France.'

She looked up at him quickly, her eyes alarmed and huge.

'When?'

'Tomorrow. I'm going to Basil's squadron.'

She stared at him for a moment longer, then she spoke quickly.

'You don't have to. Father could pull strings for you. Get you a staff job.'

'He didn't get one for Francis. I don't think he'd want to.'

'He would if I asked him. You'll be killed.'

'No, Nancy. Not me.' Try as he might, Ira couldn't even now see himself dying in an aeroplane. Despite all the near squeaks he'd had and all the near squeaks he was certain would be his lot in the future, he still failed to see himself as one of the unlucky ones who lost their lives.

She began to cry again in soft muted whimperings and he took her in his arms to comfort her, harrowed by her tears and able only to say, 'Please don't cry,' and stroke her hair. But he couldn't change the decision that had been made for him, and had no wish to give up flying to sit in an office pushing pieces of paper about—not even for someone as loving, warm and intelligent as Nancy.

After a while she calmed down and tried to smile. 'One day,' she managed, 'when you've grown too fat to fly, I'll look more kindly on you.' Then her eyes filled with moisture again and she sighed. 'I wonder how much difference it'll make when it's all over *who* won,' she said. 'Who'll be better off in all the poverty and debt?'

They ate a silent meal together and when they'd finished they walked in the grounds, hand-in-hand, neither of them speaking much.

The late sun had thrown a golden haze across the sweeping folds of countryside and the thick Sussex clumps towards the sea. At the top of the hill, where the Kestrel had crashed, they stopped. They could still see the fragment of wing impaled on the top of the tree, sticking out like a flag.

Nancy turned and Ira was startled at the passion with which she returned his kiss. As they walked back to the house, his thoughts were turbulent in his mind, and their talk was brittle and stilted.

'Can I come and see you off, Ira?' she said.

'Why not? Other people will.'

The flame in the west had burnt itself out now and the luminous blue of the evening had covered the folds of countryside. The scents of the summer day had gone except for the smell of newly cut grass that came across the fields towards them, strong and perfumed. Massed foliage loomed heavily on either side, darkening as the light went out of the sky. The moment's perfection made them silent. The sun was going down and the day was more remote than it had been five minutes earlier. The evening was full of small sounds and Nancy's eyes were large with listening as she gazed at the distance.

As the place began to drown in shadow, he noticed she was standing still and upright and he saw her breast rise quickly, then she turned and stared at him, her eyes big and bright and steady as though she were thinking a lot.

'Ira,' she said. 'We shan't be married now before you go back.'

'No.'

She gestured at the trees. 'This seems a much better place to get married in than some potty church.' She indicated the vault of the trees. 'It's only a man-made ritual, after all, isn't it?'

She was playing with the stem of a flower and she twisted it into a ring. 'Put it on my finger,' she said, and he smiled and did as she told him.

'With this ring I thee wed,' she intoned. 'Say it, Ira.'

'With this ring I thee wed.'

'With my body I thee worship.'

'With my body I thee worship.'

'No need to shout that bit.'

She seemed to have come out of the listless mood of the early evening. He didn't say anything and she went on in her brisk forthright manner.

'I suppose,' she said, 'that apart from the fact that we haven't had the Vicar to offer up his blessings over us, we're as married as we'll ever be—as married as Basil is, as married as Francis. More married than *he'll* ever be now.'

Her look was grave as she stared at him. 'Ira, we're man and wife now except for a mere formality.'

When Ira woke the following morning, dazzled and humbled, he lay straight-limbed under the sheet, staring at the ceiling, while Nancy slept quietly with her head on his shoulder. He was still a little surprised. If this was love, he thought, then it had been so easy. It had seemed such a straightforward, honest no-nonsense affair, after all the disasters of his last leave.

He turned his head to look at her and realised her eyes were open. As his lips touched hers, as though on an impulse her arms came up swiftly round his neck and she pulled him to her. When he next woke he was alone. He turned and saw the dent in the pillow where her head had rested, and he half-rose and stared at the tumble of bedclothes, unable to avoid a feeling that was arrogant, bold and self-satisfied all at once.

The door clicked and Nancy appeared. She was wearing a dressing gown belonging to one of her brothers that somehow made her seem smaller, and had pulled her hair back off her face with a blue ribbon.

'You look like a cat that's been at the cream,' she said.

She handed him breakfast on a tray and sat on the edge of the bed. 'Mustn't let Tickner know,' she went on. 'He'd never recover.'

She was putting on an act of extreme modernity, but he

suspected that underneath there was a small frightened feeling that she didn't like to acknowledge.

'We shall have to be careful about this sort of thing,' she said cheerfully. 'There mustn't be anything so silly as babies.'

They talked while they ate, frankly—like an old married couple, he thought. He had often felt it might be embarrassing to face a girl after your first night with her, but with Nancy it seemed the most normal thing in the world.

'It was fun, wasn't it?' she said. 'But I'm not really that kind of girl, you know.'

'Why with me, then?'

'Because you're you and I'm me. There are other boys'—she smiled—'better-looking boys, without broken noses—but nothing happens.' She gave a little lost shrug. 'And we all grow a little desperate for love these days, don't we? There's so little of it.'

They caught the train for London together, never quite looking at each other and half-imagining that the people on the station platform who raised their hats to Nancy suspected what they'd been up to. As the train started, neither of them said anything for a long time, then, without speaking, Nancy took Ira's hand and he felt her fingers tense and hard as she held it. Glancing at her, he saw there were tears on her cheeks. She turned and looked at him.

'I'm glad what happened did happen, Ira,' she said. 'With Francis dying it makes it all the more sensible that the rest of us should go on living.' She paused and stared at him with troubled eyes. 'But if we fall out of love, Ira, let's show each other the door—quite honestly and without fuss.'

It seemed a harsh attitude but he was aware that he had needed warmth and tenderness as any returning warrior needed them and that what had happened might only be the usual story of two young people brought together by the war and impatient of the cautious rules of peacetime. Hers was a modern approach and, at a time when everyone was changing all the time because of the circumstances of their involvement with death, it was more realistic than anything more sentimental might have been.

They were both trying very hard to be strong-minded, frank and intelligent and neither of them found it easy.

'It's just that—well—anything can happen, can't it?' Nancy said. 'And love's so suspect these days.'

The take-off at Hounslow was chaotic. It was a hot day and the Americans seemed to know every girl in London and they all seemed to be present to see them off. There was also a group of staff officers from American headquarters, a few civilians and a colonel called Mitchell who seemed to be crusading for air power. He was so fixed in his belief that the aeroplane would win the war and any other wars that might follow, it was almost obsessive.

As he called his pilots to him, Ira was surprised to see Forde among them, huge in his flying clothes.

'What are you doing here?' he asked.

Forde looked faintly sheepish. 'I'm comin' with you,' he said.

'Don't pull my leg, Toby!'

Forde grinned. 'It 'ad to be done,' he said.

'What the hell do you mean?'

'You need Toby to see you come safely 'ome to that pretty little chit of yours who gazes at you as though you were God almighty. Besides, didn't I once promise that Yank, Courtney, I'd take care of you? I've 'eard the 'Un's brought out a new Fokker that can run rings round anything we've got so you'll need somebody watching your tail.'

'That's not the reason.'

'Yes, it is,' Forde said, and it was hard, as usual, to decide if he were being serious. 'A promise is a promise.'

'What about Rachel?'

Forde smiled. '*My* love life's nothin' compared with the purity and tenderness of yours. *I*'m used to the bitter wrinkled truth, lad. Snow White grew old and Prince Charming grew bald and got gout. In the end she went off with one o' the dwarfs and Prince Charming consoled 'imself with a little bit of stuff 'e kept in a 'ouse in Maida Vale.'

'For God's sake, be serious! It's so bloody silly risking your neck when you don't have to!'

Forde shrugged, as though perplexed by his own behaviour. 'Of course it's silly,' he agreed. 'And I dessay no one would know if I dodged. But I notice *you* don't stay 'ome where it's safe.'

'I'm different,' Ira said.

Forde gave him a twisted smile. 'I've been aware of that, lad, for a long time. P'r'aps it's because I felt I was letting the side down. P'r'aps it's the fascination of the place. There's a terrible tragedy goin' on there, y'know. P'r'aps it's sheer contrariness because I get frightened to death and I'm no bloody 'ero, but I was one of the first out in 1914 and I think I'd like to be there when it finishes.'

Ira couldn't think what to reply and Forde laid a heavy hand on his shoulder.

'It so 'appened one of your boys celebrated 'is departure to the wars too well,' he said. ' 'E fell down the stairs and broke an ankle. They said I could come in his place.'

'Oh, God, Toby'—Ira felt irritated with him as he sometimes did when he was in his lyrical mood—'you *are* a bloody fool!'

Forde smiled. 'I know,' he agreed. 'But it's too late now.'

When Rachel appeared, she looked subdued, as though she realised that Forde was already no longer a part of her, and Nancy deliberately went out of her way to be light-hearted, in the way all the Avallons went out of their way to help others bear their unbearable troubles without considering burdening anyone with their own.

The SEs were already arranged in formation for take-off and Ira's last sight of her was of a small forlorn figure standing alone, holding a parasol. She seemed to have moved away from the rest of the spectators, as though she preferred it that way, and as the SE began to move, he saw her lift her arm and start to wave frantically.

5

They had arrived back in France at a bad time. The weather was scorching and the days were brass-bright in a clear white heat. Birds sang as the poppies flared among the clover, and in the next field the cows munched sleepily and a cuckoo was calling somewhere.

But there were eighteen hours of daylight out of each twenty-four and, with the front on the move again, there were no days off and Sillito's thin face was drawn as he led Ira into his office and sat down behind his desk. Alongside him, an elderly officer called Staines with a patch over his eye looked so much like Stoke it was almost like being at Huyzes again.

It seemed that the Germans had thrown all their resources into producing the new Fokkers that more than made up for the deterioration in the skill of their pilots, and things were different from 1917 and a world away from 1916. The days when they'd gained superiority with the arrival of the Camel and the SE5 were changing again and two men had been lost in the last forty-eight hours.

The German offensives were waning, however, and the squadron was waiting to follow the inevitable counter-attacks towards the east.

'I'm giving you A Flight, Ira,' Sillito said. 'Basil Avallon's got B and Toby'll end up with C. Milne's due home, and when he goes, Toby'll have to take over. With a new offensive coming I can't afford to waste an experienced man.' He sucked at his pipe for a moment. 'You've got all the difficult people,' he went on, 'Southey, a Canadian major who dropped his rank to fly, McAdam, an Australian who got the D.C.M. at the Dardanelles and doesn't like doing what he's told. The three new Americans. You'll be aware already that they're a lively lot. We've taken rather a knock lately and I've had to move people round a bit. They're still unsettled. I'd like you to settle 'em again.'

It was already dark as Ira and Forde began to unpack their belongings. The evening was so airless they were exhausted by it.

Avallon appeared soon afterwards, as immaculate as ever.

'You've arrived just in time for the offensive,' he said.

Forde's shoulders hunched a little as he bent over his kit. 'I *always* arrive in time for the offensive,' he said flatly. 'When is it?'

'Any day. They say this is the one that's going to finish the war.'

Forde's shoulders hunched a little more. 'They *all* were,' he grinned.

There were faint dark shadows under Avallon's eyes, Ira noticed, and he seemed tired and curiously like his dying brother, dignified, solitary and mature, as though unconsciously he were already taking over his brother's rôle and his brother's responsibilities to his family and to their caste.

'Things have changed out here,' he said.

Forde grinned. 'Yes. Nobody we know's at the front any longer. They're either under it or at 'ome.'

Avallon acknowledged the truth of the statement, his smile a little wry. 'It's not just that,' he said. 'Something's gone. The war was never anything to go into raptures about, I know, but it's become—well'—he hesitated, trying to set his thoughts into words—'well—more business-like, I suppose. That's what it ought to be if we're to win, of course, but it's drained it of something that was there before, that helped you to endure it. It's the massed formation tactics Richthofen started. We don't even go out in flights these days. We go out stacked one squadron above the other. Sometimes you can't move for aeroplanes.'

He seemed faintly depressed, as though something had moved beyond his comprehension.

'It's no longer a simple thing of dim military types like us setting about each other,' he said. 'All heroic but a bit romantic with noble old-fashioned ideas. It's political nowadays. Big business. Efficient killing done by numbers. Suspect I'm not making myself clear.'

Despite his incoherence, Ira saw a glimpse of what he was

trying to say. As far as the war in the air was concerned, it had grown too big to be individualistic any more. When he'd first arrived in France in 1915 it had been an affair of single machines, two pilots and two observers circling slowly in sedate combat in a lonely sky. Now vast air fleets were engaged and the fighting in the air had become as impersonal as the fighting on the ground.

Avallon made another attempt at explanation, 'After Richthofen went,' he said, 'it seemed to knock the stuffing out of the Germans. We've got some good chaps now, of course—Jimmy McCudden, Collishaw and this chap Mannock. Bishop's back again, too, I've heard, but they've all had to change their tactics. You can't nip out on your own and knock down a two-seater after supper like you used to. Not any more. The only way to survive now is to work as a team, and there's no nonsense about dog-fighting these days. The new Fokkers are too good. We just dive and zoom because the DVIIs can outwaltz and out-climb us any time.'

As they talked, they heard the low roll of engines above them and Avallon looked up. Above the muttering they heard distant explosions, then there was a tremendous crash that seemed to lift their feet from the floor. The hut fittings shook and a shower of dust fell from the cracks in the roof.

'Next field,' Avallon said. 'They're getting better. They're after the bomb dump at Morchain. Belongs to Independent Force. *They*'re always going over, too, and the Hun keeps trying to stop 'em. It'll probably grow worse as autumn draws in.'

The Australian, McAdam, was waiting by the hangar entrance with Southey, the Canadian major, and he studied Ira's ribbons with a contemptuous expression.

'Another boy wonder,' he commented, with no attempt to lower his voice.

It wasn't hard to see that he'd been in the habit of saying exactly what he thought and when he gathered the flight round him, Ira was determined not to be rattled by him.

'We'll fly a loose formation,' he began, and McAdam interrupted at once.

'The last joker always flew a tight one,' he growled.

They went out at squadron strength, led by Avallon, and it was almost like slipping into an old jacket after leaving it off for months. The sky was as vivid as ever, with thousands of little clouds like puffy dumplings at four thousand feet, and another layer in lines at a height beyond all imagination above. The landmarks came up one after another as they headed east—Albert and Warloy close by, the river at Peronne, Havrincourt Wood to the north, and the crawling festering sore, like the trail of a giant slug across the earth, where the lines wandered from the coast down to Switzerland, torn, brown, and ugly, with the rusty shadow where the wire lay.

Glancing back, Ira noticed that the flight was straggling badly, and he waved to them to pick up their places. They took time and he watched with an irritation that surprised him as he found himself comparing them with the flight he'd led from Huyzes.

His hands moved expertly over the instruments and switches in the cockpit, his eyes flickering about the machine. He had removed the windshield because it set up ripples that hurt the eyes when he pushed his goggles up, and had taken away the streamlining behind his head because it obscured his rear vision. Both guns had been adjusted to fire from the same trigger before he'd left England and, as he stared about him now, he was considering how to raise the compression on the engine and the possibility of polishing the ports and streamlining protruding fittings to produce a still better performance.

The sky seemed full of aeroplanes, formations of all types appearing and disappearing as Avallon crossed the trenches and penetrated into German territory. Ira's eyes were flickering about the sky and the earth below and over Arvoingt he saw the flash of a tilting wing reflecting the sun. Avallon saw it, too, and began to climb at once and, at twelve thousand, Ira could see the Germans clearly, four thousand feet above them, silver-blue and translucent against the darker hue of the sky.

Avallon turned after them, but the Germans were not

seeking trouble and vanished east in a long dive. As Avallon turned west, Ira spotted a group of Albatros DVs over Estourmel, but fuel was running short by this time and Avallon left them alone and headed towards Tertry.

As he signalled the final turn home Ira saw one of the machines behind him break away in a tight bank and recognised it at once as McAdam's machine. For a moment, in a surge of irritation, he felt inclined to let the Australian go alone, then against the herring-boning of the cloud above, his sharp eyes caught a group of minute silver specks and, realising that McAdam was heading for serious trouble, he signalled another turn, and breaking away from the rest of the squadron, began to climb as fast as he could, angrily waving at the rest of the flight to close up.

Unconcerned for his own safety, McAdam was trying to get into the sun above the DVs and had obviously not seen the higher machines in his eagerness to give battle. Climbing fast, Ira was hoping that his very presence would dissuade the upper flight of Germans from attacking but now, squinting into the sun again, he saw there were two flights, not one. McAdam had led them into a trap and Avallon was far to the west now.

They were on the same level now as the first of the two upper flights, which he could see were the new Fokkers, with aileron extensions and the extra lifting surface between the wheels. Still intent on the DVs, McAdam was banking now and pushing down his nose, and almost at once, as Ira had expected, the Fokkers dipped their snouts and he pushed the stick forward and headed after them.

McAdam was well below now, with the Fokkers screaming down behind him. They seemed well drilled because they saw the flight of SEs at once and the rear flight broke off the dive and swerved outwards, while the first flight continued down after McAdam.

As the DVs scattered in a hubbub of whirling machines and the diving Fokkers drifted across his front, Ira kicked at the rudder and pressed the trigger and the leading machine began to smoke and went into a dive that grew steeper and steeper until it was practically inverted. As the Germans broke up, the SEs went through them, guns clamouring. Machines flashed past, painted all the colours of the rainbow, and, ruddering frantically, Ira saw that McAdam had taken advantage of the diversion to bolt for safety.

Then a whole new formation of SEs appeared and he realised that Avallon had seen the fight and turned back. The Fokkers vanished eastwards and McAdam led them home, waving cheerfully. At Tertry he was the first to touch down and as Ira rolled to a stop and the mechanics came running forward, he appeared alongside, grinning.

'You seen the holes in my bus?' he asked enthusiastically. 'Those jokers were hot stuff.'

Ira climbed from the cockpit, white with rage. Forde was quietly unbuckling his flying suit with a wary expression on his face, waiting for the storm to break.

'Quite a little fracas, that, lad,' he said gaily.

'McAdam's a damn' fool,' Ira snorted. 'And I've never seen such bloody awful flight discipline in my life. We'll have to see that it's put right. As for Mr McAdam, one more go like that and I'll see he's posted to an artillery squadron.'

'You can do anything you want with 'im, lad,' Forde encouraged, 'except give him a baby.'

Ira scowled. 'Basil was right,' he said sharply. 'This war *has* changed. There are more bloody fools trying to win it than there were. Tell McAdam I want to see him.'

Mail had arrived when they returned to the hut, and there was a letter from Nancy lying on Ira's bed.

She was depressed by her brother's death; and her concern for Ira's safety, though it had an oddly flattening effect as he realised how much more difficult it was to fight with a woman waiting at home, made him think of her with a warm and unique tenderness. A second letter was from Felton Courtney, the American. He was joining the American Air Force now that it was at last in action, but since his wound he seemed to have lost a great deal of his old zest.

Newspapers had arrived, too, with their rantings about chasing the Germans back to their holes and their demands that they should be made to pay for all they'd done. There were hastily drawn maps on the main news pages to show how their spring offensive had been turned into a retreat, and how the blockade was growing tighter. According to the leader-writers, Berliners were spreading candle-grease on their bread now instead of butter and making coffee out of burnt crumbs. Only in Russia were things going wrong and the new revolutionary government had taken the country out of the war for good and German troops were pouring into Finland, Lithuania, the Don and the Ukraine, to grab as much food as they could to combat the starvation at home.

The newspapermen seemed uncertain who was winning and it was fortunate that in front of Tertry they could see the lorries moving forward in the late summer sunshine, and dusty columns of marching men. Despite the Russians, on balance, for the first time in four years, there seemed to be a gleam of light at the end of what had been a long dark tunnel of suffering and scarcity.

'Perhaps we're actually winning the war at last,' Forde said cheerfully, and Ira noticed that he had taken down his books on land and stockbreeding and machinery as though he were beginning to plan for the future.

There was little peace that night again because when the bombers weren't overhead, the guns in the east kept up their constant roaring and the clouds were tinted with the glare and flash of explosions. The angry red of flames filled the sky and they could hear the ominous tapping of machine guns on the wind.

The heat continued in a breathless emptiness and their few off-duty hours were spent in deckchairs near the huts or swimming in the River Somme. But the staff were pushing for absolute command in the air and the long hours of daylight and perfect weather with no days off brought casualties from sheer fatigue. Then the Army took a sudden aversion to enemy balloons and there was a concerted effort to get rid of them along the whole front.

The whole squadron went up—'A sledge-'ammer to crack a nut', Forde observed—and though they swamped the defences and all returned, Southey's machine stood on its nose as he landed and they found he'd been shot through the leg. When they assessed the damage, it was hard to decide if it had been worth while.

A week later, as though this were just the interlude before the main performance, a colonel arrived from Wing for lunch bringing news of a new offensive. He arrived in a car which, in a mistaken excess of high spirits, A Flight used to practice ground attacks. Ira had been sitting with Sillito on a court of enquiry and the flight had been led by Forde. On their return from the front they had been hedge-hopping, pouring their machines into the valleys and soaring up the other side, watching for telegraph poles and horses which, unlike men, didn't duck, lifting them over chimneys and tall trees in the most exciting thing you could do with an aeroplane. For ten minutes they had scared lorry drivers out of their wits, made even the stolid French peasants look up from their labour in the fields, and finally dived on the staff car because the red hat bands in the rear seat acted on Forde like a red flag to a bull.

He arrived at Tertry with a length of telegraph wire trailing from his wheels and was still laughing when Sillito appeared from the telephone. Foolish and shamefaced, he was handed over coldly to Ira.

'You picked the wrong chap,' Ira said quietly. 'He's coming here for lunch.'

Keeping his face straight, he managed to berate Forde—not so much for what he'd done as for not checking whom he was doing it to—and at lunch the staff colonel didn't fail to comment on A Flight's fecklessness.

'I don't like that feller,' Forde muttered darkly. 'Looks an oily beggar. I bet 'e's not just come to pass the time of day.'

He hadn't. He'd brought news that the Germans were expected to try to get across the Marne to threaten Paris.

'We've got to do all we can here,' he said 'to stop them withdrawing troops.'

'*We*'ve got to do it,' Forde commented as they left the mess. 'I bet *he* never did anything harder than shove a pen around.'

Late in the afternoon, a Bristol arrived to take away the colonel by air, and, donning a sidcot and helmet, he climbed into the pilot's cockpit.

They all streamed on to the field to watch him take off. It was a lovely evening with the sky splashed with pink and purple, but as the Bristol lifted clear of the farm buildings at the end of the field, they heard the engine cough, twice, like pistol shots, and saw the nose dip. It lost speed at once but, despite all the teachings of thousands of instructors, went into a flat bank to turn back towards the field.

'Oh Christ!' Forde said. 'The bloody idiot's going to try to get in.'

Knowing the dangers of turning downwind with a failing engine, they watched with baited breath and, as the Bristol laboured at a speed just above stalling over the farm they saw it waver in mid-air and drop abruptly. Ira was running even before the sound of the crash came.

Forde had jumped into the tender with Sillito as it roared past, and when Ira arrived on the edge of the field, he was startled to see him staggering about, bent double, his great shoulders shaking with laughter.

'Oh Gawd,' he was moaning. ' 'E couldn't steer a bike into a barn! Straight into the muck 'eap!'

The aeroplane was practically undamaged but the dung heap seemed to have been distributed over a great deal of the surrounding countryside, and the staff colonel, wildly berated by the furious farmer and surrounded by honking pigs and startled cows, was just wondering how to reach shore.

'What an invention!' Tears were streaming down Forde's face. 'A flying muck-spreader!'

Though the colonel finally had to sacrifice only a pair of shoes, Forde made a great show of checking the wind direction as he made his way to safety, and he was so delighted with the way the tables had been turned he started a binge in the mess as soon as the Crossley tender had roared off with him to headquarters.

'All 'elps to level the score a bit,' he said, pounding at the piano keys. 'We ought to make this a night to remember.'

But the noise of the guns in the east grew to such intensity it eventually stopped the singing and they all moved outside in ones and twos to stare as the horizon bubbled and flickered with the sustained shell fire. The iron chorus seemed more violent than anything they'd heard in the past four years.

'The Hun's last effort,' Sillito said.

'I don't like last efforts,' Forde growled. 'Fellers 'ave a 'abit of getting killed in 'em.'

The following day ground-strafing started once more, and there were several casualties immediately. Then Sillito devised the idea of setting A Flight above the battle as a protective cover and sending the other flights down with the Cooper bombs to do the strafing. Forde was exultant.

'What filthy rotters they must think us,' he gloated. ''Arvesting all the glory while they do all the dirty work.'

The artillery duel south of St Quentin made the air bumpy with the flight of high trajectory shells as the countryside below was hammered to pieces. Villages crumbled even as they flew over them, churches, farms and houses blazing furiously, the earth leaping under a pall of dust and vari-coloured smoke.

Casualties in B and C Flights jumped overnight. Two machines simply vanished and two other pilots disappeared to hospital, but Sillito stuck to his policy of using the most experienced flight leader for top cover, and even the new chastened McAdam began to consider himself lucky.

Through the smoke Ira caught brief glimpses of square-snouted machines moving across the brown surface of the earth, appearing and disappearing among the clouds and passing over the ragged line of guns that sparkled and flashed as they hurled their destruction against the enemy. There was surprisingly little opposition from the German Air Force, though occasional groups of Fokkers made hesitant passes at them as they waited. They seemed loathe to go down into the murk after the low-flying machines, however, and more than unwilling to try conclusions with the protective flight sitting above.

In the late evening light, however, they caught a flight of six Pfalzes which failed to see them and dropped down in the hope of picking up a victim. When they counted their score they found they had shot down four of them.

'I begin to feel dangerous again,' Forde said gaily.

When they reached the squadron office, though, his smile died. Milne, the leader of C Flight, had been hit by ground fire and his machine had flown into a house and been seen burning among the debris of bricks and timbers.

Forde had been given C Flight in his place.

6

Forde's first day as leader started with a golden morning, with cumulus piled lumpily in the sky to catch the sun and a strong westerly breeze bending the trees at the end of the field. Avallon returned from Saulnes with holes in his machine and the information that he had run into a flock of red-painted Fokkers.

'Richthofen's old lot, shouldn't wonder,' he said.

His pilots were all excited and just a little too talkative as they pushed through the circling dogs—as though their brush with the Fokkers had been a tense affair that had left them limp and sweating with reaction. One of them had collapsed his seat with the violence of his manœuvres and had escaped only by the skin of his teeth.

'That's all I want to make my cup o' bitterness full,' Forde commented, chivvying his fitters and armourers in a short-tempered way—like Wyatt who'd disappeared the previous year—and badgering his pilots to keep their eyes open.

'Not that it does much good.' He was smiling but there was

a trace of edginess in his voice as he turned to Ira. 'Three of 'em have only just arrived.'

His smile flickered across his lips again. 'And what about *me*?' he demanded in mock woe. 'What can I do for *me*? I always felt safe with you, lad. You're a sort of talisman to me. If I could I'd wear you round me neck.'

It was impossible to be over-optimistic with him because he was far too intelligent to escape the grim sardonic feeling of everyone in the mess that their most dangerous enemies had arrived opposite once more.

His first patrol was a disaster. He came back short of two men and climbed from his machine with a strained grimy face, his eyes white-edged from the excitement.

'Tomorrow,' he said angrily. 'Or the day after when I'd 'ad a chance to settle down—that would 'ave been all right—but today, my first trip! Two men gone I'd not even got to know. I can't even remember what they looked like.'

Dinner that evening was a quiet affair with the empty chairs, and while they were eating, Sillito arrived with the orders for the next day. The French were going over to the offensive and all flights were to carry bombs.

'Ground-strafing,' Forde muttered, his head down.

No one spoke much for the rest of the meal and later, lying awake in the darkness, Ira became aware that Forde was awake, too. They lit a candle to hide the shadows and Forde grinned.

'Afraid of bogey-men,' he admitted.

The morning was cool and overcast, with a strong west wind pushing a blanket of misty cloud before it, and Ira found he couldn't get above a thousand feet without losing sight of the ground. The front line was marked with the grey wool of smoke from exploding shells streaming before the wind, and as he led his flight north it became difficult to tell exactly where the line was. Then he saw swarms of khaki-clad figures edging forward in little groups and clotting at the wire or behind ridges or ruined buildings; and, behind the German lines, troops moving up with columns of carts and gun-limbers. Near Folembray, he caught a battery of guns in a sunken road and, narrow-eyed, watched the horses fall in a tangle of harness and guns.

Refuelled and rearmed, they took off again at once, until, by the end of the day, they were all worn and edgy, their eyes shifty with strain. Molynow, one of the Americans, was fidgeting with a cigarette with restless fingers, and he tapped Ira's ribbons with a twisted smile.

'If this is what you have to go through to get that lot,' he said, 'you're welcome to 'em.'

The evening patrol was a high one and seeing a large formation of Fokkers to the south of St Quentin, Ira linked up with a flight of Camels that were hovering nearby, to make the numbers even. For once, the Germans didn't disappear eastwards and he saw a Camel spin away. A brown Fokker slid across in front of him, looking exactly like a partridge rising out of the heather, and as he fired at it automatically, it flopped on to its back and hurtled downwards like a square-winged coffin.

The next day it started all over again. The Allied generals were scenting victory and were throwing everything they had at the Germans and, with brilliant weather, there were no periods of calm. Machines began to falter and nerves grew ragged, then an order appeared for British experts to pass on their know-how to American squadrons and, despite his protests, Sillito suggested Ira should go.

'Why not send Toby?' Ira suggested. 'He could do with a break.'

Sillito's eyes flickered. 'What can Toby tell them that they don't know already?' he said. 'They want an expert. That's why I'm sending you.'

The Americans put a car at Ira's disposal and it was Courtney who accompanied it, pale and limping in an American uniform with a major's badges.

'No flying for me these days,' he said. 'I guess that bullet in the chest finished me. I just do the boob jobs—like showing people round and pouring the drinks.'

The tour was a waste of time and both Ira and the Americans very quickly came to the conclusion that they were each conducting their own war very efficiently, and down near Metz, a tall ex-racing driver with a hawk face and a German-sounding name was destroying Fokkers with remarkable rapidity. As it drew to a close, a signal sent Ira on to a group of French squadrons at Trecon, where a slim young killer called Fonck was making inroads into enemy squadrons, but when he received instructions to continue to Belgian squadrons in the north, he screwed the order up and headed back to Tertry.

The first person he met on arrival was a man who'd been sent home injured after flying into a tree at Huyzes the previous year. He'd just returned to France, and he told Ira that he'd heard at St Omer that Mannock had been killed by machine-gun fire from the ground.

'There's no doubt about it,' he said. 'They saw him hit the ground and burst into flames.'

C Flight was flying, so Ira went to the hangars to watch them return. Forde arrived some time behind the rest of the flight, and Ira saw him walking away from his machine, bulky in his flying suit, his head down, his gait slow and heavy. He looked exhausted, but when he saw Ira a spasm ran across his face and he grinned. As though with an effort, his whole expression lifted and he explained his pale face by saying that his eyes were sore from too much flying and that his ears were giving him trouble.

'You 'ave to go twenty miles into 'Unland to find anything these days,' he said with an artificial briskness. 'God knows what they think they're doing *there*.'

In the hut he threw his clothes, revolver and cap on to his bed and sat down lumpily, making no attempt to change. Two new pilots, neither of them very old, watched him silently from their corners.

His tank had been hit and he hadn't yet got over the shock.

'Why do they 'ave to put the bloody things so near the exhausts?' he said in loud puzzled tones. 'The first I knew I was blinded by petrol. I was expectin' the thing to go up any minute and 'ad to go right down before I dared switch the engine on again.'

He'd had a bad fright and that night he woke shouting with a nightmare. As he lit his lamp, Ira saw the two new pilots sitting up, too, staring from their bunks, puzzled and worried.

'Been 'avin' 'em some time now,' Forde muttered shamefacedly. 'I keep dreaming I'm on fire. If I do it again, 'it me, for God's sake. It's so 'umiliating in front of those two kids.'

The following evening, as though to prevent a recurrence, he started a singsong in the mess, hammering at the piano with his huge fingers as though defying the Germans to break his spirit. He had just got everyone shouting with laughter when orders arrived to inform them that the squadron would leave Tertry the following morning and land at a new field at L'Ecoupil further north.

'Trust those oily beggars on the staff to spoil the fun,' he said heavily as they trooped off to their huts to pack.

The British advance on the Somme was going so well the whole weight of the allied army was to be thrown behind it and so as not to waste flying weather they were to fly a patrol on the way north, with B and C Flights low with bombs and A above guarding them from prowling Fokkers.

It was a cold morning with ragged cloud bustling before a strong wind. The new airfield was a bleak place behind the Somme uplands, without a tree or a bush for miles, and was surrounded by sunken roads that the newcomers eyed with dismay.

When A Flight arrived, the other flights were already down, making out their reports and eyeing the field with displeasure. Avallon was smoking a cigarette outside the office, staring across the stubbly grass with a heavy frown. Forde, just emerging, pale and shaken, forced a grin.

'I expect you've come 'ome covered with glory,' he said to Ira. 'I wish I was Deadshot Dick and could always draw the top patrol.'

They settled into their new quarters, conscious of missing

furniture. No one had had time to get hold of anything to drink and the stock from Tertry was on a lorry which had broken down en route.

Then Manners, one of Ira's pilots, brought the news that Monkey Brand, Sillito's dog, had been killed. He had been frisking with one of the other squadron mongrels on the lorry which was transporting them from Tertry and had fallen off into the path of a staff car hurrying to pass. They had buried him at the roadside and no one looked forward to having to inform Sillito.

Forde seemed more moved than anyone. 'Poor old sod,' he said. 'It 'appens to us all. Ball, Guynemer, Voss, Richthofen, Mannock. Now Monkey Brand. I thought *he* at least was immortal.'

Monkey Brand had been in France so long and was so much part of the squadron they were all a little depressed, and their low spirits weren't helped when the mess lorry finally turned up, bringing the news that McCudden had been killed, too. Coming as it did so soon after Mannock's death, they all imagined there'd been some confusion over names, but Sillito arrived later and confirmed it. 'His engine cut taking off,' he said. 'He lost flying speed and went into the ground.'

He also brought the information that Atwater had died in England in a collision with a Handley-Page.

'Well, at least,' Forde observed unsmilingly, 'the 'eavenly choir's picked up a good recruit.'

He crushed out his cigarette, pale and shivering, and Ira thought he'd been drinking. That night he had another nightmare, starting bolt upright in bed, yelling at the top of his voice. By morning he looked awful.

'I reckon I'm dying,' he said with a crooked grin. 'Probably of sheer funk.'

The doctor arrived from Wing, like all Service doctors brisk and perpetually cheerful.

'How do you feel?' he demanded.

Forde eyed him sadly. 'I think I'm in pup,' he said.

'Cheerful?'

'Not a smile in me.'

He launched into a diatribe of his woes, but the doctor silenced him by thrusting a thermometer into his mouth.

'Nothing to get worked up about.' he said. 'It's flu. It's all over Europe. It's supposed to be killing 'em off like flies in Germany and half the squadron will be down with it by next week. It's going through the Army like a dose of salts.'

Forde seemed grateful and relieved. 'I thought my nerves were getting 'old of me,' he said gaily.

He spent a wretched night in a twilight zone between sleep and wakefulness, one moment shaking with fever and the next sweating violently in a temperature, and within twenty-four hours five other men had gone down with the disease and the mess had suddenly become remarkably quiet. The rest of the squadron was formed into two flights to work alternate patrols, sharing the work with a squadron of Camels across the field.

The gunfire towards the east seemed to be increasing every day, shaking the hut and rattling the door on its hinges and Forde thoroughly enjoyed his illness.

'Trust you to pick the worst time of the war to be ill,' Ira said.

'I didn't pick it,' Forde grinned. 'It picked me. What's all the row outside?'

'Tanks knocking hell out of the Hun.' Avallon was staring through the window at the flickering sky. 'Rumours are that we're due to move forward again soon. We'll be taking over old German aerodromes from now on.'

'Hope they leave some 'ock,' Forde said. 'How's the rest of the war?'

'Still going on,' Ira said. 'The French are knocking hell out of the Hun near Soissons.'

'What about round here?'

'We've recaptured Meteren. They say it's the beginning of a general offensive to finish the war.'

'I 'ope I survive to get drunk.'

They rarely flew much higher than two thousand feet these days, tearing along the Arras–Bapaume road, shot at by machine guns. Though the Fokkers didn't worry them much, there was another flurry of casualties from ground-fire. One of the Americans crashed on landing and Avallon lost a man who flew into a tree. The same tense atmosphere started again with small irritated disputes about nothing in the mess.

Forde was recovering quickly now, however, and even seemed eager to get back to flying, as though the rest had done his nerves good.

'How's the fighting?' was his sole theme when they returned.

'Mostly at altitudes of eighteen inches,' Ira said. 'And getting more crowded every day. The Hun's feeling his oats again, too. McAdam's gone. He slipped off on his own again and this time he didn't come back. We tried to get to him and I nearly hit Cluff in the scuffle.'

'Which is Cluff? They come and go so fast I can't keep up with 'em.'

'Fair-haired actor-looking chap. Likes drink and girls and seems a bit careless with his flying. He was going one way and I was going the other. I could have spit in his eye.'

Forde studied Ira, his bulk huddled on his bed.

'Give you the wind-up?' he asked.

'A bit.'

Forde's expression was blank. 'More'n a bit, I dessay,' he suggested.

Ira nodded. 'Yes,' he agreed. 'More than a bit.'

He was still shaken from the near-miss. His controls as hard over as he could get them, he had felt certain they were going to collide, yet there hadn't been a thing he could do but wait with stopped heart for splintering oblivion. When they had missed each other—so close he saw Cluff's open wind-blown mouth shouting with horror—he hadn't been able to believe his luck and as they had made their way home, he'd still been slumped in the cockpit, wet with sweat, reliving the stiffened terror and the knowledge that he hadn't been able to do a thing to save himself.

The strong upland wind had been blowing across the field at L'Ecoupil when they had returned and he had landed badly, a thing he couldn't remember doing for years. Cluff, an impetuous young man not noted for his sensitivity, had made a joke of it and Ira had snapped his head off and had walked to the office, obsessed with a sullen feeling that they were being asked to endure too much to bring a quick victory.

Forde was watching him with concern. 'Go easy, lad,' he urged. 'We need chaps like you for generals after the war. So the politicians won't make a mess of flying.'

'I'll make a fine general,' Ira said. 'What'll I be flying? A tractor?'

Forde avoided his eyes. They still continued to talk about their farm but they both knew now that they were each only acting out the dream for the sake of the other.

'How's Basil managing?' Forde asked.

'He's got the willies, too,' Ira said. 'But, then, haven't we all?'

For the first time in his life he was sleeping badly, with dreams containing all the men he'd ever flown with, all clearly recogniseable but quite unnameable. The inability to remember them always worried him and left him tired in the mornings when he woke.

'It's a funny feeling,' Forde said, 'to think that one day it'll all stop. I wonder what it'll be like to be at peace again. I just can't imagine it any more, can you?'

He was already feeling better and his spirits were lifted further by the announcement of a batch of decorations for the squadron.

'Me, you, Basil and Sillito!' he said wonderingly. 'A prize from the lucky dip for all of us.'

He was tremendously proud of himself. 'Amazing what a warrior it makes you feel, to put a bit o' ribbon on your chest,' he said. 'I feel I could go up at this moment and shoot 'Uns down in dozens. I couldn't, of course, because I can never 'it 'em but the feeling's there all the same. It'll be just the thing to plaster across me chest when I open the 'unt ball after the war.'

7

It was unusual to get so many decorations at one go and Staines laid on a celebration. Even the invalids managed to stagger in, and Sillito, his face as straight and cold as ever, announced at dinner that a Portuguese general and his chief of staff had arrived to congratulate them.

It was Forde and Molynow who entered, dressed in uniform jackets and striped pyjama trousers and with their persons festooned with coloured sashes and medals made out of cog wheels, Lewis drums and dials from air-speed indicators and altimeters. Round his neck, Molynow wore a bully beef tin on the end of a watered silk ribbon, while Forde wore a small tin chamber pot decorated with an R.A.F. rondel. It seemed impossible that the frosty Sillito was in the joke, too, but he was, and the binge that followed was riotous, with Forde upside down at the piano at the singsong which followed.

But, almost as though it had happened deliberately to cast them down after their high spirits, the following day—even before he'd put up his new ribbon—Sillito was killed.

He was leading the lower half of a two-flight patrol, making one of his rare appearances in the air in an attempt to swell the numbers of those who weren't sick, and Ira saw the formation of red Fokkers sitting above the lonely two-seater long before he led his men down on it.

The idea of his being dead seemed impossible. He'd been at the front since 1914 and they fully expected him to telephone in his frosty tones for the squadron tender to pick him up. But during the evening Wing rang up with the information that he'd been found in his burned-out machine by advancing Australians and Forde winced at the news.

'I just can't think of 'im on fire,' he said, visibly trying to shove the idea from his mind. He seemed inconsolable and almost on the point of tears.

The place seemed strange without Sillito's frozen face, and

Ira was surprised to discover how much he'd liked him. He suddenly also began to see the cause of his blank and chilly detachment because he found himself acting Commanding Officer, occupied with all the trivia of reports, returns, records, and the problems of replacements and repairs; the worries of Staines and the N.C.O.s and armourers; the shock of casualties and the worry of new pilots who needed practice. He still had to fly, too, because, although Forde had returned to duty by this time, other men were now showing symptoms of influenza, and there were never enough of them for the work they were expected to do. Survival suddenly seemed a very chancy business again. Theirs was a generation that knew no such thing as a peaceful passing away and, as faces came and went and Ira spent more time in the squadron office than he did in his own quarters, he noticed that Forde was looking nostalgically at his farming books, sad-eyed and strangely lacking in enthusiasm.

'I was thinking about the farm we planned,' he explained.

'What about the farm?'

Forde gave him a sad betrayed look, 'I have a feeling, Sunny Jim, that p'r'aps it was just something that sounded nice and won't ever come off.'

'Of course it will,' Ira said stoutly, but Forde shook his head.

'You're goin' too fast for me, lad,' he admitted. 'I can't keep up with you. You're making your career in other directions. You can't be keen on farming. Not now.'

Ira denied it loudly, but he knew Forde was right. The enthusiasm had gone. His spell of testing had given him a whole new set of attitudes. He had always thought deeply about aeroplanes and the future of flying and he had now started to approach it with a sort of academic interest.

He felt lost. He had thought about the farm with Forde for so long he had almost begun to believe it was a fact and the new certainty that it would never come off left him bewildered.

The following morning Avallon announced that the new major was on his way. 'Temporary,' he said. 'Chap called

Worthing. Gather he's not much of a flier, but, then, neither was Sillito.' He glanced at Forde. 'Thought they'd give it to you, Ira,' he said. 'Ought to, actually.'

Forde smiled. 'Chap came from Wing while you were flying, he said. 'Talked to Staines and Basil and me. Asked us if we'd any preference and offered us a few names. We told him to give it to you, but 'e said you were still too young.'

'Thought we were being quite witty, actually,' Avallon said with an apologetic smile. 'Rather fancied having a major who was still a minor.'

The idea of entering the select ranks of the upper hierarchy startled Ira a little. While he'd grown used to command, he'd never thought of himself as a leader of men, but now he began to turn over in his mind an idea that Sillito had once tried on him—that he ought to be prepared to become a Regular after the war. Inevitably the thought led him back to the idea of farming with Forde and he finally and firmly rejected it. Flying seemed to be the only future left.

There was a lunatic binge in the mess that night and even Forde seemed to have forgotten Sillito. Things were thrown and chairs smashed and the songs grew noisier and wilder. But during the night the dream of colliding with Cluff came again and Ira woke, whimpering with fear. As he lit his lamp he was thankful he hadn't wakened Forde and he lay smoking a cigarette, faintly ashamed of himself.

There had been more truth than he'd realised in Avallon's words when they'd arrived. Things were more changed than he'd understood and a need for increased comradeship had come at a time when there was less than there had ever been. With the German collapse, everyone was making plans for after the war, and their minds were too full of what they were going to do when they were civilians again to be as aware as they had been of their friends. They all knew the break-up of their world was near and friendships were suddenly less profound.

Even flying seemed to have lost what romance it had had the previous year when there'd still been some faint trace of honour. Though he'd often jeered at the word, he had still half-believed the newspaper's descriptions of them as 'intrepid knights of the air' and had tried to live up to them. Now flying had become just a cheerless, crowded, workaday chore in which they'd had to come down from their untainted heavens to try conclusions close to the soured earth.

Worthing, the new major, wore the uniform of the R.A.F., which was rumoured to have been designed by an admiral and an actress, and he looked like something out of a musical comedy.

'Only here temporarily,' he was quick to point out. 'Holding the fort until they decide who to appoint, because I'm due to go to Wing.'

He took Ira on one side and talked to him earnestly. 'Men like you can run up a tremendous score these days,' he said. 'The Hun's beginning to lose his nerve, so I'm getting you one of the new machines with the Viper engine and the streamlined nose.'

He seemed a fire-eater eager to see Ira kill Germans for the honour of the squadron and the new machine was flown in the next afternoon. Ira worked on it for some time, adjusting the guns and fitting the gadgets he liked to have with him when he flew and, when he finished, he took it up to test it, contour-chasing for a while, catching some of the old joy of leaping over hills and clumps of trees and doing turns with one wing-tip scraping the ground.

The new machine appeared to be a good one and he climbed to see how high he could go. After the work he'd put in on it, he found he could get it up to twenty thousand feet before the controls began to grow sloppy and as he turned for home he saw three Rumplers in a vee below him, scuttling eastwards after doing their job. They were still west of him and had their noses down, and he went almost vertically into a long shaft between the clouds and came up on the starboard side of them, where only one observer could bring his gun to bear and where, if he fired, there was a danger of shooting off his own wing.

He fired at once and the outside machine went into a bank and gradually turned over on its back and began to fall. As it swung aside, trailing smoke, he bored in close to bring his sights on to the centre machine and saw it flop over in a fluttering spin, throwing out clouds of steam so that he knew that that one was finished, too. It would have been just as easy to hit the third machine because the pilot seemed so startled by what had happened to his companions he made no effort to take avoiding action, but suddenly sickened, Ira turned away and headed home, almost unaware of the last panic-stricken burst of fire from the survivor.

Worthing was pleased to see him back. 'I see you've been up to your tricks again,' he said gaily. 'Two two-seaters have just fallen behind our lines. Were they yours? Nobody else seems to be responsible.'

'Yes.' Ira nodded. 'They were mine.'

He was unable to find much enthusiasm for what he'd done. Flying seemed to be slipping from his grasp, somehow. While he'd always given it everything he'd got, it was suddenly lost in a strange sort of yearning that was compounded of youth, frustrated hopes, ambition and the impenetrable shadow that lay across the future.

One of the Rumpler pilots had managed to land his machine and, with an air of triumph, Worthing produced him in the mess that evening. He was a pale-faced boy with yellow epaulets who spoke English well. He had his arm in a sling and for the life of him, Ira could find no other emotion towards him than sympathy.

They got the boy pleasantly drunk before sending him off to join the long grey-clad columns of men filling the roads to the rear and Worthing studied Ira with a sort of surprised resentment.

'Aren't you interested in your victories?' he asked sharply.

'Not very,' Ira said.

'You should be. Do you know how many you've got now?'

'No.'

Worthing told him: Forty-one. It was a formidable figure

'That puts you pretty high on the list,' he said, stalking away.

Forde smiled at Ira's expression. 'It's a football league to some people, lad,' he said gently. 'They're great enthusiasts, but they're never the ones who're living with a thin 'ot wire threaded through their guts.'

8

The sound of the guns to the east came nowadays almost continuously and, with the Americans pouring into Europe, no one believed that the war could go on very much longer.

With the cooler weather of autumn, places which had resisted for four years all allied attempts to capture them, fell at long last and the squadron's duties lay wherever the German infantry tried to make a stand, flying low over the greenish smoke of gas shells, dropping bombs and machine-gunning until Ira was sick of the killing and numbed by narrow escapes.

Forde was shaken, sullen and a little bewildered. 'Perhaps I was too enthusiastic,' he said. 'I shoulda stayed in England where I was.'

'Why don't you ask for a home posting?' Ira suggested. 'The Doc knows about strain.'

Forde climbed heavily from his machine. 'Not with it almost over,' he said. 'A comforting worm of 'ope tells me I can see it through.' He grinned. 'Mustn't cry,' he went on cheerfully. 'Got to be a big boy. Especially now I'm a prefect.

'I can't back out now, lad,' he insisted. 'If I go 'ome early somebody else'll 'ave to do the jobs I'd 'ave done. Might even 'ave to pay something I couldn't repay. Like Sillito did when I 'ad the collywobbles.'

The argument seemed irrefutable and Forde went on with a grin. 'Thank God it'll soon be over,' he said, 'and then we can all go 'ome to our womenfolk and all the hatreds'll be lost in a warm bed as they always are.'

So many men had been lost in the recent fighting the mess had been transformed. Faces appeared and disappeared, those who vanished coming back only after they'd been dimmed by the gentleness of memory, so that their quarrelsomeness, their stupidity, their tediousness and their noise were forgotten and they all seemed sentimentally brave and true and good.

The continued low flying stretched Ira's nerves to bowstrings and he found he was doing his work with a numb indifference. Towards the end of October, he was instructing a group of new pilots in formation flying when one of them flew into his tail. He was able to descend in an uneven jerky spiral, aware of the other aeroplane passing him with a strange whirring sound as it fell, and by the grace of God, his last swooping turn occurred just as he was putting the machine down for a landing. Though it rolled itself into a mass of crumpled wreckage, he was able to step from it with nothing more than a grazed elbow.

Forde came running towards him with an expression of agony on his features that changed to a shaken relieved grin as he stood up among the debris.

'You were born to be 'anged, lad,' he said.

To Ira's annoyance, Worthing insisted on his going to base for a check-up. 'I'm all right,' he said indignantly.

'That's what they all say,' Worthing commented dryly.

Forde seemed more upset by the accident than Ira and fussed round him like a huge mother hen as he climbed into the waiting tender.

'You'll be all right, lad,' he kept saying. 'You'll be all right.'

'I know I will,' Ira retorted hotly. 'I'm not dying!'

But he was kept at the base hospital overnight and, though the doctor found nothing wrong with him, he was not very willing to allow him to return to the squadron. In the tender on the way back, even Ira had to admit to himself that he was lethargic with fatigue and growing jittery suddenly with an insidious weakening of the will to try his chances, in case his luck happened to be against him for once. He seemed to have been flying in battle half his life, and though his score had crept steadily upwards, only Worthing, anxious for the record of his squadron was gleeful. For the first time in his career, he felt vulnerable.

Back at L'Ecoupil he found that the squadron had been ordered to move further east and, from then on, they moved from one field to another, never stopping long enough to unpack properly, so that he lived in acute discomfort most of the time, just waiting for the fighting to be over. Sleeping and eating arrangements were always bad, and the mess was never again as he'd known it at Huyzes or Tertry. Men and spares failed to turn up because they were moving forward so fast, and half the time he had to fly under strength because the depots were unable to find the squadron to replace damaged machines.

The long agony in the trenches seemed to be over at last and all the fighting now was in the open and often done by cavalry or tanks. Lorries and cars moved ahead of the aeroplanes, the drivers arbitrarily selecting fields and preparing them for the squadron's arrival by simply removing neglected corn stooks and farm equipment, burying an occasional corpse and sawing down a dangerous tree. They were passing now through country that had been occupied for four years by the Germans, and Ira saw inscriptions on the shutters of the houses, with sometimes the words '*Gute Leute*' to indicate how well they'd settled in.

There were other inscriptions, too, redolent of despair and disgust. '*Deutschland Kaput*' he read, and over one Mairie there was a wooden shield, looted from its last occupants, with a Bavarian coat of arms on it, decorated with black crêpe.

Occasionally, he saw German artillery horses being driven back by grinning British soldiers, and once even by three young French boys wearing German helmets several sizes too big for them. Shells still whimpered about, however, and there was an occasional vicious spattering of bullets from a clutch of Germans determined to make a fight of it, and once, in the village near a new field, he came across a huddle of hairy bodies where an explosion had wiped out a gun team. The ground around was pitted with huge holes, overgrown with blackened vegetation among the concertina wire, with a dead German's boots among the undergrowth near a charred tank and the last rose of the year on a lopsided pergola.

It all only served to add to the growing feeling of emptiness that worried him. He wanted to go on living and hoped desperately that he would, but he was suffering from a lost lonely feeling that he had lived too long when so many had disappeared.

October waned in a damp flush of bronze sunlight that faded rapidly into mist. He heard that Jacobs had been killed instructing at Shoreham, then Molynow flew into a hill after shooting down a Fokker. Khaki-clad troops were all round the airfield now, all moving forward—thousands of them, British, American, New Zealanders, Australians, South Africans, Canadians, all of them flushed and excited at the prospect of victory. Occasionally German bombers still came overhead, their Mercedes engines beating irregularly, the crashes in the distance shaking the huts.

It grew colder and wetter and more difficult to get supplies. Shops had been looted of food by the Germans but the damage didn't seem to be deliberate and no one complained of the atrocities that the newspapers still tried to make them believe in.

Once he found himself on an old German airfield, in a mess still decorated with salvaged Lewis guns and the rondels and numbers of British machines and smelling of the sour lingering scent of cigars. Photographs of the former occupants had been arranged over the bar, and marked with dates to indicate when they'd been killed.

It was an odd way to decorate a mess, an obsession with death that was foreign to him, and it depressed him a little, but there was also a stock of wine and German brandy that had been left behind and it gave them an excuse for a celebration.

By the end of October, they were beyond Sedan, where the French civilians were almost speechless at a liberation they'd long ceased to hope for, and as November began a procession of misty days, Worthing eyed Ira gloomily as he landed.

'Any luck?'

'One. Manners got one, too.'

Worthing nodded disinterestedly. 'Well, you won't have many more chances,' he said. 'It's all over bar the shouting.'

He seemed depressed that he would no longer be involved in the competitive element of aerial fighting. 'The war's finished,' he said. 'The Hun's thrown in the towel. They say he's asking for peace—any kind of peace. The soldiers are refusing to fight.'

'Not 'ere,' Forde pointed out. 'They still keep coming up from that field at Beauraing.'

Peace just didn't seem possible after four years of war and it was hard to believe that Worthing's news could be true. There had been rumours of peace ever since 1916 but nothing had ever come of them and, while it was obvious the Germans were beaten in France, no one had ever really expected them to demand terms before they'd reached their own frontier.

They discussed the possibility excitedly and what they'd do when the killing was done. Avallon said he was going to stay in the Service, but Avallon had always been a quiet, dedicated individual and even Forde felt he belonged.

'Basil'll lend tone,' he said. 'It always seemed more of a vulgar brawl when 'e wasn't around.'

The discussion set Ira wondering about his own future. He knew now that it lay not in farming but in the air. It might take a few years, he realised, but he was still young and there was plenty of time and he couldn't imagine life without flying and the smell of dope and hot oil and metal. It had been a part of him ever since he'd been at school and, though it would include a great deal of uncertainty before it showed any kind of profit, it was in his blood, and had been ever since he'd first realised the purpose of the strange constructions his father had built.

Civilian flying was going to be hazardous business for some time, he knew. There'd be too many at it and he suspected he wouldn't be skilful enough as a businessman to compete with them. He couldn't even see a bank advancing money at his age and he had no qualifications whatsoever except those he'd learned in the war. But he had no doubts now that the dreams he and Forde had had about a farm had never been more than dreams all along. Perhaps neither of them knew enough or were wealthy enough to make of them what they'd hoped. It had been just another of those fantasies that had sprung from comradeship and the war, like his affair with Nancy, something warm and comforting to cling to in the misery.

Because he knew now that she had been right to doubt and her letters only served to make him more certain.

'Imagine,' she wrote enthusiastically, like everyone at home caught up by the thought of peace. 'Imagine, when it's all over, being able to go to parties at the Cri again, having horses to hunt and a motor car to drive!'

There'd be precious little hunting and precious little in the way of parties, horses and motor cars married to him, he thought. Once he'd yearned for nothing more ambitious than to have a girl of his own, and then, as that period had passed, for a future, for a plan, an ambition. Now he simply yearned for peace and the chance to go on living.

He knew well what was missing between them. Though he wore a chestful of ribbons, his glory was already departing and the only thing he'd have to offer afterwards was flying. He was as out of place as a brontesaurus in the new world of peace that was round the corner and he was still unconsciously reaching out in the disintegrating world for the idealism that had sent him off in 1915 to join up, for the comradeship he'd known for three years and was still loathe to lose. The men who surrounded Nancy in England were men who were either too young for the war or had managed to avoid service. With the background of his life in France, he had to judge things by the standards it had ingrained in him, and living sixty seconds to the minute, he'd been divorced by a whole era from these men who were too young to have fought and by a whole epoch from those who had known life before.

It left a sense of incompleteness that was disappointing after his previous excitement in her, but not unexpected because he had suddenly become aware that the affair was leading nowhere. Nancy's ambition ran to a comfortable future while he was only too well aware of an itching foot. It was a difference that kept intruding, much as he tried to avoid it. It was simply that he had grown up.

He was still absorbed with his thoughts, impervious to the noise in the mess, when Worthing arrived with the next day's orders.

'There's to be a final all-out effort to knock the German Air Force out of the war for good,' he said. 'The armies are to advance from now on without harassment. I've offered to set up a two-squadron raid on Beauraing.'

There was a shocked silence, through which Forde's indignant bleat burst like a bomb.

'For God's sake,' he said, 'I thought the war was over! Do you want to kill us all to prove it?'

Worthing gave him a sour look and turned the comment into a joke, but he took Forde on one side later and left him looking angry and bitter.

'What chance 'ave we,' Forde asked, 'when there are fools like Worthing about preaching 'oly war all the time?'

He suddenly looked old and beaten and Ira slapped his great shoulder.

'You'll grow hoary with age,' he said. 'You'll be a general in the next lot and live in a château.'

Forde gave him a twisted grin. 'I expect you're right,' he said. 'But it's the way people go. One minute you see a feller. The next you don't. It's like some sort o' vulgar sleight-of-'and performed by people like Worthing.'

The weather was heavy with mist and flurries of rain and Ira waited hopefully for news of a cancellation to come through. But Worthing was still busy on the telephone arranging final details and, because he was edgy and uneasy, he went to the hangars and worked over his machine, checking the guns and the engine, and going over and over again the instructions he'd received. It was Worthing's idea to catch the Germans on the ground at lunch-time, so he ate early and went to his hut for his flying clothing. Assembled at A Flight hangar, Worthing addressed them all.

'The war's as good as over,' he ended.

'What, *again*?' Ira said.

Worthing heard him and frowned. 'If it's any interest to you,' he said as he turned away, 'I've just had orders to report to Wing immediately and they're giving *you* the squadron. When you come back *you*'ll be the C.O. and can do the worrying.'

While Ira was still staring he went on maliciously. 'Pity that in a month or two everybody'll be demobilised and there'll be nothing left,' he said.

He had organised an official photographer to take their picture before they left—as though determined to set on record his period of command—and he posed in his new R.A.F. uniform in the centre of the squadron leaning on a stick.

Forde hooked an arm through a strut, not even looking at the camera and clearly uninterested in the whole proceedings. 'You'll be able to stick it up on the wall with all the ones you 'ad taken at infants' school,' he said to Ira. 'To remember the war by.'

As the photographer began to pack his equipment away, they collected in a group, checking map references and instructions. Nobody pretended it was going to be easy because these days the German airfields seemed to have more machine guns on them than men and the jokes about the holes in their machines and the bantering remarks about narrow squeaks had long since worn thin. But Ira buckled his belt carefully and adjusted his helmet and scarf with a consciousness that Worthing might well be right and this really was the last time.

Forde grinned at him, vast in a Sidcot suit that Avallon always swore had been made out of one of the Bessoneaux.

'Fit to kiss the ladies,' he said, as he pulled on his gloves. 'Strong clean and cheerful, and ready to get on with the washing. If it really is the last time, then I reckon I can manage to oblige just this once more, and then a plague on both their 'ouses.'

Shouts preceded the swinging of propellers and the roar of

engines being started, and the air was filled with blue smoke and little clouds of moisture whipped up from the grass to hover over the field like patches of mist. Glancing round, Ira noticed that almost everyone on the squadron had turned up to see them leave—clerks, storemen, cooks—all believing they were witnessing the final take-off of the war.

Worthing was standing with a stop watch and Ira saw he had a Very pistol in his hand. He glanced down the line of machines on either side of him, and beyond and behind to where the other two flights waited.

The cloud level was solid and he had decided to fly the whole operation at low level. As he waited, Worthing's pistol went off and the Very light curved into the air and, as the mechanics dropped off the wings, he opened the throttle and the SE began to bump forward, its wings rocking. Glancing backwards, he saw everyone else moving behind him, rolling forward one after another and swinging into position.

At two thousand feet they began to reach the cloud and he decided to stay just below it. It was so unbroken they were unlikely to be pounced on, and as he glanced around, he saw the second squadron of SEs moving into position behind them.

As they reached the front, he saw uncompleted German trenches, broken trees and burning brushwood where shells had fallen, and lopsided guns and dead horses and men. Ruined buildings with shattered windows like blind eyes reared their rafters to him as he roared over them and a village burned steadily, under a pall of smoke. All along a pavé shining with the recent rain and mist, the sky shone in great pools of water like splinters of grey light.

There were other flights of British aeroplanes about and the number had stirred up a ferocious barrage from Archie which filled the air with black smoke puffs. The second squadron of SEs was closer now, slotted in behind and they were heading over undamaged countryside with only a few straggling columns of men heading eastwards below.

Rocreux came up, and then Gevet, and then they were turning in a big circle to hit the field at Beauraing from the east where they wouldn't be expected. Through the mist the German hangars appeared in the distance, drab and ugly as slugs, and Ira saw a line of Fokkers and Pfalzes all mixed together with a few other machines that he didn't recognise because it was growing difficult these days for the Germans to muster a whole squadron of like machines. He glanced behind him. Forde's flight was still on his right and Avallon's on his left, and he reached into the cockpit for the Very pistol.

With the flare curving into the air, he dropped to ground level, and as they went racing through the tree tops, he caught sight of empty roads bordered by poplars with the last of the leaves spiralling downwards in the misty air. The glimpses came in clear crystal flashes with the thudding of his heart as he roared over them and the thing that imprinted itself on his mind about it all was the emptiness.

A quick glance behind him showed the two squadrons following him in a wavering line, strung out over the bare trees in little groups, then he swung into position to fly down the line of parked aeroplanes. As he pulled the wire that released his bombs, he felt his machine leap at the freedom from the weight, and he slid to starboard to evade the blast. Swinging back on course, his guns rattling, he saw a Fokker on the ground ahead of him begin to smoke and the next one in line disappear in a burst of flame, then he was racing through the puther and climbing again.

The Germans had wakened up at once and he saw men running and lines of tracer criss-crossing from the ground as the other aeroplanes roared down behind him. As he climbed, splinters holing his wings, and banked for another run, he saw Forde's flight swooping across the field on his left like a lot of drab dragonflies. Bullets rattled and clicked on his machine as he roared down again and he caught a brief glimpse of an SE smashing into the line of German machines in a flare of scarlet from which the pilot couldn't hope to survive, wiping off two of them in a shower of fragments and smoke before it came to a stop and, as he banked away, another burning in a field beyond the trees. Tracers flashed past his head and fragments leapt from a centre section strut, and he saw men running frantically for aeroplanes and lorries. Several of the German machines and one of the hangars were burning fiercely now, and as one of the Pfalzes began to move across the ground in an attempt to get into the air, he fastened on its tail and it dropped again, touched its wheels and rolled into a ditch at full speed in a flurry of collapsing wings and showering clods of earth.

As they climbed away and clawed for height, nothing followed them from the wrecked field and he began to count. Two machines at least had been lost but as his eyes flickered over them, that seemed to be the lot. It was impossible in the straggling line trying to form up behind him to decide who was missing, and they roared together towards the lines, passing over shell-torn ground, smashed trenches with scattered sandbags, and broken lorries, carts and guns and the stark legs of dead horses.

He felt listless and his limbs seemed heavy so that it was hard work even to move, but the Germans—young boys of seventeen these days, he'd heard—were cowering in their shell holes from the whine and rattle of bullets, and a tank appeared out of the murk below, waddling along like some prehistoric monster over the yellow, gas-stained vegetation to stop the ground-fire. As he climbed again, a big flight of Fokkers came down on them head-on from nowhere with a desperation that was terrifying and suddenly there seemed to be far too many aeroplanes in the sky and he was ruddering frantically in a sweat of fear to avoid a collision.

A bullet whined off the cowling and went through the top wing, tearing a jagged sliver of fabric, but as the Fokkers pulled up he lifted the nose of his machine and pressed the trigger and he saw a small glow of flame start at once under the leading plane. Even as the Fokker turned on to its back and flew into the ground in a smother of flame, a second drifted across his sights and he saw it crash into a field in a crumpled heap of torn wings and steaming engine. The pilot scrambled clear, holding his arm, and he thanked God he'd spared him to enjoy whatever peace the present chaos in Germany would permit.

Then a flight of Camels came down on them from a gap in the cloud and another flight of SEs, until they were all getting in each other's way and the ground was littered with wrecked Fokkers in a pointless and nauseating slaughter.

As they flew homewards, Ira was limp with exhaustion and when he saw men in muddy grey uniforms tramping eastwards, their figures bent with indifference, he hadn't the strength to fire at them and they didn't even bother to look up.

The light was so bad now it seemed almost dusk and he could see the flare of his exhausts against the drab sky, and the rain beginning to fall in long swaying lines that burst outwards from his propeller. Then he was down and, as he rolled, wings rocking, towards the hangar, he saw groups of men talking together, and the mechanic leaning against the wing shouted something to him and grinned. He couldn't hear what was said but as he cut the engine Staines came towards him, smiling all over his face and waving his arms in a wash-out signal.

'It's finished,' he shouted. 'It's all over! All operations to cease from eleven o'clock on the eleventh.' He paused and smiled. 'Worthing's gone, by the way. The place's yours.'

As he turned away to greet the other aircraft, Ira sat in the warm air from the exhausts as it drifted through the cockpit, indifferent to his news and his new rank. There was no feeling in his arms or legs and, dully, he realised that instinct had at last taken over and his senses were refusing to function. Indifferently, he fought to make his mind direct them but it was as though they were dead, and he had to sit, slumped and lifeless, knowing he'd returned to the front once too often.

He became aware of a mechanic staring at him over the edge of the cockpit. 'You all right, sir?' he asked.

Ira nodded, forcing his head to move with difficulty. 'Yes,' he said. 'Just tired, that's all.'

After a while, he dragged himself like a crippled animal from the cockpit and slowly pulled off his helmet. Other machines were coming in now, their wings and tails and fuselages torn by bullets. He counted them numbly, identifying the pilots and watching them jump from the cockpits, gleeful and capering, still on edge and incredible that at last it was all over.

While they'd been up, the evening had acquired a peculiar light that changed to a sinister purple full of evil so that there seemed to be some warning in the growing gloom. Avallon appeared, his face grimy and, as they talked, C Flight began to drop down behind the trees to the east and he turned as though he were drugged to welcome Forde back.

But the mechanics were staring into the sky, frowning and looking anxious. Only three machines were turning into wind, and all eyes were strained for the letters on the fuselages.

One by one the machines headed towards the hangars, mechanics hanging on to rocking wing-tips. They were all badly shot up and as the mechanics began unfastening cowlings, there was a burst of noisy talk, with hands moving in patterns then angry comments as Staines' news reached them.

Forde's fitter and rigger were standing alone, still staring towards the east, and long after C Flight had vanished to make out their reports, Ira and Avallon went on staring at the sky with them, neither of them with much hope in their hearts. They had waited too often for aeroplanes to appear that would never appear again.

Almost as though the menace had been lifted the purple had vanished from the heavens and the colour had changed to amber and then to bronze, and the trees at the eastern end of the field became black-purple against a yellow band between two layers of cloud, and the air was bathed in luminous light.

It still didn't seem really possible that the fighting had ended, that men would no longer die because of some stranger over the horizon. Ira felt dazed, fully expecting that someone would denounce the armistice before long and that the war would start again, until they'd forced their way across the Rhine.

Now that the killing was done, it left him with a sense of emptiness and a feeling of futility. Things had already vanished that he had expected always to be there, and that bright image of the future he'd cherished for when the war ended seemed dulled, and pangs of intense loneliness came, as sometimes came on a still night when an owl hooted in the distance. The standards by which he'd lived so long had been abruptly replaced by others of which he knew nothing and it gave him a feeling of uneasiness because he knew he still belonged in the past while the rest of the world had already rolled on to the future. It would take time even to realise he *had* a future again.

It seemed silly that men were dead because their luck hadn't held out and sillier still that Forde, who'd served since 1914, had not lived the last few hours. It was pitiful and sad enough to laugh at.

Despite the shouts from the mechanics' quarters and the sound of a binge already beginning in the mess, the field seemed empty. All round him, all the way from the coast to Switzerland, the land seemed deserted and he stood for a while in the darkening afternoon, not speaking, staring at Avallon with bewilderment and relief. With the sound of the motors silent, the war seemed years away already, and all round them, among the wreckage, the litter of ruined equipment, the shell holes, the splintered trees and charred houses, and the graves gathered in little groups behind buildings, in gardens and in hollows where their occupants had been dragged out of the storm of bullets to die, the silence seemed to be spreading.

He smiled painfully at Avallon, knowing that Avallon was thinking the same as he was. *They* had made it. *They* were the lucky ones and had come out of it alive. *They* had lived to see flying change because of the war from the week-end sport of enthusiastic amateurs like his father, who'd been regarded as fanatics, to a profession that was safe and the territory of experts. The future lay ahead of them when they felt able to face it, and they were harder, tougher and more able—again because of the war—to deal with it.

He drew a deep breath that wracked his whole body. There *was* hope. There had to be. And at last he knew what he was going to do. After a void of uncertainty he knew where he was going and he was certain that he knew how to travel. It wasn't the end after all. It couldn't be. In spite of Forde, in spite of Nancy, in spite of everything, it was only the beginning.

It was only the beginning.